The
UNDYING
W E S T

A Chronicle of Montana's Camas Prairie

Carlene Cross

Fulcrum Publishing
Golden, Colorado

To my family—
Salish, Kootenai, Nez Perce, Iroquois, and Homesteader

Grateful acknowledgment is made to the following for permission to reprint previously published material:

"Coyote & Rattlesnake," from *Coyote & . . . : Native American Folk Tales*, by Joe Hayes; Santa Fe, N. Mex.: Mariposa Publishing, 1983, p 57. Copyright © 1983 by Joe Hayes. Used by permission of Mariposa Publishing.

"Ceremony," from *Ceremony*, by Leslie Marmon Silko. Copyright © 1977 by Leslie Silko. Used by permission of Viking Penguin, a division of Penguin Putnam, Inc.

Library of Congress Cataloging-in-Publication Data
Cross, Carlene.
    The undying West : a chronicle of Montana's Camas Prairie / Carlene Cross.
      p. cm.
    Includes bibliographical references and index.
    ISBN 1-55591-432-2
    1. Camas Prairie (Mont.)—History.   2. Camas Prairie (Mont.)—Social life and customs.   3. Natural history—Montana—Camas Prairie.   4. Cross, Carlene.   5. Country life—Montana—Camas Prairie.   6. Camas Prairie (Mont.) Biography.   I. Title.
F737.M6C76   1999
978.6'833—dc21   99–16314
                                            CIP

Project editor: Daniel Forrest-Bank
Editorial services: Heath Lynn Silberfeld
Designer: Bill Spahr
Cover illustration: Jim Hays
Interior photographs: Carlene Cross, unless otherwise noted

Printed in the United States of America
0 9 8 7 6 5 4 3 2 1

Fulcrum Publishing
350 Indiana Street, Suite 350
Golden, Colorado 80401-5093
(800) 992-2908 • (303) 277-1623
www.fulcrum-books.com

Contents

Acknowledgments, v
Preface, ix

Chapter 1
Seasons of a Prairie Wind   *1*

Chapter 2
A Perfectly Preserved Fossil   *36*

Chapter 3
The Fur Trade   *72*

Chapter 4
They Overran the Land   *104*

Chapter 5
Dividing the Claim   *121*

Chapter 6
This Century   *143*

Chapter 7
History as Story   *178*

Chapter 8
The Undying West   *212*

Notes, 209
Index, 220
About the Author, 226

Acknowledgments

B *ooks are rarely the work of a lone individual;* so it is with this one. My mother combed libraries, retrieved community documents, and unearthed photos when distance made it impossible for me to do so. As always, her support has been that of a dedicated mom and dearest friend.

My father convinced his sod-busting friends to reminisce into my tape recorder, earnestly arguing that there were people who wanted to read about such things. He happily repeated his own homesteading, Prohibition, and Depression stories and provided a wealth of information about cattle futures and land preservation.

Without the help of my sister, I would have made some embarrassing mistakes. Melanie understands farming better than I ever will and is the only woman I know who can differentiate between knap weed and fan weed or can tell me that my long-horned antelope should have been prong-horned. She is just as much fun today as she was thirty years ago when we swam in the horse trough together.

My teenagers, Carise, Mi'cael, and Jason, graciously listened to rough drafts and fretted about my reclusiveness. They are wonderful people and raising them has been the proudest thing I've ever done.

My Uncle Bud shared his wealth of Indian and homesteader history with the delightful good humor for which he is known throughout the area. My cousin, Tammy Beerntsen, loaned her beautiful photographs, and my grandfather recalled his homestead days. Grandpa is responsible for a large and colorful family, which has supported this project like they always do one another.

Camas Prairie residents Johnny Stanislaw, Arthur Argo, Jim and Theresa Holland, Vera Burgess, Ed Sipes, Chuck Hunter, Morland Neiman, and Herb Cross offered great help. They gave me pictures and wonderful tales of life in the valley.

For years, Al Listen sent books and news articles from Missoula about Montana history and current events. His friendship and timing have always been perfect.

One of the greatest rewards of research is meeting the fascinating and generous people along the way. Jack Nisbet gave me insightful suggestions on the chapter about David Thompson. Brian Dippie of the University of Victoria shared his extensive knowledge of western art and Charlie Russell. Paul Fugleberg, George Knapp, Dan Vichorek, and Lon Johnson were of immense help with their understanding of Montana history and pictures from their private collections. Jim Hays magically translated my clippings of color and texture into a beautiful cover illustration. His deep understanding and love of the West is evident in it. Other talented artists who shared their work were Jacqueline Moore, Jack McMaster, Tom Bauer, and Ben Marra.

I received tremendous help from the people of the Confederated Salish and Kootenai Tribes. Velda Shelby sent me invaluable packets of information. Tony Incashola, Johnny Arlee, Frances Vanderburg, Micky Pablo, Marsha Cross, Bill Swaney, and Alec Quequesah talked to me at length about the tribe's past and its future.

Librarians at the University of Washington, Seattle Public Library, University of Montana, and Salish Kootenai College were gracious and helpful.

Ivan and Carol Doig, Ben and Linda Marra, and Richard White generously assisted me through the publishing experience.

Publisher Bob Baron and his staff at Fulcrum were an honor and delight to work with. Sam Scinta, my editor, is a man of abundant patience and skill. He gently prodded me to take a set of musings about the land and turn them into a book. Marlene Blessing, Bill Spahr, and Daniel Forrest-Bank worked diligently to see the final copy coalesce.

Mindy Clemmer, Kevin Kawamoto, and Ed Bassett read the original manuscript and gave insightful suggestions. Mindy edited it with the kind of exacting precision and sense of humor that has kept her, at the company we work at, the well-liked director of quality assurance—a difficult combination.

Others who read all or parts of the manuscript and made perceptive comments were Diane Milton, Dave Porubek, Lois Tuengel, Michelle Babcock, Bill Pitlick, Roger Simpson, and Jeff Cantrell. I am thankful for their support and friendship.

Preface

When I was eight years old, I awoke one hot August morning to the sound of muffled voices. I couldn't hear what they whispered, but the tones that seeped through the walls of my bedroom awakened and startled me. I jumped out of bed and, without grabbing my bathrobe, sneaked down the hallway toward the unnerving sounds. I knew something terrible had happened. The sheriff and my father had already moved out onto the porch. Standing motionless in our farmhouse kitchen, I strained to listen to the frightening tale.

Joe Curley, a Salish Indian our family had known for years, lay dead in our wheat field. The previous evening, he and his buddy Joe Jacobs left the Perma Bar, drinking their way across Camas Prairie. For some reason, Joe Curley was riding in the back of the pickup when Joe Jacobs ran off the road. Once Jacobs realized Curley had fallen out, he circled the field in search of his companion. As he looped around, he drove over his friend several times before killing him.

The morning breeze swept off the prairie land and played with my soft cotton nightgown. It carried the luxurious smell of a summer meadow, a fragrance bursting with life and ripe to harvest. Now, alongside that warm breeze, ran the image of Joe Curley dead among the stocks of grain. In the midst of the West's inspiring landscape, beauty and tragedy mingle in a region that holds more than its share of heart-ache, suffering, and unfairness.

Such hard-edgedness prompted me to leave Montana and move to Seattle when I reached adulthood. In the years that followed, I never thought much about the culture and land that reared me. How-ever, like a bird whose instincts cannot be erased, something always pulled me home. In the spring, as I walked on the city pavement, I could smell the Camas Prairie wildflowers budding five hundred miles away. In the fall, migrating Canada geese called out to me above Seattle's traffic.

Over the years and from another perspective, I began to see the rural West in terms deeper than merely its toughness. Once I became a single mother and began raising my children in suburbia, I sensed the importance of keeping them linked to their Montana roots.

In early summer, we'd pack our rattletrap Ford and head out at 5:00 A.M. On the Seattle side of the mountains we'd play Kenny G— in honor of the culture we were leaving and so whoever wanted to could sleep. Once we reached Ellensburg everyone woke up, and John Denver took over—in anticipation of the culture we were heading into.

It was on the eastern side of Snoqualmie Pass that we all agreed the real West began. For us, the boundary was not political or geo-graphic, but dictated by the wind. With a gust that dried the soul, the hot breeze of eastern Washington distinguished itself from Seattle's humid air. As we raced out across I-90, and through the open farmland that flanked it, the arid western wind escorted us like an old friend, carrying a wild freedom that smelled of openness and community.

During those years, as I watched my children delight in our ritu-alistic trips to Montana and in their experiences on the farm once we got there, I became more deeply aware of the battle my parents waged to continue farming amidst the encroaching world of agribusiness. Their struggle was more poignant to me now that I had children of my own. The importance of keeping the land my great-grandmother homesteaded grew in the face of their future.

I also became acutely aware of the struggle the Salish and Kootenai people waged to preserve their past while adapting to the modern world. Many of my friends and relatives were members of the tribe and part of its efforts to continue vital into the new century.

I began to see the cultures of the West in a new light—instead of severity I saw strength, rather than bull-headedness or tragedy I saw incredible adaptability. Even in the midst of great trial, both the native and farm communities were constantly adjusting and evolving. I wondered how they remained so tenacious and spirited in the face of a modern onslaught that deemed them obsolete.

I came to believe that it was their love of the land and sensitivity to its voice that kept them alive. Both the native and white cultures of the rural West find healing and joy in the earth. They recognize the land's restorative powers and understand the great solace of its force and rhythm. Both cultures also possess a strong appreciation of community. Their customs and stories connect them to place and to each other. Instead of facing the world alone, they move into the future tied to, and celebrating, a collective past.

Today, many people in America feel little need for a land ethic or cultural identity. In the process, we have forfeited our stories, living in a mythless world where nothing but scientific rhetoric is considered truth. The mystery of life has been replaced with the Newtonian steady state theory of the universe. Folklore has been transcended by scientific rationalism. In the post-modern world we have stacked levels of concrete between us and the soil and then marvel at our angst. We grieve our hyperactivity and alienation and then feed them with noise and pavement. We sterilize our fingernails from dirt and our hands from difficult physical labor. The chasm between us and the earth's wisdom widens as we literally lose touch with the natural world.

As a result only things remain—so we hoard everything we can lay our hands on. Yet, in our techno-cities, where we surround ourselves with convenience, malaise spreads. Gadgets bombard us with racket, and automation litters our atmosphere. Excessive sound dulls our genetic earth-instinct. Quiet space makes us nervous; we fill it like an empty coffee cup.

By neglecting to cultivate a relationship with nature, are we not denying ourselves the only mentor capable of tutoring us back into contentment and sustainability? With all the wonderful things science has given us, hasn't it also taken us too far afield from the enchantment of creation and the ancient practices that have sustained us through the ages?

I set out to trace the history of Montana's Camas Prairie and the people of the rural West who still cling to meaningful story and land knowledge. By giving both storytelling and history a voice, I hoped to paint a fuller picture of the West's past and present. Such a tale might help us discover some of the wisdom that has kept Native and white alive and evolving even in the throes of great upheaval and change.

Does the earth and storytelling have power to revive our spirits? Can such customs have meaning in a modern age? The answers reside in the people who practice them. Their ongoing fortitude has been achieved through an understanding of the physical world and of one another. This gritty way of life and attachment to community has sustained them through plenty of history. The success of their evolution brings a message of submission to the earth and respect for one's culture.

During a recent visit to the farm, I went out to help my father fix fence. He was born on the family homestead seventy-six years ago and has farmed the land his entire life. Even after having hip and knee replacements and surviving a heart attack, he refuses to slow down. He jumps from tractors and barn roofs and chases cattle when he clearly should refrain from doing so.

He and I drove up into the hills, miles from the house, and hopped out. We lugged the wire stretcher, box of nails, and 80-pound bucket of tools over to the fence line. He then attacked the job with vigor. He pulled and shimmied the wire until it snapped and gouged a cut across his arm, which he ignored. He talked about Chuck Stipe's calf crop and rotating the Argo Place from hay to grain—the good year we'd had for water, and the terrible price of beef. He pulled and heaved on the wire stretcher like a teenage wrestler. I said nothing but thought about the heart attacks that killed his father and, last year, his brother. He must have read my mind because suddenly, and uncharacteristically, he said, "Fixing fence is my favorite thing to do. I hope when I die it's somewhere out here fixing fence."

Since then, I rarely worry about my father. He has lived a life extravagant with meaning. For seventy years, he has chased cows and repaired fence on Camas Prairie. Like many in the rural West, his journey has included plenty of hardship, but also immense purpose and connection to the soil that he loves. His gifts of tradition are intertwined with the deep-seated legacy of the West, in which we are rooted perpetually to the land.

Chapter 1

Seasons of a Prairie Wind

*C*aptured within the Rocky Mountains of northwestern Montana rests a vast grassland called Camas Prairie. Trees are scarce here. When they do exist, it's merely to announce a group of worn-down buildings—farmhouses sheltering equally weathered inhabitants. To the stranger's eye, the meadow rolls on hypnotically in waves of drab monotony. But to its longtime caretakers, the land holds as many nuances as Eskimos see in what others simply call snow.

Such people are the Hollands, whose great-grandparents home-steaded here, or the Marrinans who followed—leading the way for the Jorgensons and the Argos. Today, three generations later, these aging men and women work the same soil their great-grandparents laid claim to a hundred years ago. Alongside the whites live Native Americans with names like Red Crow, Stanislaw, and Big Crane, folks whose connection to the land predates the homesteaders, going back to what anthropologists call "time immemorial."

Even though these cultures are separate and, at times, suspect of one another, this rugged country whittles similarities between them. Through the years, the earth coaxes them to submit to its rhythms. They are molded by its whims and change in tandem with its seasons; their attachment to the land goes beyond reason—as love does.

This strong alliance with the soil enables both Indian and white to survive and pass their understanding on to a new generation. They are hands-to-the-earth, ear-to-the-ground people, with fierce identification with place, memory, and community. Each finds rootedness and healing in quiet. Nature's intelligence has mentored them, and in the process they have developed a deep loyalty to the earth and their traditions. Even in the midst of predicted extinction, through tenacity and adaptation they have continued to endure. Their survival has been earned through the feel of their hands and ceremony with the seasons.

In the summer, the valley bursts with harvest as farm families reap the hay crop. Once the stock is down, they work long into the evenings getting it baled. If exposed to an impetuous thunderstorm, protein washes from the alfalfa, stripping it of nutrients needed to keep cattle healthy through the winter.

As a child, my favorite time of summer was August, when we would cut the grain. In the distance, our bright combine devoured rows of wheat that swayed with the grace of a revival-meeting choir. The dust rolled off the dirt road into the sweltering heat as we raced toward the field in our battered truck. Once we bounced onto the stubble, the noisy auger moved toward us like a gigantic steamboat coming into port. We would throw our blanket onto the sheered-off stock, which immediately poked its way through the cloth, and use the prickly surface as both table and chairs for a picnic lunch. I didn't mind the discomfort; a great adventure was about to begin.

Once the combine dumped the grain into the truck, we headed out of the valley to the elevator in Perma. The first challenge consisted of getting across the churning Flathead River via the Perma bridge. The bridge, built in the 1920s, was suspended with slide hangers, causing it to swing when weight was applied. The architect felt that if stressed the bridge would rock rather than give way. His calculations were a bit off. In 1942 a section of the bridge collapsed immediately after Ted Shaeffer drove his load of lumber over it. The damage was repaired, and until 1967 it remained the only passageway across the river.

My mother's normally fearless face always drained of color when we approached the swinging contraption in our overloaded grain truck. Once safely on the other side, she swore (which was also unusual) about how much she hated the damned thing. Horses, having more sense than people, refused to step onto it and had to be led. The experience always prepared us for the elevator.

The huge red wooden silo, built about the same time as the bridge, stood taller than any building on the reservation. The chaff-filled place fascinated and frightened every farm kid who entered it. The floor shook as belts and pulleys noisily clanked the bins of wheat upward, far above our heads. We knew someone's limb would be torn free at any moment or the walls, acting as the belly of the terrible monster, would open up and we'd be lost in a rolling sea of grain.

My father drove the truck onto a wobbly scale and Al Olsen, a hunched-over, hurting old man, hollered out the weight. Dad moved the vehicle forward and pulled his handmade hydraulic hoist, which then dumped the box of wheat into a bin. Farmers less resourceful than my father had to shovel their wheat.

If we didn't cause any trouble, we'd get to stop by the bar/grocery store for a quick soda. The establishment was more bar than store and the only other business in Perma. My father's patience wore thin during harvest season, so we'd tumble out of the truck, racing against time. Ignoring orders, I always ran to peek inside the bar. It never disappointed me. Compelling characters filled the place, whites and Indians dancing and playing pool to honky-tonk music: toothless, loud, and shameless—slugging whiskey in the middle of the afternoon.

Today, the old bridge, elevator, and bar in Perma are gone. As an adult I drive the isolated stretch of highway past the place and each time am amazed that nothing is left. Even in the midst of such change, however, plenty remains the same. The valley's rugged inhabitants continue to be tutored by the elements. The wind is their greatest instructor. In the summer, the dry breeze seduces the flintiest of characters, calling to them to relax into its musky warmth—to feel the

Perma in 1967.

strength of its heat through the gentleness of its movement. People lift their faces to it. In return, it breathes into them its own need for the open.

Over the wide emptiness the parched breeze pours, caressing every crevasse and ravine, ruffling the curlew and swelling the grain. It laughs at the stable world, mocking the responsible fence posts that try to bind in wire the ebb and flow of prairie life. The sky's unrestricted territory further encourages the wind's independence, free to tutor the westerner in stubbornness.

This fragrant air hints of the centuries that have passed. Swirling across the land and through the exhausted walls of abandoned homesteads, it whispers secrets of the long-dead pioneers who built them, performing a time-honored dance that smells of distance and history. From room to room it explores, remembering the sounds of lovemaking and happiness or defeated, quiet desperation when the Montana winter had become too long, its hunger too great, and its confinement too unending. The breeze retells such tales, having witnessed the original event through cracks between the boards.

As a girl, I ran from our quiet farmhouse across the short-grass plains to meet the wind at these destinations. My favorite rendezvous was the Parkses' place. It was unique among simple homesteads, like that of my great-grandmother. Even in its dilapidated state the Parkses' house hinted of sophistication: crumbling plaster walls and sections of beautiful mitered trim, worn-down cedar shakes and exposed pipes that in 1912 made its owners the only homesteaders on Camas Prairie with running water. The wind guided these tours, moving through the huge picture window that looked down across the valley and up the staircase that carpenters built.

Unlike the prairie's sod-busting bunch, Wade and Rebecca Parks did not attempt to disturb the desert meadow into productive farmland. It was why they had money. Wade worked as the county attorney, leaving Sunday afternoon in a thoroughbred-drawn buggy down Cottonwood Road and out of the valley to the town of Wild Horse Plains. Each week he left Rebecca, surrounded by rattlesnakes and wolves, in their fashionable homestead without children.

In the 1920s my great-grandmother Anna herded turkeys across the hillside and used to stop and visit Rebecca. She didn't stay long; Grandma was an immigrant and did not speak much English. I wondered if the pioneer women longed to trade places on occasion. Down in the grassland, Anna's homestead lacked even crude amenities. During empty winter nights, Rebecca might have wished for Grandma's shack filled with laughing Bohemians.

Homesteads like Rebecca's and Grandma's pepper the valley. Extracting clues from them filled my lazy summer afternoons with what seemed to me noble archaeological adventure. I'd climb into the ancient jalopies that landscaped the house like shrubbery. In the intense heat, the rust, decaying wood, and rubber smelled of sadness. These early pioneers, with their dwellings every 160 acres, had disappeared from the Camas Prairie grassland like an extinct species of wildflower. The only thing to speak for them were the trinkets they left behind—on purpose, it seemed, as testimony to dreams unfulfilled.

I'd dig up cups and bottles blued by the sun, turn-of-the-century magazines, and linens. I'd collect rotting newspapers and farm journals that, mixed with straw and dirt, carpeted the living-room floors. I read them in search of what these early pioneers sought—which in later years I learned was the secret of how to trick this dry soil into fruitful yield.

Many of these early pioneers endured less than a decade. Others, like Claudia Nickerson, stayed a lifetime. For years, from across the fence, I admired Mrs. Nick's crumbling shack with its steeple roof leaning into the rolling landscape like a sailboat going down. Early in the century she had come to the valley with her husband, Joe. After he died, she stayed on and over the years earned the reputation of a very eccentric character—a notable distinction considering the local competition for such a title.

Mrs. Nick grew up on the East Coast, in a household with lots of money. Lovely furniture once filled her homestead. As a girl she was trained as a classical pianist, and in the evenings she entertained her guests by playing the Underwood piano that sat in the corner. However, after Joe's death, she also fed her own cattle, harvested her own crops, and mended her own fence. In the winter, she took her herd down to the lowlands where her hay was stacked, and she holed up in a little hut and fed her cattle through the blizzard season. In 1933, when the snow drifted impossibly high and no one had heard from her for months, my grandmother sent my uncle Gordon on horseback with groceries. Mrs. Nick was grateful; she couldn't get out and was down to a box of cake mix.

This hard life sanded her exterior to a rough edge. When I was born in 1957 she handed my mother a delicately frilled pink chiffon dress and gruffly instructed her to "put this on that child." Several months later Mrs. Nick died. Apparently hepatitis killed her, contracted from the swamp water in the shallow drinking well near her winter hut. After her death, relatives found money stuffed in her mattress and deposited in banks from Wild Horse Plains to Missoula. Claudia Nickerson hadn't lived on Camas Prairie out of poverty. She had stayed by choice.

I knew this complicated woman would have left remnants of intrigue, but exploring her homestead was simply out of the question. After Mrs. Nick passed away, Phil Pelley, whose ten thousand acres butted up against ours, bought the land. For years he and my father had feuded over unfixed fence and wandering cattle. More than once they had nearly come to blows; now, to keep peace, they never spoke. As an adult, I realize this battle was probably not as serious as I'd thought. To my ten-year-old imagination, however, trespassing on Pelley land seemed an invitation to get shot.

One hot summer day, the wind convinced me to follow it there. I snuck under the fence and sped across the quarter mile toward the house. The land felt oddly alien under my feet. I was an invader on the wrong side of allied territory. Even so, I wasn't going to make it easy for Pelley. To shoot me, he'd have to hit a moving target.

Just as I'd suspected, the venture was worth the risk. Except for the evidence of time, it looked as though Mrs. Nick had left yesterday and in a hurry. Unlike the rummaged-through homesteads on our land, it appeared as though no one had laid eyes on it since she died in 1958.

The breeze blew through the open window, as it had fifty years before, carrying its bouquet of summer. Instinctively, I walked into the kitchen—a farmwoman's happiest room. A shred of curtain swelled gently in the wind. As the waving heat beat through the pane, it instantly created a mirage of Claudia, the company she congregated with around her table, her coffeepot, and the smells of her fresh bread. There they sat, a much younger version of the same old farmers who frequented our kitchen. Their faces were pinker and lineless, but their talk of cattle prices and lack of moisture remained the same. I also imagined her well-heeled sister from California arriving after Joe had died to plead with her to flee this godforsaken place—to return to the conveniences of their childhood. There was no reason to hang on now. Something, however, kept Mrs. Nick here for a lifetime.

Upstairs, the floor was scattered with editions of *Ladies' Home Journal* and mail-order catalogs inflated twice their size with moisture. *Montgomery Ward* was gummed open to a page featuring elegant ladies in feathered hats and doeskin gloves, dresses with long rows of buttoned backs and inlaid bodices. The sophisticated high-heeled boots would have been downright silly on the Montana prairie. This wardrobe didn't fit the description of the toughened Mrs. Nick I imagined. Then I saw her dress in the corner. It was simple but tailored and lovely. The buttons still shined, although the brown pleated suede had advanced into disintegration. Claudia must have been a small woman who couldn't have weighed more than 120 pounds soaking wet. I held up the dress, imagining Joe, with softness in his eyes, giving it to her.

In an instant I decided to rescue it. My conscience shook its head and reminded me that trespassing was one thing but stealing was quite another. I determined, however, that Mrs. Nick would not have wanted her beautiful dress to rot there alongside rubble. Several more seasons in this damp and it would be a handful of cobwebs. I wrapped it gently, stuffed it inside my summer blouse, and ran down the stairs.

I started out toward the distant fence line when I heard the unmistakable roar of a pickup crashing over the hills. My father was right; sooner or later my disdain for obedience was going to catch up with me—today, I resigned, would be that day. My only hope was to reach the rock pile that lay a hundred yards ahead. I flung myself beneath it, convinced that the rattlers living there would be more gracious hosts than Pelley. I listened and heard nothing, peered up and saw only the yawning hillside to freedom. Maybe he was waiting for me over the ridge. If so, I would not only be branded an intruder but a thief as well. If he didn't kill me, my father would.

To avoid such disaster, I decided to bury Mrs. Nick's dress in the rock pile and come back for it later. I made a desperate run for the fence line and dove through. If Phil saw me, he never told my parents or took a shot. I decided not to push my luck and never went back. Today, thirty years later, like Joe and Claudia Nickerson, her beautiful dress has become part of the Camas Prairie meadow.

I left our Montana farm more than twenty years ago in pursuit of a more exciting lifestyle. However, after another frenzied year of Seattle living, I see the wisdom of Mrs. Nick's choice. Although drinking swamp water doesn't appeal to me much, her quiet existence, connected to seasonal rhythms, does. In metropolitan life, we rush to embrace the mechanical while losing touch with the organic. Many attempt to cajole, transplant, or buy meaning for their lives with title or possession. Days reverberate with the sounds of horns and bells, alarms, sirens, and whistles.

The landscape of the West forces a different existence. It watches and waits with a quiet nearly vanished from the modern world. To those not accustomed to this stillness, it's almost claustrophobic. Void engulfs, forcing them to listen to it and their own heartbeat as one. Silence strips the ornamental from us. In its presence, we are compelled to housekeep the soul—the first step in reconciliation with ourselves and nature. In this starvation from noise, we develop an insatiable appetite for life. Instead of striving to find contentment, satisfaction, and meaning from without, the soul is filled from within.

If we are to regain this health, we must seek these places of quiet. In the West such land still exists as it did more than a hundred years ago when William Butler wrote, "No solitude can equal the loneliness of a night shadowed Prairie; one can feel the stillness and hear the silence, the wail of the prowling wolf makes the voice of solitude audible, the stars look down through infinite silence upon a silence almost as intense."[1] The American West is a final guardian of this pristine calm. I believe it is the region's most precious resource.

This rugged country also tutors in human survival. Here, things out of sync with the soil die. Native people have always understood this and been in union with the earth. It has taken whites longer to get the lesson, but the terrain has forced them to listen. Wallace Stegner once claimed that distance and space molded people as sure as they bred keen eyesight into pronghorn antelope. Those who have remained in the rural West have evolved such fine-tuned acumen.

This keen perception took a while to achieve. In the process, plenty went wrong. These people—my people—came to the West and homesteaded on land given to Native Americans. They tore up topsoil and brought European flowers that doubled as toad flax. Yet their legacy is more complicated than what is sometimes blankly condemned. These people have learned to live in harmony with the earth and to create enduring community. Today they work to pass these lessons on to a new farm generation.

I believe there is truth and honor in both native and farm culture. In the PBS documentary *In Search of the Oregon Trail,* Patricia Limerick points out that contemplating history often leaves us seeing goodness and feeling empathy with each of two clashing narratives.

As she states, "I don't think you are supposed to reach resolution. It's something you are supposed to live the rest of your life unsettled by. Anyone who reaches resolution is cheating."

Today farm society offers important insight. Learning from the dust bowl fiasco, farmers are, by and large, jealous caretakers of the soil. And although battles like those between my father and Phil Pelley exist, a sense of community is stronger than any quarrel individuals wage. Ranchers epitomize generosity toward family and the whole.

I bring my suburban teenagers back to our farm to reinforce this connection to their ancestry and the land. Although Seattle's urban energy offers them much, the dissipate transience of modernity is not one of the city's advantages. I take them to the homestead where their grandfather was born without the help of a doctor or running water, to rummage through the dirt of their heritage. We stand in Rebecca Parks's living room and look down across the valley as she did ninety years ago. Together with their grandparents, we sit on the farmhouse porch during long summer evenings and listen to the quiet. I see them beginning to understand its rest.

Here on this grassland I am renewed, a wanderer returning to be clothed and fed. The land questions my absence, but in a forgiving way. Its gentle night touches my skin as it did when I was a child, reconnecting me to its rhythms and smells, its silence and safety. It makes me explain why I stay away so long, then assures me that although I leave, my home is here—mingled with its memories of my grandmother and her mother before. On that tired porch I am perfectly content, surrounded by the people and earth I most love. And if there is peace for me in this world, it is here embracing this ancient valley's silent voice.

In this place, where all but the core is stripped away, essentials take on great worth. I watch my mom tour my children through her cedar chest—filled with hats her mother wore tucked neatly next to the pink chiffon dress Mrs. Nick gave her own daughter—or play hours of pinochle with them. My aging father repeats tales about Camas Prairie—stories of people who, although imperfect, are connected to the land by touch and one another by community.

Because of this commitment to family and place, both white and Native American have persevered here, transferring their wisdom through example and their traditions through storytelling. Their narrative with the land is nurtured through enduring earth ritual. Such earth ceremony is the bedrock of native culture.

In June the summer breeze hints at these ancient rites as it carries the smell of ripened camas through a pure Montana sky. The Kalispel Indians named the valley for the lovely plant whose stocks carpet it in a sea of blue. For millennia they have harvested the camas bulb here. Camas stands about twenty inches tall and is topped with small, lilylike flowers. Inches below the soil lies its onion-shaped bulb. From a standing position, a shovel, once constructed of deer or elk horn and now made of metal, is thrust into the ground and the plant is gently pried out.

The Kalispel bake the fresh root by placing boulders in a large pit filled with tinder from the cottonwood tree. They set the wood afire and, when only red-hot coals remain, the rocks are covered with a layer of green willow sticks, bunchgrass, and skunk cabbage leaves. The peeled camas bulbs are placed on top. Next, a moistened layer of tree lichen or Douglass onion is added, and the steaming pit is covered with dirt. Another fire, ignited on top, burns from twenty-four to forty-eight hours. Once baked, the bulbs have the consistency of boiled beets.

In ancient times, the Indians mashed most camas bulbs into cakes. They left some whole for baking or ground them into a powder that served as a natural sugar. Along with its pleasant taste, the bulb provided a complete source of vitamins; the tribe claimed camas could sustain them longer than any other food or foods combined.

Experiments at the University of Michigan have revealed much about the plant's biochemistry. In raw form, it consists of insulin, a form of sugar the human body cannot digest. After the bulb is baked, however, the insulin breaks down into a high concentration of healthy, absorbable fructose.

Camas, Camassia quamash [Pursh] Greene. Botanical illustration courtesy of Jacqueline Moore.

11

In centuries past, the fact that camas could be preserved was as important as its nutritive qualities. Explorer David Thompson reported that camas bulbs collected in 1811 were still good in 1847, although they had lost their "fine aromatic smell." The plant provided the Kalispel with a healthy, long-lasting food, and its gathering was an important social affair. During its harvest, the old men told stories of the tribe's history and the young men related present-day hunting tales. The occasion was especially important for the young women, who competed to see who could collect the most camas. A successful dig displayed a woman's industry and increased her reputation as a potentially valuable marriage partner. At the end of the annual dig, the tribe held a small ceremony. All thanked the earth by dancing clockwise and singing the Camas Song.

The Kalispel have long cultivated this relationship with the camas plant. Anthropologists believe that thousands of years ago they belonged to a large Salish-speaking tribe in British Columbia. Around 2000 B.C., invading Athabascans pushed them south. The Salish speakers split into smaller subgroups. Some journeyed west to the coast, others east: the Kalispel onto the Columbia Plateau and into Montana, the Pend d'Oreille north of the Mission Mountains, and the Flathead to the central plains.[2] For centuries the Interior Salish maintained these territories and, except for battles with the Blackfeet from Canada, lived in tranquillity.[3]

The Kalispel traveled with the seasonal cycle of hunting and gathering. They migrated between eastern Washington, Idaho, and western Montana. Groups, or bands, of Kalispels moved up and down the Clark Fork River, which functioned as a major east-west Indian trade route. An inland trail also ran alongside the river and veered off through Camas Prairie to avoid impassable rapids north of Perma. Although the bands spent much time traveling, each called a specific location home. Indians descending from the great Kalispel chief Ambrose claimed Camas Prairie as their territory.

In addition to this dependence on the land for subsistence, the Salish also placed great value in the act of communicating directly with the animals of the valley. When they reached adolescence, Salish boys and girls obtained their spirit guardians. Cold-water baths and

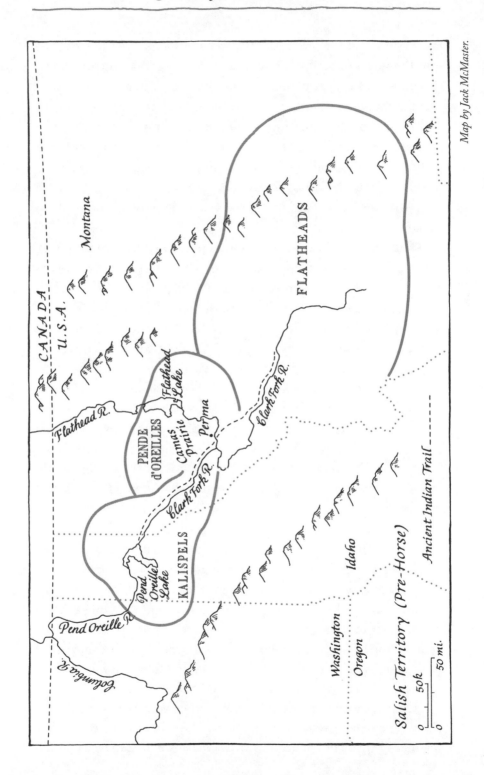

Map by Jack McMaster.

CANADA
U.S.A.

Montana

Flathead R.

PENDE
d'OREILLES

Flathead
Lake

Camas
Prairie

Perma

Clark Fork R.

FLATHEADS

Clark Fork R.

Pend
Oreille
Lake

KALISPELS

Pend Oreille R.

Columbia R.

Washington

Oregon

Idaho

Ancient Indian Trail - - -

Salish Territory (Pre-Horse)

50k

50 mi.

fasting initiated the process. Next, teenagers journeyed individually into the surrounding hills, built low stone walls around themselves, and prayed for the spirit guide to introduce itself. In time, the animal mentor appeared, announcing something like "You have sought me and I have sought you. Now I will tell you something good." The animal gave its student a personal song, which invoked the ally's protection, guidance, and power. The youth also received a feather, claw, or other representation of the animal guide's body, which the youth wrapped into a medicine bundle, carried throughout life, and took to the grave.

This process imparted the medicine power or *sumesh* of the guide. Recipients often relied upon this power and adopted characteristics of the protector, such as the strength of Bear, the speed of Deer, or the guile of Coyote. In 1958 Lasso Stasso talked about his sojourn to a nearby cliff and his guide's appearance. "All kinds of spirits are there: birds, animals, rocks, everything. Coyote spoke to me up there one night. He gave me a song. It is a song which contains the power."[4]

Salish culture was magical. Its world was awake, and spirit guides and animals talked. Native people understood such things because they knew how to listen. As they attuned themselves to quiet, their senses became acute. Creatures spoke, knowing the Indians could hear them. The tribe celebrated this unity with the animal world through ceremony. Animal spirits gave the Salish many of their dances and the inspiration for their costumes. Some dances imitated animals or birds and were performed in honor of them. The Buffalo, Owl, Eagle, Fish, and Snake Dances reflect this interaction.

In the Snake Dance, a chosen man assembled participants at the chief's tent and began dancing toward the center of the camp. The warriors followed him in single file, weaving and doubling back in the fashion of a snake, while drummers brought up the rear and chanted the Snake Song. When a man sang, he not only chanted the words but lived the song as well. He sang to transform himself into accord with the Spirit, the universe, and his fellow man.

Once the warriors arrived in a pavilion previously constructed for the occasion, they began the War Dance. The women stood to the side, undulating their cries of acclaim as the men exhibited their individual styles of war dancing while chanting of past coups and petitioning their animal spirits to protect them in future battles.

These powwows consisted not only of dancing but also of parades and games. In the afternoons, the Salish dressed in their brightest clothes of exquisitely beaded deerskin, porcupine-quilled breastplates, and bird feathers. Mounted upon fully decorated horses, they marched row upon row, a proud nation under an ageless sky.

Today, Camas Prairie is part of the Flathead Indian Reservation and the Kalispel, Pend d'Oreille, Flathead, and Kootenai still hold such powwows. As a little girl, I was both petrified and enchanted with these beautiful dances. Drums opened the ceremony with textured throbs that vibrated the entire heaven. The ground obeyed and sent pulsations of wonder up my toes. Drummers, singing alongside a voice that emerged from deep within the earth, wailed stunningly wild and pure. Like wolves recounting the story of a famous battle, they cried with horror and splendor. Magnificent spirit creatures entered and circled in eagle-feathered headcrests and hawk bustles, bone breastplates and bird claws that rattled ancient secrets of quest. The scent of buckskin filled the air as geometric beadwork splashed and blurred vibrant primary colors into a rainbow of one. The dancers waved hoops and ornamented rawhide shields, dance sticks, and bird-quill fans. Bells jingled in rhythm with the heavy cadence of drum and soul their feet followed. Painted faces shone transfixed with pride and fearlessness that sent tremors of terror through my skinny spine.

In days past these dances originated when warriors, returning from battle with scalps tied to their belts, celebrated victory over the enemy. I was convinced nostalgia might break out any minute. Most of the time powwows were held outside, where a girl could run for her life if she had to. When I was in the first grade, however, the entire community entered the old gymnasium for a performance that was to be given by champion dancers from across Montana.

The drumbeat threatened to collapse the place, as piercing howls of fearlessness opened the ceremony. The most frightening and glorious dancers I had ever seen encircled the old wooden floor. As they moved with energy and grace, I became convinced that ancient spirits possessed them. And here I was, a white kid trapped in this mystical

*Photo of the author as a young girl and her powwow
dance partner in 1963, taken by Grant Preston.
Courtesy of Dwight Preston.*

whirlpool with no way out. Then a boy of about twelve heard my fascination and terror and looked right at me. He left the circle and, in a gym of two hundred people, reached out, grabbed my hand, and pulled me into the whole.

I felt transported into the outer world. Through rhythm and ritual, I transcended oceans of time as though my feet had partaken forever in this sacred custom. In the midst of these breathtakingly beautiful people, I danced, a small blond child overtaken by the voice that has spoken to them since the beginning.

Today the reservation's oldest powwow is held every Fourth of July in the town of Arlee, located on a plain where, in prehistoric times, fierce battles between the Salish and Blackfeet occurred. It was named after a Salish chief named Arlee, and his descendants still participate in the event. Here, the dances and stick games continue in much the same fashion and resonate the union of human, animal, and earth.

In the fall, Camas Prairie enters a time of crisp beauty tinged with sadness. The range wind transforms into hollow loneliness and stirs the nomadic tumbleweed to begin its pilgrimage. The spindly zealot pushes across the land headlong in humble devotion on a mecca of unknown destination. The chilled air calls to the Canada geese on Kennedy's Lake, instructing them to assemble for their long journey south. They honk and carry on, flying in sickle-section formation for trial runs across the graying sky. Summer's clear light lengthens to cast languid shadows across the valley. A faint overripeness mixed with autumn chill hints of harvest closure and elicits a mature tint from the timothy grass and willow tree. Like a mother resting after childbirth, the tired earth quiets for winter.

Among the ten-foot cattails along the creek bottom, beavers prepare for winter. They rush to finish constructing their shaggy domed huts but in the process watch carefully. Their fur has grown thick for winter and is valuable to trappers. The fuzzy rodent has lost much ground to humans. In 1832 Nathaniel Wyeth trapped it on Camas Prairie and wrote that the Montana beaver's coat was excellent and so abundant that he had "taken a pack of them in less than a month."[5] The Salish used the beaver for medicine. They also ate their tails, which were considered a great delicacy. Today the animal is scarce and rarely pokes its head above the bullrushes.

Like chameleons responding to change, the weasel and jackrabbit exchange earth-toned fur for white coats. Their new vestments protect against subzero weather, and the color increases their winter life expectancy. But more foolish creatures worry less. Having fattened themselves on summer plenty, Hungarian pheasants strut across meadows with no talent for alarm. They are completely unaware that by spring they will have served as winter feed for the barn owl, marsh hawk, and coyote. Field mice scamper through recently mowed stubble. Without cover, they become hors d'oeuvres for bald eagles that perform in the updrafts and overhead breezes. Neither carefree nor careful, the rattlesnake and woodchuck simply burrow into the meadow floor.

For domesticated animals, fall is a time of gathering. Calves are weaned from their mothers and shipped to market; yearling bulls and horse colts are sold. The rancher's fiscal year ends, and the verdict of whether he will prove up on this year's interest payment or move deeper into an uneven partnership with the Production Credit Association (PCA) is imminent. Whatever the outcome, the family heads to the county fair in Wild Horse Plains.

Amid carnival criers and the muffled sounds of the never-ending rodeo filtering over the grandstands, the tired cattlemen sit in the shade, hats tipped back—sporting slow grins. Their wives and children rush to enter pies, quilts, and squash in contests in the appropriate barns. The judges arrive early on Wednesday to stroll through the straw-floored buildings. In each category, purple ribbons go to the grand champions: blues to first, reds to second, whites to third, and greens to fourth, which at the county fair is the color of embarrassment and not envy. Unlike the Oscars, where the loser can make a quick party appearance afterward and a short night of their humiliation, the county fair encourages far greater character. During the entire week, accusing green is pinned to the creator's work for every relative, friend, and acquaintance to see.

One year I entered a family tree quilt I made for my daughter. As soon as I handed it over to the aged sewing bee panel, I realized my recklessness. With a berry pie or knitted mittens, one can survive an honorable mention and still maintain a guarded level of respect in the community. A brave soul might even, illegally of course, sneak the condemned item out of the place. But a family tree quilt reeked of potential disaster. I instantly envisioned it hanging from the 4-H barn rafters, every blood tie listed backward to Prague, with a green ribbon attached. The thought induced a thorough cleansing of the system. Thank God my karma held. Even a respectable blue was little reward for such suffering. I promised never again to tempt fate so egregiously and left the barn glad I hadn't showered shame on the entire clan.

The ribbons awarded and stories exchanged at the county fair constitute serious business. The ranchers from Camas Prairie congregate with those from Garson Gulch, Little Bitterroot Valley, and Lonepine to gossip and discuss the year's business. After consideration of the season's hay and calf crops, they begin their storytelling.

A seasoned storyteller has a certain cadence to his voice (I say "his" because usually the men in Montana do the storytelling). When a teller introduces a line like "Remember the winter of '53? Was the goddamndest thing—so cold the bulls' testicles froze. Fell plum off the poor sonsabitches," you know to keep quiet and listen. Expert storytellers follow the same rhythm as Pachelbel's "Canon in D"—simple, well-timed genius.

The country incubates such tellers. Its harsh climate and complex past encourage a certain eccentricity in them. Adornment has been chipped away from them like soil from a rock-ribbed cliff. To outsiders they seem an uncomplicated lot; in reality their simple, direct language reflects years of silent contemplation. The aloneness and tangled history of the West create people who say little and consider much. Here, on the Flathead Indian Reservation, it is no different.

And like its people, the history of the West is far from simple or romantic. In 1855 the government prodded the Salish to abandon their wandering by giving them the land bordered east by the Mission Mountains and west by the Cabinet Range. To the north, the boundary cut through Flathead Lake, to the south through Evaro Canyon. The Flathead Indian Reservation was two thousand square miles of pristine beauty with Camas Prairie nestled in its southwest corner.

The government fully expected the ancient nomads, whose original territory encompassed twenty-three thousand square miles of Montana, to become tillers of the land. But by 1910 the Salish were still not farmers and the United States opened the reservation to white settlement. It reasoned that, by working alongside the Native Americans, the whites could teach the tribes agrarian skills needed to survive on a closed frontier. It always seemed curious to me that the reservation's farmers mostly ended up being the whites. Many of the Indians sold their allotments and worked as laborers or drank their government checks up at the Pioneer Bar. The white man's burden had fallen on unresponsive ears.

Before opening the reservation for white settlement, the government sent out thousands of pamphlets and newspaper advertisements describing it as fertile, virgin farmland—a place of endless possibility. The government believed it was in everyone's interest to see the area developed. The railroad wholeheartedly agreed. The Northern Pacific completed its line through Montana by 1883 and, to stay solvent, coaxed greater numbers of people into the isolated region.

Like my family, thousands headed to the rural West; over the years, few stayed. In reality, the place fit John Wesley Powell's description better. In 1878 his U.S. Geological Survey report described much of the West as too arid for farming. He argued that the sparse prairie land should be divided into large tracts, which could support grazing herds and not agricultural yeomen on 160-acre plots. It wasn't a popular theory. However, by the 1920s many homesteaders had converted to Powell's view. As one settler wrote in a self-published book titled *Cry of the Homestead:*

Montana Land

I've reached the land of drought and heat,
Where nothing grows for man to eat.
We do not live, we only stay,
We are too poor to move away.
Oh, Montana land, bare Montana land.
On your burning soil I stand.
I look away across the plain
And wonder why it never rains.

Scores left Camas Prairie after the grasshopper plague of 1916; others gave up during the droughts of 1917, 1918, and 1919. Yet a remnant remained and with each year grew more stubborn and attached—some too bullheaded to leave, the rest with nowhere else to go.

Today the descendants of these hardened souls are the valley's family farmers. They have survived winters like those in 1953 and the drought and insects that followed. Most do not overgraze (doing so would remove all possibility of avoiding bankruptcy). They are responsible caretakers, laboring to pass the land on to their children. Over the years they have received some government assistance—but not enough to matter much or keep most here for long. Those who have stayed are proud and independent; some say they are the last remnant of a dying breed.

Before the whites came, the Kalispel harvested their berry crop in the fall. They picked the huckleberries, chokecherries, and servi-ceberries that filled the prairie's hillside. Within weeks, they obtained enough to last the entire year. Most of the berries were dried, pounded into patties, and stored for later use in cedar bark bags sewn together with strips of willow.

October brought the fall hunt. To capture deer, the Kalispel of-ten drove their prey up a canyon into a corral made of tree branches. The drivers shouted as they advanced, flushing the animals forward. With various whistles they communicated to the hunters who waited in the bushes surrounding the trap. Once they captured the deer, they killed only enough for the tribe's use and, with another whistle, let those remaining go. The men packed the meat to camp, where the women sliced and dried it and divided it equally among the people.

As the snows approached, the tribe formed a winter camp. The intensity of labor slackened as hunting and gathering and, along with it, the setting up and taking down of the tents and the packing and unpacking of the bags and ponies came to an end. The people quieted and prepared for the long Montana winter.

By the first snowfall, the Salish had their food stored away, after which tales filled the evenings. The Salish called November "Storytelling Month," and throughout winter the tribe gathered around huge fires and told stories of creation and the unity of life. Many legends centered on Coyote, the most important of the animal people.

In the beginning, the stories related, the Spirit Chief appointed Coyote to improve the plight of creatures on Earth. Sometimes Coy-ote lived up to this commission, sometimes he didn't. With a mis-chievous nature and the name Sin-ka-lip', meaning "imitator," the wily dog was the world's first antihero—one minute a yellow-eyed Solomon, the next a trickster creating all-around havoc.

The storytelling explained why Coyote, because of his foolish-ness and anger, was responsible for the lack of Salmon in the Clark

Fork River and for Old Man Buffalo staying east of the Rocky Mountains. However, Coyote could also be helpful. His tricks humbled proud Badger and eliminated the people-eating Elk. And Coyote fought wicked monsters that threatened human beings—turning the evil creatures into rock cliffs.

Although he was often brave and generous, Coyote also spent much of his time in trouble. Sometimes his misadventures got him killed. That's why the Creator, being omniscient, sent Fox to Earth. Each time his brother Coyote died, Fox resurrected him by stepping over his bones.

Many tales spoke of this cultural hero. Others explained why Marten's face, once smooth and handsome, was now wrinkled and homely, and how the sweat house came to be. The spoken word retold the story of the tribe, of past leaders, heroes, and enemies. It reinforced religious and moral teachings, reminded the Salish of their connection to Earth and its creatures and of the magical possibilities of life.

Today, both the native and white cultures on the prairie continue to be peoples of oral tradition. Their myths are passed on through folklore and poetry. Their communities are held together with the glue of storytelling. Instinctively, they respond to the tactile and the verbal. In this rugged, breathtaking country, both whites and Native Americans speak a sensual dialect born of the earth and memory. For instance, February, usually Camas Prairie's coldest month, is called *Cqwosqnsp'qni* in Salish, meaning "curly." The weather is so cold it literally curls the ends of the grass. The range wind swirls the snow into sparkling ballets of crisp, light dryness. Its beauty is deceiving, however. As the bulls in the valley can attest, the snow, coupled with a negative wind-chill factor, quickly freezes anything exposed. As the snow drifts across the valley, creating bridges over the fence posts, human impotence is obvious. A northerner moaning down from Canada exposes the delicacy of the human condition. Nature shows off, and the valley humbly submits to its authority.

For the rancher, it's calving time. The little creatures are introduced to the place during its harshest season. On nights when the snow is too deep and the cattle cannot smell their calves, some refuse to "mother up," which consists of licking the afterbirth off a tiny, shaking calf and letting it nurse.

I remember bringing such orphans into our house. My father, who was up every two hours to check the herd, laid the calves next to our potbellied stove or, if they had been exposed too long, we filled our only bathtub with hot water and "soaked" them warm. In the morning the infants would lie contentedly around the kitchen floor as we hopped over them on our way to the school bus.

To get a cow to claim her calf, my father milked the mother and fed it to the newborn. Once the liquid had passed through the infant and the mother's smell remained, they inevitably made up. If a cow had twins and refused one of them, my father skinned the body of a recently dead calf and tied it around the hungry baby like a new winter coat. The dead calf's mother recognized her offspring's scent and usually adopted the abandoned one as her own.

Both animal and human fight the winter as the eternal cold drags on, stark and piercing. The coyote is the only creature brave and foolish enough to venture out. At night, across the white-as-death and twice-as-cold stillness, he and his kind slink their impossibly skinny frames over the frozen snow. Their ribs testify to the season's cruelty and that all living creatures must be content simply to survive.

Winter in Montana can defeat even the heartiest of spirits. Earth's frozen hibernation waits with exhausting stillness and patience. Its stubbornness compounds the isolation of the place. However, about the time this battle with the elements seems endless and winter seems holed in for eternity, the Canada geese return. Their noisy arrival announces, contrary to all indications, that life will be renewed. The reward for winter survival is to experience Camas Prairie's most beautiful, emotional season.

The Greeks believed that spring signaled the return of Persephone to earth. One day, while the lovely maiden-goddess was collecting field flowers, Hades, god of the underworld, looked on. He became mesmerized by her beauty and decided to steal her from earth. He rose up, opened the ground, and dragged her down into its core to be his wife.

For nine days and nights Persephone's mother, Demeter, the earth goddess of vegetation, roamed the world with a lit torch, searching for her beloved daughter. Once Demeter discovered Persephone's fate, she went into a rage and vowed to make the earth barren until her child's return. To appease Demeter's fury, Zeus commanded Hades to release the beautiful maiden. However, while in the underworld, Hades had convinced Persephone to eat a pomegranate, which obligated her by cosmic law to remain.

Zeus negotiated a compromise. During spring and summer, Persephone could reunite with her mother, but during winter, or the "season of death," she had to descend back into the underworld. Since then, winter's barrenness reveals Demeter's desolation. In the spring, however, when Persephone rises from the bowels of the earth, Demeter rejoices. On Camas Prairie, animal and human join in this exhilaration as the lovely maiden returns to warm the soil.

In spring, Persephone's spirit rides in on Chinook winds while the land still slumbers. The fragrant breeze whispers to the frigid earth—gently coaxing, playfully teasing. The grumpy soil, frozen solid from the bitter winter chill, stubbornly requests to be left alone. Persephone's warm breath persists, and finally, like a cold heart succumbing to unexpected love, the earth slowly and irresistibly awakens. Its body warms and quickens. Crocuses sprout and reach to the wind. The Bonner Springs bubble and flow onto the melting snow.

Those connected to the land feel this arousal and are restless in its presence. In *The Big Sky,* A. B. Guthrie describes such a Montana spring:

> *Spring made a man feel good and sad, too, and wild sometimes, wanting to howl with the wolves or strike north with the ducks or fork a horse and ride alone over the far rim of the world into new country, into a fresh life. Spring was a good hurting inside the body. It made laughter come easy, and tears if a man didn't shut them off.*[6]

Even now, twenty years and five hundred miles removed from this childhood meadow, I am awakened each March with remembrances of the smell of grassland lovemaking and must consciously resist a road trip to anywhere.

This restlessness is felt by the prairie's creatures. New foals and calves hop-dance in delight. Curlews march congenially through April's crested wheat grass. Like miniature storks, their bony legs elevate them above the new growth. Magpies, crows, robins, and bluebirds return home, chattering happily about the details of their migratory journeys.

Spring clouds streak the endless sky in shades of blue and cumulous white, casting changing light fit for Monet. The air fills with the scents of new-life spring as the meadow's flora push through the soil.

On the hills of our family farm, thousands of bitterroots emerge. The petals of the lovely pink-white flowers fan out like those of daisies. Their delicacy is deceiving, however. In 1807, when Lewis and Clark returned with samples of bitterroot to the Academy of Natural Sciences in Philadelphia, botanist Frederick Pursch honored Lewis by naming the plant *Lewisia rediviva,* referring to the plant's ability to resurrect itself and survive for more than a year without water.

The Salish found more than merely beauty and strength in the bitterroot. They used it as a medicine to combat pleurisy and heart trouble and to strengthen the circulatory system. Women boiled its roots into a tea and drank it to increase milk flow after childbirth. The bitterroot was especially important to the tribe because it represented the first fruits of spring and its arrival often ended hunger. The bitterroot's starch fueled their bodies through the long Montana winter, and the Salish believe that in ages past the plant saved them from starvation.

Long ago, when the people were experiencing a famine, an old woman, who had completely run out of meat to feed her children, went down to the Clark Fork River to weep and sing a death song. The Sun, rising above the eastern mountains, heard her cries. To comfort the old woman, the Sun sent a guardian spirit in the form of a beautiful red bird.

The bird appeared and softly promised, "A new plant will be created from the tears which you have wept upon the soil. Its petals will take the rose from my wing feathers and its center from the white of your hair. Your people will eat the roots of this plant and regain their strength. The food will be bitter to remind them of your sorrow, and each time the flower blooms they will say, 'Here is the silver of our mother's hair upon the ground and the rose from the wings of the spirit bird. Our mother's tears of bitterness have given us food.'"

From that day on, in May, also known as the Bitterroot Moon, the Kalispel, along with the Flathead and Pend d'Oreille, assembled on Camas Prairie for the Bitterroot Festival. Before the harvest began, a chosen woman collected samples to see if the root was ready to pick. If the bulb's brown covering pulled off easily, it was ripe, prompting prayers of thanksgiving and the start of the harvest.

The Salish lifted the plants from the soil with a digging stick, twisted off the tops, and placed the roots into reed baskets. At the end of the day, they peeled, washed, and spread out the bulbs on canvas. Once dry, the bitterroot could be stored for long periods of time.

Today the tribe continues to harvest bitterroot on Camas Prairie. Each spring, members ascend the hillside of our ranch and repeat the ancient ritual they have performed here for millennia. Salish and Kootenai people arrive from across the reservation. The tribe's Culture Committee oversees the event. Organizers direct waves of vehicles up to the site. Like a gigantic snake winding toward heaven, the convoy inches its way up the rugged dirt road.

The tribe invites our family to join them. My children and I try to make the trip from Seattle. I am honored and delighted to have the chance to witness the sacred gathering, yet I am hesitant—feeling somewhat like an eavesdropper on an intimate family conversation. However, once I arrive I

Montana bitterroot. Photo by Tammy Beerntsen.

A 1910 Edward Curtis photo of a Salish woman digging up bitterroot. Courtesy of the Special Collections Division, University of Washington Library.

am overtaken by the beauty of the gathering. It seems that the valley itself, after extensive preparation, waits expectantly for the ceremony to begin. Yarrow and sage have worked their way through the soil—filling the landscape with a hallowed, mossy incense. Like exuberant flower girls, yellow bell, dog-tooth violet, and shooting star splash petals across the hillside. As humans approach, Hawk cries a greeting, while Killdeer and Meadowlark dart throughout the grassland, proclaiming that Bitterroot's welcoming ceremony is at hand. Wind calls back for silence—then reverently stills itself. Earth follows into absolute hush.

An aging woman pulls a plant from the soil. Once it's declared ready, Culture Committee chairman Tony Incashola explains the importance of the bitterroot to his people. It provides both sustenance and guidance. As a friend and caretaker of the tribe, the plant must be honored, spoken to, and handled with absolute respect. To prove its vitality, he peels away a layer of the root to reveal a tiny red heart buried within. Participants then form large circles around the plant, join hands, and Johnny Arlee recites a prayer in Salish and repeats its meaning in English: "We thank the Creator for this

27

Photo of the Bitterroot Dig on Camas Prairie. Courtesy of Tom Bauer.

beautiful day, warm enough for us to come out and begin a new season in our lives. We thank the landowner for his permission to let us here. We ask the Creator to put back in our hearts the wisdom of our ancestors."

In this lifetime, union is rare. We are given brief flashes—glimpses—when our souls join with the earth and each other. This transcendence keeps us mindful of what is and what isn't important, what will fade and what will exist forever. The bitterroot ceremony is such an occurrence.

Meaningful rituals spark these exceptional experiences. Many of us despair from seeking them. For us, traditional piety is dead—or worse, promotes division from, and judgment of, our fellow humans and nature. As children of the Enlightenment, we feel we've evolved past rituals. However, if those who study myth are correct, these brief moments lead us to the collective experience during which we realize that, no matter what our Judeo-Christian heritage proclaims, enmity is not the true state of affairs. Separation is an illusion. We are part of the whole, and as part of that perfect unity we must view the world differently. Whatever is done to the part will affect the whole.

Native Americans have celebrated this harmony since the beginning. Such ceremony has ages of history behind it—history that connects a unique people to a specific place. The Salish and Kootenai have cultivated their alliance with the bitterroot and Camas Prairie for endless decades. The observance of this bond evokes powerful earth-memory. In *God Is Red,* Vine Deloria, Jr., discusses this union: "Thousands of years of occupancy on their lands taught tribal peoples the sacred landscapes for which they were responsible and gradually the structure of ceremonial reality became clear. It was not what the people believed to be true that was important but what they experienced to be true. Hence revelation was seen as a continuous process of adjustment to the natural surroundings."[7]

Native religion is not an abstract set of laws but a set of beliefs and rites fine-tuned to the rhythm of nature. This unity comes from ancestral dependence on the land, from living in the wind and weather and using the senses to embrace every seasonal nuance. Early Indians obtained their food, clothing, and shelter directly and exclusively from the elements of the earth. Such reliance is hard for us to imagine today.

Because of their religious heritage, whites seem to have a harder time nurturing this union. The legacy of the Judeo-Christian bible condemns the earth and dictates that humans take dominion over rather than revere it. Such emphasis is judicial and moral rather than celebratory and unifying. The white holy land is half a world away instead of on the soil where whites have endured for generations. Whites rely on a two-thousand-year-old rulebook to guide their footsteps rather than on revelation from the environment. No wonder many have a difficult time treating the land and others with respect. This mind-set of judgment and transcendence comes with a considerable price. To celebrate the type of connection native people enjoy through inheritance, whites have had to rely on nonreligious earth traditions. In the American West, they have instituted such ceremony when planting and harvesting or during events that bring the community together, such as county fairs and branding.

In May the ranchers of Camas Prairie congregate for their annual ritual of branding. Each family chooses a different day to perform the task so that they can help one another. It's farm country where, in *Land Circle,* Linda Hasselstrom claims, "neighbor is a verb."[8] Every person excels at a job—such as vaccinating, dehorning, castrating, or branding—and usually ends up performing the same work at all locations. Others help by chasing cattle and cooking. The children run after strays and watch the gates.

My parents and crew run their herd down into aging corrals from the same bitterroot hills used by the Salish. The calves are separated from the cows by an expert herder and gatekeeper. The herder singles out a pair from the riled-up bunch and heads them toward the gate. The gatekeeper stands behind the swinging wooden gate and pulls it open at just the right moment—after the mother runs by and before the calf does. When this works as intended, the calf passes through into a pen.

While growing up on the farm, I hated gatekeeping and wasn't any good at it, probably because I had a tendency to daydream, an activity my father insisted didn't mix well with much in life, especially branding. One spring when I held the gatekeeper's position a particularly wild cow was in the corral. She had decided, whatever the cost, that she was going into the calf pen. My job was to keep her out.

The female could smell my weakness. About the time I began to contemplate Paris in springtime, she got a running start and, with the force of a twelve-hundred-pound tidal wave, hit the swinging gate located two feet from my head. There were positive aspects to the incident: The manure on the other side of the corral was soft and I was relieved of my duties.

Once the cattle are separated, the calves are run down a long chute. They charge toward a small deceiving hole at the end of the tunnel and, as they try to jump through, are snatched midair. As the snatching device opens, the calf is conveniently pinned to its side and the aged ranchers descend to perform their assigned tasks. Within minutes the calf is "worked" and on its way.

Branding gives the stockmen a chance to take inventory of their herds. They know each cow's calving history and health record. The details help them decide whether it will be kept another year or culled out of the herd. The process is physically taxing for both rancher and animal and forces the cattle growers to reconsider the price paid for their independence.

Many times, land payments alone are more than profits can stand. The North American Free Trade Agreement (NAFTA) and the General Agreement on Tariff and Trade (GATT) have opened the borders of trade and, with beef streaming in from Canada and Mexico, have signaled a fifteen-cent-per-pound drop in price. Although over-the-counter meat costs have stayed relatively stable, U.S. ranchers receive substantially less for their cattle. The rugged lot lie awake at night, considering reasons to abandon the struggle Jeremy Rifkin has yet to imagine.

The small rancher is also pitted against the practical sterility of twentieth-century corporate agribusiness. In its churning path, the hand-to-the-plow fellow seems sorely anachronistic. Like the Camas Prairie Kalispel, the twentieth-century farmer participates in life's dialectic clash. The "progress" that has visited Indian culture now knocks at the rancher's door.

And yet, although reduced in numbers, the community remains strong. Ritual and land link them. As they gather, they discuss new farming techniques and ways in which they can prevent the their own extinction. In *The Solace of Open Spaces*, Gretel Ehrlich aptly describes the lifestyle:

> *Implicated as we westerners are in this sperm, blood, and guts business of ranching, and propelled forward by steady gusts of blizzards, cold fronts, droughts, heat, and wind, there's a ceremonial feel to life on a ranch. It's raw and impulsive but the narrative thread of birth, death, chores, and seasons keeps tugging at us until we find ourselves braided inextricably into the strand.*[9]

Also like their Native American counterparts, ranchers are connected to place—land that gives them identification. Much of modern society no longer enjoys such kinship. In the past century, most have moved off the soil and away from community onto asphalt and into clatter. What their grandparents, or even parents, experienced is completely foreign to them. Today, modern man is even deeper in "future shock" than when Alvin Toffler coined the phrase twenty-eight years ago.

Many placate this trauma with things, adopting the mantra of modernity—add on, use up, consume. Or they insulate themselves in more noise—against their own knowing. As William Kittredge claims in *Who Owns the West?*, "Isolate us from nature too long, as individuals, as societies, and we start getting nervous, crazy, unmoored, inhabited by diseases we cannot name, driven to thoughtless ambitions and easy cruelties."[10]

Although it is impossible for many to return to this existence, we need to cultivate ceremony of our own, to spend time in quiet and in nature, observing the seasons. We must teach our children to honor the earth through experience and then memory. In reviving our shriveled instincts, we will renew our alliance with the soil and one another. When we can hear the earth's voice again we will be capable of saving it from further neglect. Only by cultivating an attachment to the land and an understanding of its history, can we renew our relationship with it. Many in the West have enjoyed this liaison for centuries—a connection that has enabled them to adapt and survive.

Chapter 2

A Perfectly Preserved Fossil

*A*lthough human history on Camas Prairie is one of constant adjustment, the land remains unchanged. We know how the valley appeared in prehistoric times because, according to geologist David Alt, "It is a perfectly preserved fossil that looks almost exactly as it must have 2 to 3 million years ago."[1] The prairie's landscape is petrified because of its dryness. Water changes things, and because a river hasn't run through the place since the Pliocene era, the geology remains untouched by time.

Belt rock juts from the hillside—sharp, ancient, and ragged. It was pushed here when a series of slabs peeled off the earth's floor and shoved eastward to create the Rocky Mountains. These stones are part of the Prichard Formation and originated in the continental crust more than six billion years ago. They have seen the beginning of time and now stand as sentinels guarding the meadow basin.

Beneath the valley floor rests a deep accumulation of coal, limestone, and gravel. Ages ago, Montana resembled Death Valley. Without water to drain eroded sediment into the ocean, it collected in the state's lowlands. Adding to the thick dust, eruptions from the Cascade Mountains spewed volcanic ash into eastern winds and blanketed the Northwest. This collection, called the Renova Mass, runs thousands of feet deep on Camas Prairie and has also been undisturbed for millennia.

Glacial Lake Missoula. From David Alt, Roadside Geology of Montana *(Missoula: Mountain Press Publishing Co., 1986), p. 49.*

The valley's only major geologic change occurred fifteen thousand years ago with the advent of Lake Missoula. During the ice age, glaciers covered British Columbia and a cube twenty miles wide pushed south into Idaho's Lake Pend d'Oreille. The entire flow of the lake's tributary, the Clark Fork River, backed up behind the dam, creating a body of water five hundred cubic miles in capacity. It covered northwestern Montana from Noxon to Hamilton, with Camas Prairie centered in the heart of this phenomenon.

Eventually, because ice is lighter than liquid and does not constitute trustworthy dam material, the cube broke, rushing its contents with a spectacular two-thousand-foot-high torrent into the adjoining states. Boulders of ancient Montana belt rock have been found as far south and west as the Willamette Valley in Oregon. Once drained,

The giant ripples that encircle the valley are clearly seen during winter.

the ice dam created itself anew and Glacial Lake Missoula deepened. Geologists believe that in its one-thousand-year existence, as many as forty-one fillings and drainings occurred.

The hills of Camas Prairie hold the record of this ancient spectacle in giant waves of soil called "varves." As the floodwater poured west across the valley it scoured the hillside, dumping ripples of sediment thirty-five feet high and three hundred feet from crest to crest. Evidence of the churning catastrophe rests embedded in the calm, scar-faced hills. Horizontal shorelines ring the valley in perfect circles.

As a child, I remember buses filled with sober archaeologists braving a long field trip from the University of Montana. They'd politely file out of the vehicles to take pictures and confer. Later we'd receive their articles stating that the event was "beyond any doubt the greatest flood catastrophe of which we have certain knowledge." All I knew was that when it snowed, huge bathtub rings appeared around the hillsides. The archaeologists' reports made me wonder if the ancient flood was why we struggled to grow things; we'd given our good soil to Oregon.

After the ice age cleared, around 10,000 B.C., the land dried out and the Salish journeyed into Montana. However, they claim that they were not the first human beings on Camas Prairie. When they arrived, a group they called the "Foolish Folk" already inhabited the valley. Anthropologist James Teit named them the Semte'use.[2]

The Foolish Folk had short, muscular bodies and darker skin than the Salish. They had bowlegs and flat feet that made them poor runners. The little people didn't wear clothing and dwelled in underground huts. The Salish, along with other Montana tribes, intensely disliked them, claiming they were stupid and cruel beyond comprehension. In 1915 an old Indian told Teit the story of one such instance.

Not far from Camas Prairie three Semte'use brothers went hunting. They soon happened upon a tree that had been hollowed out by a recent forest fire. Seeing live coals at the end of the stump, one brother said, "I will now smoke and will crawl up this burnt log and light my pipe from the embers at the other end." When the squatty man wedged himself into the opening and blew onto the coals, the entire stump ignited and he was trapped inside. Instead of saving their brother, which they easily could have done, the others laughed uproariously at the sounds he made while he burned to death. Still chuckling about their adventure, they reported the incident to his wife, telling her he had "roasted himself beautifully." When, in a storm of tears, she refused to be consoled, they comforted her by suggesting she marry one of them because they all had larger private parts than her deceased husband.

The Salish cited instances like these to illustrate the meanness of the tribe. They claimed the Foolish Folks' only redeeming quality was their fearlessness. The little people were great warriors and never retreated, even from the gravest of danger. It was this recklessness, however, along with their witlessness, that eventually caused the Semte'use to die off. The Salish were glad to see them go, as well as the tiny horses they didn't ride—but ate.

Anthropologists don't know where the Semte'use came from, but they do have a clearer picture of Salish origin. Linguistic evidence indicates the Salish migrated from Canada after Athabascans pushed into their territory thousands of years before Christ. The disbursement sent the Snohomish, Skagit, and more than twenty other Salishan tribes to the West Coast. The Kalispel, Pend d'Oreille, and Flathead moved east into Montana. The Salish people parted as friends and soon established vigorous trade relations. The coastal Salish bartered shells and sea products to their interior cousins for tule baskets and dried bitterroot.

A trail passing through Camas Prairie connected the exchange route. North, the road led to the Clark Fork River, which served as a major thoroughfare onto the Columbia Plateau and to the West Coast. The trail led south to the Flathead River and onto the Great Plains. This

A 1910 Edward Curtis photo of the sturgeon-nosed canoes of the Kalispel. Courtesy of the Special Collections Division, University of Washington Library.

passageway also facilitated trade with other tribes. The Salish obtained salmon products and painted leather from the Thompsons in Washington, watertight bags and baskets from the Nez Perce in Idaho, and, during times of truce, pipestone pottery from the Alberta Blackfeet.

Along a tributary of the Clark Fork, several miles from Camas Prairie, Edward Lozeau discovered an ancient burial site. The fossilized skeleton there was adorned with virgin copper beads of great antiquity. These beads were of high purity, indicating they originated outside the area because copper can be found in Montana only in ore form. Next to the skeleton lay an abalone shell earring, and around its neck lay a dentalium necklace—both deep-sea materials of coastal origin. The grave also contained arrowheads believed to have originated in the Yakima Valley or at Port Hammond in British Columbia.[3]

The ancient Kalispel traded with their cousins and neighbors throughout the Northwest but possessed a distinct territory. Because the land acknowledged as their domain ran from Lake Pend d'Oreille down the Clark Fork and they fished and traveled these waters in canoelike boats, they were known as "canoe people." The boats built by the Kalispel possessed bodies of white pine bark and ribs of cedar, sewn together with black pine roots. The builders fashioned the ends into low snouts. These "sturgeon-nosed" canoes allowed paddlers better visibility and greater control in high winds.

The Kalispel traveled and fished in these sturdy vessels. Using dip nets made from hemp or three-pronged spears called "leisters," they caught whitefish and trout on the Clark Fork and brought them back to the prairie in woven tule bags.

The women braided these tule bags, as well as willow and birch bark baskets and mats. They tightly secured their woven articles with sinew thread made from the backs of elk and deer and painted them with geometric squares of red and blue. In addition to weaving, the women also dressed animal skins, made clothing, and constructed and erected longhouses.

The conical longhouse was the common shelter for Kalispel families. Women owned the dwellings and congregated to help one another construct them. To prepare the foundation, they dug soil away from the earth in a long, shallow rectangle. A foot inside the foundation and running parallel down the length of the opening, they tamped two rows of ten-foot lodge poles into the ground. Inside these lines they inserted another row of poles fifteen feet high. To these they attached a row of braces, forming rafters. Next they secured poles to the outside perimeter and propped them against the ten- and fifteen-foot poles, giving the structure a lean-to appearance.

The women covered such shelters with bullrush mats constructed by laying cattails on the ground in parallel bunches, with the lower end of one bunch next to the upper tip of the next. Using the twine technique of basketry, they weaved silver berry branches or sinew thread through the cattails. Once secured, these mats were sturdy and waterproof. The woman arranged and overlapped them horizontally to cover the longhouse, with a gap at the top for a smoke hole. They made the dwellings draft-tight by laying brush around their bases and banking them with dirt. Three to four families could live inside one of these roomy lodges.

Women also gathered the vegetable foods. They collected leaves, mosses, nuts, and the inner bark of trees in the wooded southern hills of Camas Prairie and roots and berries in the meadows.[4] The vegetable food list of the Kalispel tribe included more than fifteen hundred items and comprised fifty percent of its diet.

Leaves, such as those from the Oregon grape plant, were eaten or boiled into a tea to alleviate kidney and stomach troubles and reduce fevers. In modern times, pharmacists have discovered that Oregon grape is rich in a bitter alkaloid called berberine. This chemical contains antiseptic and antibacterial properties that are acknowledged for their healing abilities.

The Kalispel also smoked leaves. They dried leaves of the kinnikinnick plant into a sweet tobacco. In *Native Plants and Early Peoples*, Camas Prairie Kalispel John Pelkoe recalled the ancient process: "The best way

Black Tree Lichen (Alectora fremontii Tuck). *Botanical illustration courtesy of Jacqueline Moore.*

to prepare the kinnikinnick leaves is to hang them up in the sweat house. When the heat dries the leaves you take them out in the open and squeeze them."[5] This reduces the plant into a coarse powder. Because kinnikinnick did not burn easily, the Kalispel mixed it with ground-up dogwood or willow bark and the roots of false hellebore and sweet cicely.

The Salish gathered black tree lichen from the mountain conifers surrounding the valley. Baking transformed the dark hairlike growth into a sweet, gelatinous mass. Processing was begun by cleaning and soaking the lichen in water, then baking it for several days in underground fire pits in the same manner as, or along with, camas. Once the lichen was reduced to a jelly, it was eaten or sundried into a powder. In winter, women prepared it with dried camas, adding water and boiling the mixture into a thick mush. The Salish considered tree lichen more a treat than a staple, and each family consumed about twenty-five pounds a year.

The women collected seeds from the buffaloberry plant by thrashing the nutlike fruit off its branches onto deer hides. They cleaned and placed this bounty into a water-filled container. Using a special whipping stick made of grass, they then beat the berries into a frothy mixture the tribe considered a great treat. Wild sunflower seeds were also collected, which were dried and powdered. In winter, boiling water was added to the material to create gruel.

Although many native peoples ate tree bark, the Salish apparently relished it more than most. They gathered it until 1910 when the reservation opened to white settlement and Indian agents discouraged the practice because it was deemed injurious to commercial species of timber. The tribe's favorite bark was that of the cottonwood tree. It held the sweetest inner bark of any they gathered. To peel it, they used tools made from the ribs of elk. After they stripped one side of the tree—leaving the other so as not to harm the plant—they hollowed out a passageway through which to collect the sap. In addition, cottonwood leaves were useful for making infection-drawing poultices and tea for treating colds, and cottonwood itself was an excellent, clean-burning firewood for enclosed lodges.

Ponderosa pine provided a pleasant-tasting inner bark. The women pulled it from trees in May when the sap flowed abundantly. They used a chisel-like instrument made of flattened juniper that was strong and limber enough to follow the curve of a trunk without breaking. Peeling long strips of ponderosa pine required great strength and stamina, characteristics the small but sturdy women possessed. They rolled the tender bark into balls and packed it in green leaves to prevent drying.

They used ponderosa pine for medicine as well. Camas Prairie Indian Mitch Small Salmon claimed that by placing heated pine needles on the abdomen of a laboring mother, the baby emerged more quickly. Probably learning from the Indians, Lewis and Clark also used the tree for healing. On June 5, 1806, Lewis wrote in his journal, "I applied a plaster of salve made of resin of the long leafed pine, bees wax and bear's oil mixed, which has subsided the inflammation entirely."[6] Larch, quaking aspen, and lodgepole pine are other trees that provided the tribe with valuable medicines and tasty barks and saps.

The main root foods on Camas Prairie were bitterroot and camas, and the native fruits were chokecherries, huckleberries, and serviceberries. To prepare these latter foods for storage, the Salish mashed the berries on a flat rock and pressed them into patties. They also created puddings and cakes from the berries or added them to meat stews, and boiled chokecherries into a delicious broth. Chokecherries possessed great medicinal qualities as well. When Meriwether Lewis became ill with abdominal cramps, he brewed a tea made from chokecherry twigs and recovered by the next day. Resin from the plant's bark healed eye sores and burns. Kalispel women spent much time gathering these plants for food and medicine.

Along with this time-consuming job, women also made the tribe's clothing. For fathers and husbands, they constructed fringed leather shirts and long leggings, breechcloths, and moccasins. For themselves they made simple, elegant shifts and decorated the bodices with porcupine quills, elk teeth, and hawk feathers. They painted their dresses in blues, reds, and yellows—or tanned them into pure white. Each woman had several outfits, which she regularly cleaned with pipe clay.

The male tribal members made weapons and tools, painted robes and shields, and obtained the meat supply. To hunt game, they used sinew-backed bows made of syringa wood or—for a shorter, more powerful bow—the horns of mountain sheep. With these weapons they hunted the deer, antelope, moose, bear, and caribou that populated the valley's mountainside. Once an animal was killed, its eyes were closed and it was honored for the sacrifice it had made to feed the tribe. Further, children were never allowed to make fun of any part of an animal. The Indians prevented such behavior because they believed it might offend the animal's spirit and that future hunts could be spoiled.

The Kalispel believed that the grizzly's spiritual strength was equal to its physical might, so before stalking grizzly bear in the nearby Mission Mountains, the hunter observed special rites. After preparing himself with prayers and a sweat bath, the hunter announced his intention to the village. So that he might not be bitten, his wife fasted during his absence. After the kill, the hunter talked with the bear, calling it "Grandfather" and thanking it for its sacrifice. In honor of the animal, he was careful never to break the bear's bones during butchering or cooking.

Both men and women worked hard. In 1811 fur trapper Ross Cox wrote that the Salish were industrious people and that "laziness was a stranger to them." He described their physical appearance as "rather slender and remarkably well made. Both sexes are comparatively fair, and their complexions are a shade lighter than the palest new copper. They are honest in their dealings, brave in the field, quiet and amenable to their chiefs, and fond of cleanliness."[7]

Rocky Mountain Juniper (juniperus scopulorum Sarg.). *Botanical illustration courtesy of Jacqueline Moore.*

The Indians washed their hair with honeysuckle and made perfumes and insect repellents from the prairie's abundant native grasses. They crushed yarrow and meadow rue seeds into an aromatic powder and folded it into their clothes or rubbed it onto their skin. They stuffed their pillows with sweet-smelling pineapple weed and hung fur boughs or mint leaves in their lodges.

Scents also held meaning in religious ceremonies. To welcome benevolent powers and bring blessings, the Salish burned sweet grass, fir, and juniper. Because juniper branches were strong and flexible and remained green and fragrant year-round, the Indians believed that Great Spirit had blessed the plant with eternal youthfulness. Therefore, they placed it centrally in many of their purification rites.

Colors, as well as smells, were important. Alder bark created red dye, Oregon grape root and pine moss colored items yellow, and black came from charcoal. Buds from cottonwood trees produced red, green, yellow, purple, or white dyes.

The Salish wore bright, neat clothing and enjoyed times of lighthearted teasing and lovemaking. Although not promiscuous (in *The Columbia River,* Cox also wrote that the women were "excellent wives and mothers, and their character for fidelity is so well established, that we never heard an instance of one proving unfaithful to her husband"),[8] they viewed sexual passion as natural and enjoyable. The journals of fur traders who took Indian wives tell of the delightful companions they made. Salish women were completely loyal yet hardly boring. Their lovemaking was skillful and varied—sometimes downright ingenious.

At night, when the tribe gathered around the campfire to play games or tell tales, the woods began to echo with the calls of young men beckoning their sweethearts to leave the fire and join them. Each couple had a special signal. Sometimes it was a whoop or a cry (the Salish word for the call shares the same linguistic root as "war cry"); other times it was the sound made by blowing a whistle made from the bone of a bird or by using both hands to form a sound box and blowing through bent thumbs.

The tribe celebrated sexual passion but did not look kindly upon adultery. Once a couple married, they were to remain faithful or seek divorce. Under law an offended husband could kill his wife or her lover or destroy his rival's property and the offender's family could not intervene.

As with most other offenses, the Salish council oversaw discipline. When a matter needed to be addressed, the august group painted their faces and assembled in a circle. They wrapped themselves in their robes, thrust their honor sticks into the ground next to them, and discussed the issue at hand. A council was called a "talking" and the location a "talking place." Once the group reached a decision, the chief pronounced the verdict. In council, the chief wore a bonnet of feathers or a red sash and held a whipping stick that could enact punishment. Most times, however, a stern verbal reprimand was all the offender needed.

Although the chief acted as judge, his primary role was one of father (his name pˑgˑt denoted parental guardianship). The people showed him great respect and were taught from infancy to honor and obey him. In return, he was responsible for acting with modesty and temperance and never speaking in a loud voice, quarreling, or showing anger or jealousy. The chief's wife was expected to act in a quiet, dignified, and hospitable manner and never to disgrace her husband.

Each hereditary chief led his band, a subdivision of the larger tribe. Socially, bands were held together by blood and dialect—emotionally, by tradition and storytelling. Stories instructed the people and warned them of danger. Coyote's adventures held lessons in both—like the tale of his interaction with Rattlesnake.[9]

Long ago, Coyote, the Imitator, who loved to play games and have contests, came across Rattlesnake. Coyote especially enjoyed challenging animals who were smaller than he, and the skinny creature seemed a good candidate. When Coyote approached Rattler, the snake's black tongue darted out of his mouth.

Coyote laughed. "Rattlesnake, is that your tongue? It looks like nothing more than a dead piece of grass." Coyote hung his big, pink tongue from his mouth and said, "Now, this is a tongue."

Rattler spoke not a word but raised his tail and shook it— wwhhhrr!

Coyote howled with glee. "Is that all the sound you can make? Just listen to this!" Coyote threw his head back and howled to the wind. "Now, that is music," he mocked. Coyote, feeling quite superior to the small reptile, tossed dirt in Rattlesnake's face. Rattlesnake arched his back and opened his mouth. When Coyote saw Rattler's two fangs he shouted uproariously, "See what a fine set of teeth I have!"

Rattler remained silent, slowly coiling into a circle.

Confident in his evident physical superiority, Coyote decided to get a meal out of the adventure and said, "Let's play a game. We'll bite each other and see which one hurts the most." Rattler followed the dog with his beady eyes.

"What's the matter, Rattlesnake?" Coyote taunted. "Don't you like games? Let me show you how much fun they can be!" And he jumped forward and bit Rattler in the middle of his body. The snake whipped around and sunk his long fangs into Coyote's shoulder.

"Yipe!" Coyote jumped back. That hurt more than he thought it would. Shaken but still confident, he laid down under a nearby bush to wait for the intense ache to subside. After all, Snake had only two teeth.

When the sun set and the air cooled, Rattler slithered away,
but for three days Coyote lay racked with pain under the bush.
Coyote recovered from his snakebite. However, he never again
offered to play games with Rattlesnake.

Tales like these not only reveal Salish wisdom but also convince anthropologists that the tribe has occupied northwestern Montana since prehistoric times. The anthropologists argue that myths are centuries old, indicating the location of a people at least that far back. Also, Kalispel myths do not include migration stories or speak of animals outside the region. For instance, they rarely mention the buffalo or salmon except to explain why they did not inhabit their land. Indigenous animals such as the rattlesnake, coyote, beaver, and blue jay dominate their storytelling.

The Blue Jay Dance also is unique to western Montana. Once a year, generally the week after the turn of the year, the Blue Jay Ceremony was held. By January, winter had drawn upon the people's store of light, and the ceremony was performed to renew their strength. The Salish assembled, cleared a chosen area, and constructed a medicine lodge. Several days prior to the ceremony, the shamans gathered and began purifying themselves. They baked in the sweat house, abstaining from food and drink, and implored Blue Jay to reveal himself. Once the ceremony began, the people abstained from eating and congregated in the medicine lodge. The shamans dressed only in breechcloths, blackened their faces entirely with charcoal, and danced down the center of the lodge. The tribe, doing their utmost to increase the shamans' hysteria, encircled them while singing and shaking deer-hoof rattles.

The tribe danced all evening and, although overtaken with exhaustion, were not allowed to rest or sleep without the holy men's permission. On the second night the sick were laid before the shamans. By this time Blue Jay's magic was strong and the holy men began to perform cures. The dancing continued into the night until the elders suddenly extinguished the fires burning down the length of the medicine lodge. Then the shamans became completely possessed with Blue Jay and began to "go wild." They began to speak in the bird's tongue, chirping and talking backward. Certain onlookers were delegated to remember their words, which were later interpreted as prophecies. No one touched the medicine men while they were in trance because the magic they emitted was so strong that any contact caused the toucher to faint. The shamans agilely ascended the lodge poles, chirping and cawing. They ran along the narrow rafters with the grace of Blue Jay. While seized with the bird's spirit, they tried to escape the lodge. Even though every effort was made to keep them inside, some fled into the night. Swift runners followed them because, overcome by Blue Jay, they could disappear into the surrounding hills and die eventually of starvation and the medicine power of Blue Jay.

In the morning, the people collected the shamans from the lodge and took them down from the trees they perched in. To smoke out Blue Jay's spirit, they held the shamans over a fire of burning sweet grass and gave them drinks of holy water, which returned them to human consciousness. The Blue Jay Ceremony renewed the people and, following the rite, the medicine men's healing abilities were especially strong.

This powerful medicine allowed the shamans to perform other miraculous feats, such as riding with impunity into enemy fire and, as long as they chanted their spirit songs, emerging untouched. Some carried searing rocks by hand from the fire to the sweat house without being burned. Others walked across the thinly iced Clark Fork River without breaking through—leaving tracks as proof of the accomplishment.

Each medicine man was a specialist. A seer could pierce the veil of space. He could tell where herds of buffalo grazed, observe the approach of the enemy, or predict the outcome of future battles. One shaman's medicine was so strong, the Blackfeet refused to attack or even spy on a camp where he dwelled. They believed he could journey to listen in on even their most secret councils.

Other shamans were healers. These experts sucked illness out of their patients and blew it out of affected body parts while uttering incantations, shaking rattles, and chanting. Sometimes they wore elaborate costumes; other times they performed stripped to breechcloths. They often colored their faces to match the spirit animals that gave them their shamanistic gifts. In later years, such shamans claimed that the whites' interference had weakened their power, and they insisted that nothing of white manufacture be allowed around them while they officiated at a ceremony.

They also worked as herb doctors, prescribing agrimony for sore throats and yarrow tea for colds. They used wormwood to reduce the swelling of injuries and kinnikinnick leaves to promote the healing of burns. They covered sores with herbs, dung, pitch, or mud poultices and inserted a woodpecker's beak or rattlesnake fangs into infected gums and decaying teeth (or simply pried out rotten teeth).

The people also diagnosed themselves. They chewed the dried roots of lovage for relief from headaches and toothaches or made salves from lovage for earaches. They also boiled it and inhaled the steam for sinus infections and congestion. For seizures, Camas Prairie medicine woman Sophie Adams claimed the Salish chewed the root and rubbed it on the ailing person's body. Lovage's curative powers were famous among Montana Indians. Because it did not grow in the eastern part of the state, Cree and Crow tribes eagerly sought it in trade.

The Salish distilled biscuit root into a soothing lotion and heated yellow pond lily and bathed in it to ease rheumatism. A hot horsetail poultice relieved bladder and prostate pain, and yarrow leaves doubled as a disinfectant and blood clotting agent. Alumroot alleviated the diarrhea occasionally occured the tribe in the summer from eating so many vegetable foods.

Anthropologists believe that for thousands of years the Salish thrived on their diet, stayed robust from their herbal cures, and lived in peace. Then in the 1700s, Salish life changed dramatically. The tribe obtained modern horses and came into contact with foreign diseases. From then on, adaptation and change would be the norm— even until today.

The horse began its journey northward in the early 1600s when Navajos and Apaches raided Spanish ranches in New Mexico and seized their first horses. In 1680 the migration accelerated during the Pueblo revolt. After driving the Spanish out of New Mexico, rebels

The northward spread of the horse in the western United States. Lines indicate the approximate routes followed by horses and the approximate dates the horses reached each area. From Francis Hanies, "The Northwest Spread of Horses Among the Plains Indians," American Anthropologist, Menasha, Wisc., 1938, vol. 40, p. 430.

captured thousands of horses and traded them to Plains Indians. The migration of the animals followed the Santa Fe River to the Snake River and proceeded up the headwaters of the Colorado, Grand, and Green Rivers. Along this pathway the Navajos and Apaches traded the horses to the Utes, who sold them to the Shoshones of southern Idaho. The Utes, Comanches, and Shoshones, all of the same linguistic stock, formed a chain of commerce from New Mexico to Montana. From this line of trade, the Flathead tribe obtained the animal around 1730.

The Kalispel obtained the modern horse through their Flathead cousins and saw their first when a Flathead—proudly perched on top of his mount and smoking a pipe—loped down the banks of the Clark Fork River. The Indian crossed the river and the Kalispel gathered around to marvel at the strange creature. Initially, having no word for the beasts, the Kalispel called them "big dogs." The horse's influence accelerated the pace and extended the economic range of Salish life. The Kalispel began to congregate with the Flathead, Pend d'Oreille, and Kootenai and ventured onto the eastern Montana plains to hunt buffalo.[10]

By 1740 the Alberta Blackfeet had obtained horses from the Shoshone, as well as guns from Canadian fur traders. Once the aggressive Blackfeet had both, they pushed down onto the central plains and into buffalo country. Because the Flathead already occupied the territory, the Blackfeet waged war on the tribe. Although the Flathead were fearless fighters, the Canadian Indians outnumbered them eight to one, with firearms adding to the Blackfeet advantage.

The Blackfeet hid behind bushes and trees and picked off the Flathead. This kind of warfare made them impossible to repel. During hand-to-hand combat Salish warriors triumphed, but the Blackfeet always returned in waves, carrying guns. A century later in 1833, the Flathead recounted their movement off the plains to trapper Warren Ferris. Their chief, Big Face, gathered the tribe and announced that they would flee north to the Rockies. "Let us seek the mountains' deepest recesses where unknown to our destroyers, we may hunt the deer and bighorn and bring gladness back to the hearts of our wives and children."[11] The tribe moved to their northernwestern most territory in the Bitterroot Valley, near present-day Missoula.

The Blackfeet pursued all of the Plains Indians, forcing the Flathead north and west, the Crow west, and the Shoshone and Bannock south. Soon the old system of geographically localized bands ended and tribes grouped together for protection. Campsites dating before the acquisition of the horse are small, spread out, and numerous. Those dating after the mid-1700s are larger and less frequent.[12] Now that they lived in close proximity, the Kalispel, Pend d'Oreille, and Flathead began to intermarry, and their bloodlines and cultures reunite. Whites, arriving eighty years later, often grouped the Kalispel with the Pend d'Oreille and at times classified all three tribes merely as "Flathead."

In the 1700s, deaths from disease added to those from war. Even before the Salish saw a European, the whites' illnesses reached the tribe through neighboring Crow and Shoshone. In the 1760s and again in the 1780s, a smallpox epidemic spread among Plateau Indians. Men returning home from the buffalo hunt found tents filled with the dead bodies of women, children, and the elderly. The Salish's traditional cures of heavy sweating followed by diving into cold water raised the grisly toll. It is estimated that smallpox had cut the tribe's population in half by the beginning of the 1800s.

By the late 1700s, the Blackfeet dominated the Montana plains. They attempted to deny western Indians access to buffalo country by guarding the entrances of commonly used mountain passes. However, although sorely outnumbered, the Flathead insisted on their hereditary right to hunt bison and, accompanied by their Kalispel and Pend d'Oreille relatives, bravely crossed the mountains to the east.

South of Camas Prairie, in the foothills of the Rockies, exists a canyon called Hellgate. The Salish used this ravine as a passageway into buffalo country. French trappers named the place "The Gate of Hell" because so many Salish and Kootenai bones from Blackfeet ambushes were littered there.

Before long, the Blackfeet aggressors were not content to stay on the plains and began to raid Salish territory to steal horses. In 1858 George Stuckly wrote that for more than one hundred years in Northwestern Montana, "murders the most brutal, and robberies the most bold and daring have been committed. The word 'Blackfoot' has become the by-word of terror and fear among all the tribes of Indians west of the Rocky Mountains. The Flathead have been so greatly diminished by being murdered by the Blackfeet that at the present there remains but a handful of the noblest of the Indian tribes of North America."[13]

The introduction of the horse spurred this conflict and also initiated a new tribal hierarchy. A man rich in horses became wealthy in material goods. He could obtain a large supply of meat and trade it for other products. Some men took several wives, who then accompanied them onto the plains to skin and butcher the buffalo they killed.

In addition to social and economic change, the horse also brought changes in travel and hunting conditions, and two major bison hunts were conducted each year, one in spring and one in fall. Once the tribe arrived in buffalo country, they chose a campsite in a treed area

A 1910 Edward Curtis photo of a Montana Salish child using a buffalo horn as a cup. Courtesy of the Special Collections Division, University of Washington Library.

near a cliff. The group then erected and hid within the trees a V-shaped pen with its narrow end opening over the precipice.

Once constructed, the group elected a "Grand Master" or "Lord of the Pen." This man, who had great experience with the spirit world, soon consulted the spirits to locate the animals and determine the crucial moment of the drive. The Lord of the Pen made a medicine mast, consisting of a scarlet-colored cloth, a piece of kinnikinnick, and a buffalo horn. He placed the charm at the center of the fenced area. Its magic was used to call the animals to their doom.

On a designated morning, the Lord of the Pen awoke the sleeping camp with the beating of his drum and the chanting of incantations. He provided four swift runners with a *wahon,* a medicine ball made of skin and stuffed with hair, and sent them toward the browsing buffalo. Once the runners located the herd and the perfect time arrived—when the wind blew away from the pen and the herd grazed in a favorable position—one of the runners sped back, handing the ball to the Grand Master and proclaiming the joyful news.

The *wahon*'s delivery prompted a mighty beating of the Lord of the Pen's drum, which, in return, emptied the encampment tents. Excitedly, the people mounted their horses and took their positions along the camouflaged fence. A single warrior enveloped in a bison robe approached the herd. Once among the sea of beasts, he sounded the distress call of a baby buffalo. Slowly the herd advanced toward him. He re-echoed the call as they followed him, increasing their speed from a trot to a gallop. Soon they looked like a swelling black wave as the brave Indian, still covered in buffalo skins, ran for his life. Once inside the pen, the horsemen, and those waiting on foot, closed in around the wild herd, shouting, throwing rocks, and shooting arrows. Picking up the sight and smell of the Indians, the bison panicked. The Salish hoped the beasts' forward momentum would continue and drive them over the cliff. If all went well, hundreds would fall to their deaths.

After the kill, the women quickly cut and packed the meat. They considered the tongue, hump, thighs, and bone marrow the greatest delicacies. Some meat was immediately eaten raw. To keep the rest preserved, and repel insects, they put it in hide bags with wild bergamot, peppermint, and pineapple weed. Once in camp they cut it into long strips and dried it over a slow fire to make jerky. The intestines were cleaned and turned inside out to save the outer coating of fat. With a stone ax the women pulverized the vertebrae for use in soups and boiled the bones, collecting the rich grease that rose to the surface. They stored this fat in the stomach or, after a portion of the meat had been roasted and pounded into a coarse powder, poured the grease over it. To this mixture they added dried fruit, making a nutritious food called pemmican. They packed this staple into skin bags that kept it fresh for long periods of time.

The Salish used the buffalo for more than meat. Bison horns served as cups and shoulder blades as hoes and spades. The placenta was utilized to hold paints. They made sinew from the bison's hind legs into thread. Bones became sharp awls that could puncture holes in tough hides, making it possible to sew them into clothing.

The women softened these hides by scraping and rubbing compounds of animal brains and sagebrush into them. Skins taken in the late fall, when the bison's fur was long and luxuriant, made robes. Spring skins had less hair and were easier to scrape clean, so the Indians used them for tepees and clothing. The thick neck skin—the toughest part of the animal—was stretched around stumps to create buckets and pots. The women also cut the neck skin into wide strips, which they wrapped around trees and pounded with stone hammers into flexible, sturdy ropes. Bison flesh made an almost impenetrable shield. Upon shield surfaces, natives painted records of chases, kills, and mystical experiences.

The horse brought this nomadic buffalo culture to the Kalispel of Camas Prairie. It also changed the tribe's daily work routine. Now they spent hours guarding and caretaking their steeds. Because the valley's rich grassland and open pastures, naturally enclosed by rugged mountains, provided a perfect breeding ground, Camas Prairie became home for thousands of wild horses. Its endless meadows and those of the adjacent Wild Horse Plains became famous for their exquisite herds.

The Kalispel rode their horses bareback or with saddles of simple skin pads stuffed with grass or hair. They constructed harness bits from strips of hide or rope that they tied under the animals' jaws. The women used saddles with high pommels and cantles that reflected the Moorish-Spanish-Shoshone influence.

As the horse's importance to the tribe increased, it became a major participant in Salish celebrations. The women ornamented horse saddles with long strips of beaded skins and made stirrups of bent wood or mountain sheep horns covered with embroidery. For parades, they painted the animals' bodies and dressed them with beaded headbands and breastplates, and they adorned exceptionally brave horses with headdresses of eagle feathers. The Salish believed that the horse's tail revealed much about its character. A thin tail meant that it would be unreliable and weak. A full, strong tail brought honor. The Native Americans elaborately braided and decorated their horses' tails for each celebration.

In addition to affecting the tribe's social structure, the horse also changed the ecological balance of the land. For one thing, the mount made it possible to kill more game, and some local species became scarce as a result. Faster travel widened the tribe's trade routes and allowed the Salish to obtain flint, chalcedony, and jasper from the eastern Montana Crows, materials from which they made weapons with harder, sharper points, further enhancing the success of the hunt.

As trips onto the plains increased, the Kalispel relied more on the bison, and the culture of the nomadic hunter soon usurped that of the fisherman. They replaced their tule longhouses with buffalo-skin tepees. Although heavy, the tepee transported easily on the horse caravan, which could move thirty miles a day. In contrast to the relatively stationary longhouse of earlier times, the rawhide tepee could be erected and taken down quickly (in about fifteen minutes), thereby serving the needs of the hunt more efficiently.

Within one hundred years of the horse's introduction, not only the Salish but all of Montana's native peoples had undergone substantial change. The horse allowed greater mobility and affected trade routes, hunting practices, social traditions, populations, and even geographic locations. Camas Prairie's people were in flux, and this transformation would only continue. By the start of the 1800s, another challenge darkened the horizon: whites were making their way toward the isolated valley.

Chapter 3

The Fur Trade

xplorer David Thompson was the first white man on Camas Prairie.
In 1807 the Canadian Northwest Trade Company commissioned
him to map the Columbia River Basin. The trading company feared
Yankee trappers would follow the explorers and, hoping to exploit
the area before the United States rooted there, sent its most expert
cartographer to map the region and establish trading posts. Thompson
did so immediately after Lewis and Clark completed their successful
journey to the Pacific. Thompson had begun his trading career twenty-
three years earlier in the employ of the Hudson's Bay Company. At
the age of fourteen he had been hired as an apprentice and sailed
from England to Canada to work for the oldest, most prestigious
company on the American continent.

In 1670 Britain's King Charles II granted a charter to Hudson's
Bay with the exclusive right to establish trading factories on the shores
of Hudson Bay and its tributaries. For one hundred years the company
dominated an area of more than three million square miles. The
Hudson's Bay Company hesitated to exploit the interior of the continent, however. Before the 1760s, France ruled there and controlled a
vigorous fur trade around the Great Lakes. Even after the French
relinquished Canada to England in 1763, the company did not move
aggressively west.

Then in 1784, an enterprising group of traders formed a union to challenge the Hudson's Bay Company by conducting business differently. While employees of Hudson's Bay were controlled by a board of British elite living in London, members of the Northwest Trade Company held direct shares, determined company policy, and oversaw the trade themselves. After a successful apprenticeship, clerks who hired on could even become partners. This incentive prodded the aggressive company to push farther into uncharted territory and enterprising young men such as David Thompson to join them.

In addition to the companies' differences, however, they shared similarities. In both, the leadership themselves did not trap furs. Although Northwest Company owners traveled into the interior, most remained stationary once they arrived at their posts. They provided guidance, kept the books, and hired the French and Iroquois Indians to handle the boats and do the trapping. Once the trappers acquired a number of pelts, they brought them to the Canadian trading posts and received $1 apiece for them. The Canadians, in turn, sold the pelts for $10.

In 1797, after a successful career with Hudson's Bay, Thompson switched allegiance to the Northwest Trade Company, which soon sent him to explore the interior, map its geography, and determine the exact location of its newly established trading posts. On August 7, Thompson set out with the fur brigades from Grand Portage, Canada. Equipped with a sextant of ten-inch radius, two telescopes, a compass, drawing instruments, and two thermometers, he would become what many believe to be "the greatest geographer in the history of North America."[1]

During Thompson's first ten months, including the most difficult seasons of the year, he surveyed more than four thousand miles of uncharted territory. Northwest Company partner Alexander Mackenzie acknowledged Thompson's work by stating that he had accomplished more in several months than the company had expected in two years.[2] Thompson's discoveries had only begun. For nine years he explored the Canadian frontier. He built a trading post on Lake LaBiche and recorded amazingly accurate and detailed maps, surveys, and astronomical observations throughout the region.

In the westernmost Athabascan district, Thompson built a trading post and explored the Athabasca River. In the spring of 1799, he journeyed south to deliver his stash of furs at Ile a la Crosse. There he met a Cree girl named Charlotte Small. Charlotte was the daughter of Patrick Small, one of the original Northwest Company partners. After living and trading at Ile a la Crosse for several years, Small had returned to England, leaving his Indian wife and child behind—a practice not uncommon.

On June 10, 1799, Thompson and Charlotte were married. She was not yet fourteen; he was twenty-nine. About his new wife he wrote, "My lovely wife is of the blood of these people, speaking their language, and well educated in the English language, which gives me a great advantage."[3] Over the years he and Charlotte had thirteen children. The family remained together whenever possible, living at remote trading posts or traveling. On his trip south into the rugged Oregon Territory, however, Charlotte and the children did not follow.

In 1807 the company sent Thompson to explore the region coveted by both Britain and the United States. The idea was genius. Because of the posts Thompson constructed, the company successfully outflanked the Americans in the Pacific interior fur business. Salish House, built on the Clark Fork River just north of Camas Prairie, gave the British a trading stronghold that they retained, despite U.S. competition, until after their withdrawal from the United States in 1871.[4]

This ascendancy gave the Canadians access to a huge quantity of furs as well as products indispensable to operating the trade: dressed buffalo skins, parfleches, dried meat, pemmican, and tallow, the latter required to supply the brigades that followed. Salish House became Canada's line against the advance of U.S. trade into the region. David Thompson and his men made this dominance possible.

Within months of his departure in 1807, Thompson discovered the source of the Columbia River. In 1808 he and his companions moved down its tributary, the Kootenai, and established Kootenai House. Next, they cut toward Lake Pend d'Oreille. Here, at the mouth of the Clark Fork, the Salish eagerly awaited them. Thompson supplied the tribe with firearms and iron-tipped arrowheads, which some

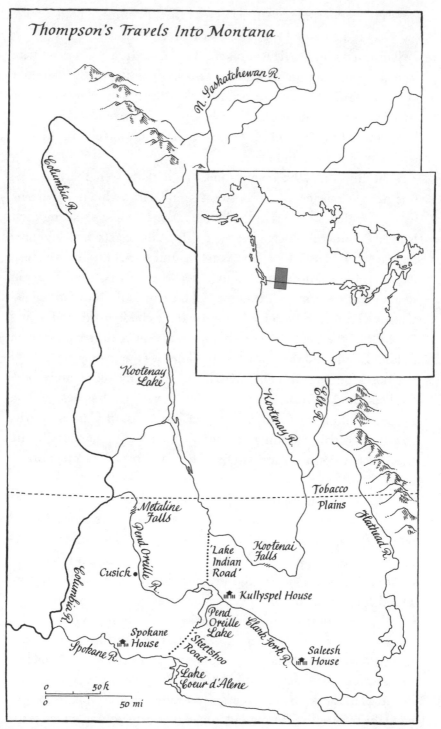

Thompson's Travels Into Montana

Map by Jack McMaster.

believe saved them from eventual annihilation at the hands of the Blackfeet. Thompson wrote, "Our arrival rejoiced them very much, for their only arms were a few rude lances, and flint-headed arrows."[5]

Thompson claimed the Salish soon became deadly shots because of the marksmanship they'd developed hitting antelope from long distances with bows and arrows. He argued that the Blackfeet, who had possessed guns for some time, could not shoot as well. They mainly fired on bison at short range from horseback. The dwindling Salish now had an advantage.

In return, the tribe gave Thompson pelts, dried salmon, and twelve pounds of camas root. Thompson liked the plant's taste and in his journal described its drying process, which preserved the bulb for years.

Thompson built Kalispel House at the mouth of the Clark Fork River. He encouraged the Salish to increase their trapping so they could purchase more guns and merchandise. Then, putting his trusted clerk Finan McDonald in charge, he traveled seventy-five miles upriver into present-day Montana. At a point in the river near a jagged cliff named Bad Rock, he built Salish House, the state's first trading post and permanent building.[6]

Thompson's journals furnish a clear description of the settlement, which consisted of three main buildings: a house for him, one for his men, and a trading post. The trappers secured the log buildings and insulated the gabled roofs with mud and grass. The plaster served fine in cold or dry weather, but when the snow melted or it rained, water seeped between the boards. To construct the floors, the men split small logs and placed the flat sides up. With stone and mud they fashioned the lower section of the chimney. The upper sections consisted of layers of grass and mud worked into crosspieces and fastened to poles inserted in the stonework. The fireplace, which was raised slightly above floor level, was four feet wide and fifteen inches deep. The living quarters had one room; the trading post had two and a second-floor loft. The trappers covered the windows with parchment paper, which they eventually replaced with skins.

After the completion of Salish House, bands of Kalispel, Kootenai, and Flathead came to camp in the adjoining meadow to trade with the men. One day Thompson received three packs—240 pounds—of furs and 1,300 pounds of dried provisions. Along with his trading record, three times a day he noted the weather, temperature, direction, and force of the wind.

That winter Thompson hired Salish hunters to supply the post with meat. After feeding themselves, the men stored the surplus in a "glacier"—an icehouse that was a necessary part of every post.[7] The Canadians spent much of the winter drying and pounding meat to make pemmican. They constructed wooden troughs, pouring melted fat into them to make soap. They also made wooden saddles in preparation for their spring expedition in search of birch bark to construct new canoes.

In March 1810, Thompson and his men made their first excursion into the Camas Prairie area, crossing Wild Horse Plains onto the prairie. On March 10 they camped in the valley with the Kalispel. Thompson called the area "Onion Plains" in honor of the meadow's abundant camas and onion-shaped bulbs. He commented that the Kalispel were a people in which confidence could be placed.

From Camas Prairie, Thompson journeyed southeast, joining a large Salish band near Dixon. The next morning Indian scouts spotted riders approaching from the east. Immediately, one hundred warriors mounted their horses and rode off to meet what they hoped were Blackfeet. Proud of their new guns, they declared their eagerness to fight the enemy on equal ground. However, they returned disappointed that the approaching men were Kootenai returning from a buffalo hunt. Thompson derived "great pleasure in seeing the alacrity with which they went to seek the enemy, when before, their whole thought and exertions were to get away from them."[8]

Within a month, however, the Salish received their chance to fight. After Thompson left for the annual meeting at Northwest Company headquarters in Canada, Finan McDonald arrived from Kalispel House to accompany the tribe on its spring buffalo hunt. McDonald had instructions to assist the Indians in the use of their newly acquired firearms, a task the fiery Highlander, who was six feet, four inches and covered with a bushy red beard and long hair, savored. In *The Columbia River,* Ross Cox described McDonald:

*To the gentleness of a lamb he united the courage of a lion. He
was particularly affectionate to men of small size, whether
equals or inferiors, and would stand their bantering with the
utmost good-humour; but if any man approaching his own
altitude presumed to encroach too far on his good-nature, a
lowering look and distended nostrils warned the intruder of an
approaching eruption.*[9]

Once the Salish and their wild accomplice reached the Missouri
River, the Blackfeet attacked. With the help of guns, the men routed
their aggressors. The armed Blackfeet tasted defeat for the first time,
and in their fury they "determined to wreak vengeance on the white
men who furnished arms and ammunition to their enemies."[10] Immediately, the Blackfeet planned an ambush for Thompson's return.
As a consequence, he was forced to travel over the rugged Athabasca
Pass and did not arrive back in Montana until 1811.

For a year after his return, Thompson lived among the Salish, per-
fecting his use of their language and providing them with guns and goods.
He frequently camped on Camas Prairie to map the area and record its
native wildlife. He guessed the route of its geese migration to be from
New Orleans between the parallels of fifty-eight to sixty-two degrees
north and five hundred miles east of the Rockies. In his journal, he questioned what guided these creatures over such a great space, crossing the
Rocky Mountains both in spring and fall. He answered that the Indians
call such ability "*manito,* which the Great Spirit has given to all creatures" and observed that the civilized world has its own *manito,* which
it calls "Instinct . . . that undefinable property of Mind."[11] David
Thompson possessed much of this unerring "Instinct" himself.

In 1812 Thompson crossed the Rockies into Canada and never
returned. There Charlotte and the children waited. He was highly
devoted to his family, and unlike some mountain men did not abandon them once his trapping days were over. Thompson died in 1857
in extreme poverty and obscurity and was buried in an unmarked
grave in Montreal. Three months later Charlotte died as well.

The explorer's lack of fame can be traced to his habit of always
sending his exquisite maps directly back to Northwest Company

headquarters. Company staff believed it was in their best interest to keep the accurate charts secret, so they hung them in a secluded room at Fort William. Thompson's name remained unknown until 1888 when field geologist J. B. Tyrell uncovered Thompson's journals. Even then, details of his accomplishments eluded Montana historians until decades into the twentieth century.[12]

Besides providing extensive details of previously uncharted territory, astronomical readings, and cartography of the land, Thompson was the first explorer to describe the seasonal flora, fauna, and customs of the continent's interior and its people. By the end of his career he had discovered the source of the Columbia, surveyed its entire course of more than thirteen hundred miles, and built the first trading posts on its upper waters, thus laying the foundation for the coming Oregon Territory fur trade.

The Americans

The Northwest Trade Company was correct in assuming Americans would follow Lewis and Clark. The 1803 Louisiana Purchase terminated French control over New Orleans and secured a U.S. grip on the fertile Mississippi Valley. President Thomas Jefferson wanted his new acquisition, as well as the land west of it, mapped. Although Jefferson admitted that Louisiana did not give the United States claim to the territory beyond the Rocky Mountains, he made clear his dream of an American empire extending to the Pacific. The president believed that Captain John Gray's discovery of the Columbia in 1792 gave the United States implied claim to Oregon. Establishing fur trade in the region would blaze a trail for eventual migration there.

One purpose of the Lewis and Clark Expedition was to determine the suitability of the Oregon Territory for this trade. Jefferson instructed Meriwether Lewis to document all fur-bearing animals, to ascertain the attitudes of the native occupants regarding trade, and to "establish the most direct and practicable water communication across the continent, for the purposes of commerce."[13]

If lore was correct, the Rocky Mountains ended at the forty-sixth parallel and a water passage existed from the Missouri River to the

Columbia River and thus to the Pacific Ocean. This route would allow goods to flow from the heartland of the United States to the mouth of the Columbia and on to India. Such a waterway would be far more efficient than any northern route the British had available to them. The explorers set out to find this mythological "Northwest Passage."

Even though Lewis and Clark failed to find such a route, they did tell of rivers, "richer in beaver and otter than any place on earth."[14] Obtaining food wouldn't pose a problem either. Herds of bison loomed so massive that the explorers feared they might be caught in a stampede and killed. They also encountered peaceful Indians to facilitate the beaver trade: the Mandans on the Missouri River, the Pawnee on the Platte River, and the Salish in Oregon Territory.

On September 4, 1805, eighty miles south of Camas Prairie, the explorers met the Salish, commenting, "They received us as friends and appeared to be glad to see us."[15] When Lewis and Clark arrived, the Indians immediately brought out their best buffalo robes, placing them around the visitors' shoulders. The explorers filled their pipes with Salish tobacco—kinnikinnick—but didn't like the taste. The whites' tobacco, to everyone's amusement, made the Indians cough. Clark mixed some kinnikinnick with his own tobacco, and both the explorers and the Indians liked the combination. The Salish enjoyed the whites' sense of humor, too.[16]

Several years later, encouraged by the success of the expedition and personally prodded by Jefferson, New York businessman John Jacob Astor entered the fur business. He set out to establish trading posts from the upper Missouri to the mouth of the Columbia. On the Columbia, his chief post, Astoria, would funnel goods and supplies into the interior. Pelts arriving from inland would be loaded onto ships and transported to Canton, China, where they would be exchanged for silk, tea, and spices. These luxuries would then be sailed to merchants in New York City.

In 1810 Astor formed the Pacific Fur Company. His first ship, *Tonquin,* sailed from New York around Cape Horn to the Hawaiian Islands, then crossed the Pacific to the mouth of the Columbia. *Tonquin* carried twenty-five men. Onboard was a young Scotsman named Alexander Ross. Ross would write *The Fur Hunters of the Far West*, one of the few existing accounts of the early Oregon fur trade.

At the mouth of the great Columbia, Ross and the crew began constructing Fort Astoria. The next year, another vessel, named *Beaver*, sailed fresh recruits over the same passageway. *Beaver* brought an Englishman named Ross Cox, whose personal account, *The Columbia River*, would be more colorful, but less accurate, than Alexander Ross's.

From St. Louis, Astor sent Andrew Henry across the Great Plains toward the coast. He reached Astoria in 1811. During his journey he sent a continuous flow of geographic information back to Missouri. Soon a visual map coalesced from St. Louis's "street corner parley." As the information passed from one frontiersman to another, a word-of-mouth cartography took form. As Bernard De Voto wrote, "rugged trappers and traders soon moved through the blank spaces of the American West, like men going to the barn."[17]

With Fort Astoria constructed and the overland fur trade developing, the future looked bright for the Americans. Soon, however, incoming news shocked Astor's men. War had broken out between the United States and Great Britain, and the British ship *Raccoon* was en route to stage an armed takeover of the post. Astor immediately sold his buildings, equipment, and pelts to the Canadian Northwest Company for a fraction of their market price and postponed his dream of a trade route to the Far East.

The Northwest Company directors gave Ross and Cox the choice of working for them or heading east. Both men took the company's offer to change alliegence. Ross remained at the newly established Fort George, near Astoria, while Cox traveled up the Columbia to spend the winter at Salish House. In his journal, Cox described the post as "a good trading store, a comfortable house for the men, and a snug box for ourselves; surrounded on all sides with pine, spruce, larch, beech, birch, and cedar. Our hunters killed a few mountain sheep, and I brought up a bag of flour, a bag of rice, plenty of tea and coffee, some arrowroot, and fifteen gallons of prime rum. We spent a comparatively happy Christmas and, by the side of the blazing fire in a warm room, forgot the sufferings we endured in our dreary progress through the woods."[18] While at Salish House, Cox recorded the story of Two Eagle.

Each year the Salish elected a war chief to lead the men in battle against the Blackfeet. This warrior was to assume supreme command during the party's campaign against the enemy. Once appointed, his comrades showed him unswerving allegiance. To meet the dreaded Blackfeet he rode in the lead, his face painted red and black. In his hand he held a long, thick spear decorated with feathers and the scalps of his enemies. Cox witnessed this election near Salish House—probably on Wild Horse Plains.

At the time Cox wrote about this custom, Two Eagle was appointed to the position for the fifth consecutive year. Cox was astounded by the man's wisdom and fearlessness—twenty Blackfeet coup hung from the pole of his lodge door. However, alongside the warrior's brave heart also ran deep sorrow. The previous year the Blackfeet had captured Two Eagle's beautiful wife and put her to death. He refused to remarry and at times, when her memory overwhelmed him, he retreated far into the woods, calling upon her spirit to appear. After his grief subsided, Two Eagle would return to his tribe with renewed determination to exact vengeance on her murderers.

During Cox's stay, the Salish had captured two Blackfeet prisoners. When they prepared to kill the unlucky souls, the fur trader reminded Two Eagle that such cruelty had taken his beloved wife from him forever and urged him to end the ritual. The warrior told the trapper, "My white friend, you do not know the savage nature of the Blackfeet. They hope to exterminate our tribe; they are a great deal more numerous than we are and were it not for our bravery, their object would have been achieved long ago."[19] Nevertheless, Two Eagle set the captives free.

During the same winter, American trappers retreated from the Oregon Territory and, because of the economic and political repercussions from the War of 1812, U.S. fur trade lapsed. Meanwhile, the British reinforced Fort George and strengthened their inland positions.

In 1816 the United States instituted a law that forbade foreign fur traders within the territory of the Louisiana Purchase. Two years later, the United States and Britain signed an agreement for the joint occupation of the Oregon Territory. These events dictated that the British stay west of the Continental Divide and that Americans could trap on land from St. Louis to the Pacific. With this advantage, discussion of the fur trade revived.

In 1822 William Ashley, lieutenant governor of Missouri and brigadier general of the state militia, entered the fur business. He hired seasoned guide Andrew Henry and advertised for raw recruits. On February 13, the *St. Louis Missouri Gazette* contained the following:

To Enterprising Young Men

The subscriber wishes to engage one hundred men to ascend the river Missouri to its source, there to be employed for one, two or three years. For particulars, inquire of Major Andrew Henry, near the lead mines, in the County of Washington, (who will ascend with and command the Party) or to the subscriber at St. Louis.

Two keelboats full of Ashley's men left St. Louis in the spring of 1822. The first departed on April 3 with twenty-six men, including Jim Bridger. A month later the second boat left, carrying Jedediah Smith.

Smith had grown up in a deeply religious family from Erie County, Pennsylvania. A local physician tutored Jedediah, introducing him to the accounts of Lewis and Clark and Zebulon Pike. The stories fascinated the boy, who dreamed of seeing the frontier. At age twenty he left Pennsylvania and headed west. Three years later, aboard Ashley's boat, he embarked on his own western adventure. Although the most rugged of mountain men, Smith did not forget the teachings of his childhood. He never smoked, swore, or drank, and he read whenever possible.

Bridger, on the other hand, came from different stock. In 1804 he was born in a tavern near Richmond, Virginia. His mother was the tavern's barmaid and his father its bartender. When the establishment failed, the family headed west and settled on a farm near the Mississippi. For years the Bridgers worked hard yet remained poor. Then in 1817, Jim's mother, father, and brother died in swift succession.

To survive, the thirteen-year-old orphan worked on a flatboat ferry—
a job even grown men considered backbreaking. He never learned to
read or write. To a boy with little future, Ashley's offer of adventure
and fortune seemed irresistible. At eighteen he became the general's
youngest recruit.

These two legends of the American fur trade came from different social ranks but entered the business on equal ground. As "free
traders" they were not salaried but paid according to the number of
skins they procured. Although Indians did sell pelts to the Americans, Ashley relied heavily on white trappers by sending them into
the mountains and encouraging them to remain there for at least
three years. Some, like Bridger, stayed longer. After leaving St. Louis
in 1822, he roamed the wilderness trapping for seventeen years before returning to civilization.

This system had advantages and disadvantages. The Americans
traveled in small groups, which provided flexibility. However, without the protection of numbers, trappers were easy targets for hostile
Indians. In 1840 Reverend Samuel Parker observed that of more than
two hundred men who began trapping in 1837, only thirty or forty
were still alive. He concluded, "It may be seen that the [trapper] averages about three years."[20]

The mountain men feared the Blackfeet most. The tribe reveled
in its infamous reputation, using the same tactics perfected on their
Salish rivals: never attacking unless they greatly outnumbered their
prey and shooting their enemies while hiding behind bushes. The
Blackfeet conducted most of their horse raids at night, swooping into
camp and stampeding the horses with their piercing screams. However, if a trapper could survive hostile raids and ambushes, the reward
was potentially high. Ashley paid $6 to $8 a pelt.

The Americans also collected furs differently than the British
did. Attempting to improve on the expensive upkeep of trading posts,
Ashley instituted the "rendezvous." These wild gatherings became an
annual affair in which a caravan of supplies arrived at a central location in July. There, the trappers sold their cache of pelts and bought
goods needed for the following year. Once they'd had their fill of
whiskey and brawling, they'd tramp back into the mountains for

another year. Ashley usually recovered most of his high costs in inflated whiskey and hardware prices. Trapper Osborne Russell estimated the markup reached 2,000 percent.[21]

Some mountain men spent an entire year's wages in a few days. Trapper Joe Meek recalled that the men were eager to purchase whatever Ashley had to offer at the value "of a year's labor, privation, and danger."[22] Others had more self-control. With his profits, Jim Bridger built Fort Bridger.[23] Jedediah Smith used his money eventually to buy out Ashley.

For the few trappers who survived and invested well, the adventure paid off. However, Ashley remained the biggest profiteer. Within four years he earned more than $200,000 in the Rocky Mountains. He then sold the company to Smith, William Sublette, and David Jackson and retired to Missouri to pursue a career in politics.

The generous pelt prices Ashley instituted produced conflict once the Americans entered the same territory as the Canadians. At British prices, the Indians went into debt for a few goods. The situation caused the Iroquois to complain that they were forever owing the English. When the Americans moved in, offering six to eight times what the British paid for furs, tempers flared. Animosity between the two countries reached its climax in the 1820s during the Snake Country Expeditions, which originated from Salish House.

The traditional British system, in which Indians delivered their pelts to the trading post, worked fine in Canada. However, it hadn't been as successful in the Oregon Territory. So in 1821, after the Northwest and Hudson's Bay Companies merged, the new Hudson's Bay Company built a larger stockade south of Salish House called Flathead Post and introduced a different strategy. Naturally loath to copy the detested Yankees, the company nevertheless made adaptations. In 1823, from the new post, it sent an expedition to trap the Snake country, assigning Finan McDonald to lead it.

Forty-four men accompanied McDonald, crossing Wild Horse Plains to Camas Prairie and proceeding to the Flathead River at present-day Perma. The route followed the same Salish trail used by the Indians for centuries. Impassable rapids raged on the Clark Fork between Flathead Post and Perma, forcing the overland route on travelers

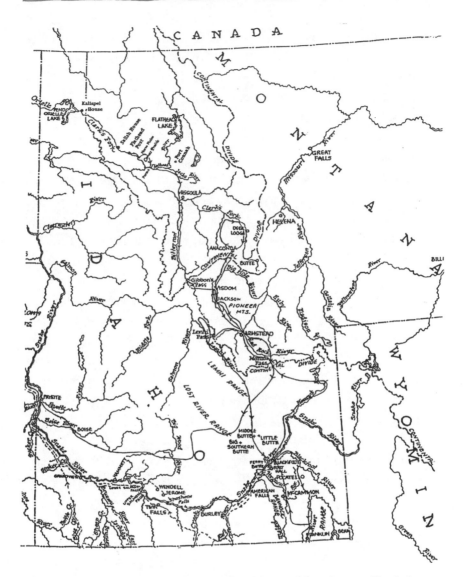

Route of Snake Country Expeditions, 1823 to 1826. Map traced from the notes of Lewis A. McArthur and Robert Sawyer. Map drawn by Ralph M. Shane, Warm Springs, Oregon, 1950.

heading south or east. From there, McDonald traveled along the Jocko River and on to present-day Missoula.

Within a few months the party reached the Big Hole River. At its northernmost bend the Blackfeet waited for their old enemy and traveling companions. Attacking the party, they shot and killed a trapper named Anderson. The Blackfeet lifted his scalp and retreated.

Shaken, the men proceeded over the Continental Divide and on to American soil, thus violating the 1816 law that forbid trapping by British citizens on land belonging to the United States.

At Lemhi Pass the Blackfeet taunted the Hudson's Bay Company again by firing on the camp. Although no one was killed, the temperamental Scotsman had had enough. Enraged, McDonald set out with thirty men to ambush the Indians. The trappers encircled the Blackfeet, who immediately took cover in surrounding bushes, screaming defiantly and waving Anderson's scalp from an uplifted pole. McDonald poured fifty-six pounds of buckshot into the bushes while the Indians fired back. Before long, twenty Blackfeet and seven trappers lay dead.

The Indians threw out their guns in surrender, but McDonald refused the offer of peace. Instead, he set the plains afire and declared he would smoke them out. From the burning bushes, the Blackfeet ran into the trappers' assault—incredibly, seven were able to escape. The flames consumed ten Blackfeet, and McDonald and his men shot another fifty-eight. The ordeal caused the party to cut the expedition short. Before they returned to Flathead Post, however, McDonald got into a squabble with one of his Iroquois men. In the fray, a gun accidentally discharged, badly wounding the Scotsman.

Although he brought 4,339 beaver out of the Snake River, making the trip a monetary success, McDonald soon retired. After twenty years of service in the Oregon Territory, he took his Salish wife and children and moved to Canada. But even on the way home, the mountain man found trouble. On June 1, 1827, near Edmonton, Alberta, McDonald tangled with a huge bison his trapping party had wounded. The bison, which had suffered less injury than expected, began chasing McDonald and overtook him. His companions had depleted their ammunition, so the trapper was on his own. Somehow McDonald wrestled the infuriated bull to the ground and held him there. Finally, after some time, the exhausted bull stumbled to its feet and walked away. Trapper David Douglas ended his eyewitness account by stating, "McDonald was fearfully injured and senseless, but received first aid and was rushed by boat to Carlton House."[24]

Amazingly, Finan McDonald did not die a mountain man. In 1843 he was elected to the provincial parliament in Ontario. The next year, his nephew Archie wrote to the trapper's old partner and Flathead Post associate Francis Ermatinger, reporting on his uncle's interrogation of the premier of the province. Archie wrote that McDonald performed the interview with "the same èlan that he did with the Blackfeet and Buffalo bull."[25]

The year after Finan McDonald's expedition, Alexander Ross led the Hudson's Bay brigade. Ross's trials would not come from the Blackfeet—who, after their bout with McDonald, left the trappers alone for several years—but from the Iroquois and the Americans. On December 10, 1823, Ross left Flathead Post with eleven men. At Wild Horse Plains, thirty-four more joined him. Ross was a bit uneasy about the eclectic group:

> *On assembling my people I smiled at the medley, the variety of accents of dresses, habits, and ideas; but above all, at the confusion of languages in our camp in which were two Americans, seventeen Canadians, five half-breeds from the east side of the mountains, twelve Iroquois, two Abanakee Indians from Lower Canada, two natives from Lower Canada, two natives from Lake Nepissing, one Saultman from Lake Huron, two Crees from Athabasca, one Chinook, two Spokanes, two Kootenai, three Flatheads, two Kalispels, one Palouse, and one Snake slave! Five of the Canadians were about sixty years of age and two were on the wrong side of seventy.*[26]

Fifty-five people left Wild Horse Plains and descended onto Camas Prairie. There they camped for two days, killing six deer to feed the group. On the prairie, Ross heard the first grumbling from the Iroquois trappers. His journal entry on December 12 stated, "Murmuring among the Iroquois, but I could not learn the cause."

The next morning the Indians demanded to see their accounts. Ross showed them the books, then ordered the camp to pack up and leave the valley. Once the party entered the Perma canyon, Ross realized the Iroquois were not with them. He went back into the valley and found that eleven of them had remained there. They informed Ross that the price paid for furs, in proportion to the exorbitant advance on goods, was so small they would never be able to pay their debts, much less make any money. They informed him they would no longer trap for the Hudson's Bay Company. Desperate, Ross promised to adjust their accounts. He wrote, "they grumbled and talked, and talked and grumbled and at last consented to proceed. Thinks I to myself—this is the beginning."

The Iroquois were wise to question the British system of payment, especially with Finan McDonald's experience fresh in their mind. Risking their lives for a dollar a pelt did seem foolhardy. The Iroquois continued to complain, asking Ross to let them separate from the group and trap on their own, thus making their individual fur counts higher and justifying the trip. Finally, the Hudson's Bay leader let them venture out on their own.

The Iroquois were successful until, near the Big Hole, Snake Indians attacked them and robbed nine hundred beaver, fifty-four traps, twenty-six horses, five guns, and nearly all of their clothing. The next day Jedediah Smith and his men found the Iroquois naked and destitute and, for a price, agreed to escort them back to Ross's brigade.

Although the diversion ended Smith's own trapping expedition, the hiatus was well worth it. It gave the American a firsthand tour of the British operation. Alexander Ross realized the implications of the escort and called the men "rather spies than trappers." He also lamented, "The quarter is swarming with trappers who next season are to penetrate the Snake country with Major Henry. . . . The report of these men on the price of beaver has a very great influence on our trappers."

Much to Ross's dismay, Smith and his men accompanied the party back to Flathead Post. Even though Ross topped McDonald's previous count, bringing five thousand beaver out of the country, Hudson's Bay officials were furious. The Columbia district was in an uproar over the American escort, and Alexander Ross hadn't returned with just any Yankee but with the famous Jedediah Smith.

During Smith's time in the West, he'd crisscrossed the country, making a name for himself as a fearless, resourceful leader and explorer. By his death in 1831 from Comanche ambush, he had discovered South Pass and been the first white to reach California by an overland route, cross the Sierra Nevadas, traverse the Great Basin, and journey up through California to Oregon.

A year before meeting Ross, while commandeering a group of trappers through the Black Hills, Smith had been attacked by a grizzly bear. The incident left him with vivid scars and an upturned eye. Companion Jim Clyman recorded the incident:

> *The grissly did not hesitate a moment but sprang on the capt taking him by the head . . . breaking several of his ribs and cutting his head badly. . . . I found the baare had taken nearly all his head in his capcious mouth clos to his left eye on one side and clos to his right ear on the other and laid the skull bare to near the crown of the head . . . one of his ears was torn from his head . . . this gave us a lesson on the character of the grissly baare which we did not forget."* [27]

Smith calmly ordered Clyman to stitch him up as best he could and to try to save the ear, which his friend did. The party continued through the rugged mountains until they reached the Wind River, where they camped among the Crows. Ten days later they journeyed on.

This daring young American offering his "freeman's wage" was a threat to the British who paid trappers far less for pelts. Jedediah Smith's very presence would inflame competition. Hudson's Bay officials knew Smith would only be the first of many and devised a plan to stop the Americans from coming. London sent word to Governor George Simpson, the company's district supervisor, to launch an aggressive and relentless campaign to exploit the area from Flathead Post through the Snake country, leaving "it in as bad a state as possible for the Americans."[28] The Canadians called this plan the "scorched earth" policy; if they could trap bare the entire area around the Snake River, the north and western sides would be protected against American ingress.

Simpson, refusing to believe that it was the Hudson's Bay Company's unfair prices that spurred unrest, blamed Alexander Ross for the company's problems. He declared that the vital Snake Country Expedition should not be left to a "self sufficient empty headed man like Ross" but to a "Commissioned Gentlemen"[29] like Peter Skene Ogden, whom he soon cajoled into leading the next brigade.

Ogden joined the Northwest Company at an early age. He fought so zealously for the company's interests that at the time of the 1821 merger with Hudson's Bay, the latter refused to admit him to membership. Ogden sailed to London to make a personal appeal on his own behalf. Because of Governor Simpson's intervention, the company reinstituted Ogden as a member of the new Hudson's Bay Company and appointed him chief factor at Spokane Post. When Simpson asked Ogden to lead the 1824–1825 expedition, he could hardly refuse.

Ogden arrived at Flathead Post on November 26, 1824. A few hours later Ross trudged in with Smith and his men. Ogden coldly greeted the Americans but said no more and immediately began preparing for their next expedition, scheduled to leave in less than a month. Before they departed, however, Hudson's Bay held a rendezvous of its own, a festival that rivaled even Ashley's best. On November 30, 860 Flatheads, Pend d'Oreilles, Kootenais, Kalispels, Nez Perce, and Spokanes gathered on Wild Horse Plains.

A Flathead garrison began the festivities. The austere collective, mounted and chanting a peace song, rode to the post. As they approached, the Indians saluted the fort with discharges from their guns. The British returned the compliment by firing the fort's cannon. Ross wrote, "The reverberating sound had a fine effect. The head chief advanced and made a fine speech welcoming the whites to these lands, apologizing for having but a few beaver."[30] The cavalcade dismounted, and the chiefs entered the post to smoke with the whites. After the women unloaded the provisions, brisk trade began that lasted until dark. Once the Flatheads finished, the Pend d'Oreille did business. In succession, each tribe dealt with the British. After four days, the Salish alone had sold 1,183 beaver, 14 otter, 529 muskrats, 8 fishers, 3 minks, 1 martin, 2 foxes, and 11,072 pounds of dried buffalo meat to Hudson's Bay.

On December 23, Ogden embarked on the last Snake Country Expedition from Flathead Post. He crossed Camas Prairie with fifty-three freemen, thirty women, thirty-five children, ten company servants, and two interpreters. After crossing the prairie, they advanced down the Flathead River (then called the Wild Horse River because of the great number of wild horses in the area). On Christmas Eve the company killed several of these horses and ate them for dinner. Jedediah Smith and his men had followed close behind and on December 27 joined the brigade near Missoula, informing Ogden they intended to stay with the British until they were safely through Blackfeet country.

As the trappers moved south, a Salish hunting party joined them. Once the large assembly crossed the Continental Divide into Big Hole country, they were not only entering U.S. territory but Blackfeet land. It did not take the Blackfeet long to make their presence known. During the night of January 31, they crept into camp and stole twenty-six horses. The next morning the Salish discovered their loss and prepared to retrieve the steeds. In *Traits of American Indian Life*, Peter Skene Ogden recalls the tragic story that followed.[31]

In council the hereditary chief Cut Thumb suggested a meeting with the Blackfeet to try and peaceably recover the horses. The great warrior and war chief Red Feather, also known as Insula, agreed. Red Feather's prized steed, "The Black," had been stolen, and he meant to retrieve her by whatever means he could.

Red Feather was highly respected by his tribe. Ogden claimed that when he spoke "every eye turned in expectation of his counsel." He described Insula in the following manner:

> *Bold and fearless and at the same time prudent and skillful beyond any Indian who roved the prairies; his renown was spread far and wide. . . . Tall, well-shaped and muscular, his person exhibited every characteristic of strength and activity; while his features distinguished him as a man of character and ability.*

The Blackfeet, on the other hand, hated Red Feather as much as his own tribe admired him. He had killed many of their warriors in battle and displayed their scalps with pride.

Ogden accompanied the Salish as they met with their enemies. When the Blackfeet saw Red Feather, they went into a rage because,

Peter Skene Ogden. Courtesy of Oregon Historical Society.

they declared, at that moment three Blackfeet scalps decorated Red Feather's lodge. The council disintegrated, and Ogden and the Salish returned to camp.

Several days later Red Feather told the trapper he was going to recover The Black himself by sneaking into the enemy camp for her. The war chief and several men then departed on foot. When they found the encampment, they skillfully maneuvered among the grazing horses. As quickly as Red Feather mounted The Black, his presence was known and a rapid chase began. However, the Blackfeet had no chance of catching him atop his exquisite steed. Once far enough in the lead, Red Feather stopped atop a ridge and, dancing The Black in a circle, screamed back at his enemies in defiance. Meanwhile, Blackfeet scouts had approached from the side and set the prairie on fire. In a wild gust of wind the grassland rushed ablaze toward Red Feather. The other Salish warriors, who had not hesitated, raced toward a strip of bare soil that the fire could not cross, reaching it with only moments to spare. Red Feather's act of defiance, however, had cost

Jim Bridger in 1866 at the age of sixty-two.
Courtesy of the Denver Public Library Western
History Collection.

him precious time and thus his life. Later, the war chief's companions returned his charred body to the Hudson's Bay camp.

After Ogden and his group departed from "the brave and hospitable tribe that had plunged into mourning," Ogden fell into trouble
of his own. As the expedition progressed, Jedediah Smith continued
to remind the trappers of the disparity in Canadian American pelt
prices, and Ogden's men began to desert. Finally, to the Englishman's
relief, Smith and his company departed at Bear River.

His good fortune was short-lived however. By late summer,
Johnson Gardner's party of Americans burst into Ogden's camp and
challenged the Canadians for trapping on U.S. territory, offering the
trappers eight times what the British gave them for pelts. The confrontation was a disaster for Hudson's Bay. Twenty-three more men
left, attempting to pillage the camp as they went. With the group
reduced to seventeen, Ogden abandoned the expedition and attempted
to make it safely out of Blackfeet country. The small party arrived
back at Flathead Post in November 1825, lucky to be alive.

Although Governor Simpson sanctioned, in fact ordered, the trespass onto American soil, London recanted, sending instructions that in the future all officers will confine themselves within the limits of the company's territories. The Hudson's Bay Company moved the Snake Country Expedition from Montana into Idaho and thereafter contained it west of the Continental Divide.

This time the revolt produced reform. The British immediately increased the price they paid for furs, even forgiving outstanding Indian debts. As a result they managed to hold onto the interior trade and keep the Americans at bay. Eventually they succeeded in trapping the area clean and sterilizing the southern and eastern sides of the Columbia Valley, thus insulating the Northwest from Yankee trappers.

Over the remaining fur-trading years, Americans did make some attempt to trap in Salish territory. In the 1830s, Nathaniel Wyeth traveled through the area, dreaming of reviving John Jacob Astor's plan of establishing a successful trade route to China. Wyeth was a young, enterprising merchant who managed a Massachusetts ice-exporting company. The expansionist proselytizer Hall Kelly inspired him to head west to seek his fortune. Like Astor, Wyeth planned to build a trading post at the mouth of the Columbia and direct his operation from there. He outfitted a supply ship from Boston and sent it around Cape Horn. He and his men then journeyed overland toward the Columbia. However, once they arrived on the West Coast, they learned their supply ship had sunk near the Society Islands. Disappointed but still determined, Wyeth remained with the British during the winter of 1831 and then traveled to Flathead Post the next spring. Still hoping to build American stockades, Wyeth took note of British strategy.

In the spring, he and Francis Ermatinger, Flathead Post's new factor, crossed Camas Prairie. Wyeth entered the valley cautiously, noting its danger and writing in his journal that Blackfeet "infest much of the country we are now entering." He described Camas Prairie as a "large open valley with little timber and much grass. Opposite our Camp is a mountain where 200 Flatheads, Kootenai, Pend d'Oreille and other Indians were killed by the Blackfoot Indians."[32] While on the prairie, a band of Salish warned them to be cautious, as the Blackfeet had recently made two successful horse raids in the valley.

After his explorations, Wyeth realized he could not compete with the Hudson's Bay Company and moved south. He eventually abandoned his dream of fur-trade prosperity and returned to Boston to make his fortune in the ice business.

Other Americans came. Warren Ferris, an associate of the American Fur Trading Company, arrived at Flathead Post in 1831. Heading across Wild Horse Plains, he "descended the mountain into a fine valley called Cammas Prairie, watered by a beautiful well timbered stream . . . while in the valley we saw wild horses galloping in bands over the plains, almost daily, several of which were caught by Indians and domesticated with but little trouble."[33]

On Camas Prairie, Ferris watched the Salish breaking wild horses. He wrote that the Indians pursued the untamed horses on steeds of their own. Once lassoed, the wild horses exerted all their strength in fruitless efforts to escape; however, they eventually became gentle from exhaustion. The Salish then bridled, mounted, and whipped their new charges into action.

Other Americans also attempted to cash in on the area by modeling their brigades after those of the Snake Country Expeditions. Jim Bridger led the efforts of the Rocky Mountain Fur Company—whose men were more flexible, self-sufficient, and capable of defending themselves against Indian attack than those of the British. Bridger, who eventually married the daughter of war chief Insula, conducted the expedition through northwestern Montana, crossing Camas Prairie in 1831 and 1832.

Bridger's Salish bride and her people accompanied the Americans, fighting alongside them during frequent Blackfeet attacks. In 1832, while near the Big Hole, the company ran into a migrating Blackfeet village. The tribe signaled to Bridger that they did not want to fight. The trapper mounted his horse and rode to meet the chief who was holding a peace pipe.

On the trappers' side a Blackfeet girl, who was married to a mountain man named Loretto, looked on. As a child she had been captured by the Crow. Loretto had bought her from the tribe and married

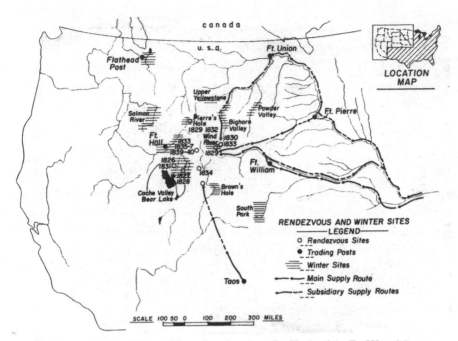

Rendezvous site. From Hiram Chittenden, American Fur Trade of the Far West *(New York: Press of the Pioneers, 1935), p. 186.*

her. The Indian girl watched from the rocks with their newborn baby in her arms. Suddenly she recognized her brother among the Blackfeet warriors; the village was that of her childhood. She handed the baby to her husband and rushed out across the plains toward her family. Bridger, startled by the commotion, cocked his rifle. The chief grabbed the barrel, twisting it down toward the ground. The gun went off and immediately two Blackfeet arrows thudded into Bridger's back. He fell forward, and the chief clubbed him across the head with the gun. Trappers converged, pulling Bridger back amid ensuing fire.

Both sides took cover and began a battle that raged throughout the day. The only break in shooting came when Loretto, knowing that the Blackfeet would never allow his wife to return to him, darted out across the prairie with the baby. Incredibly, both sides ceased fire. He handed the child to his wife and ran back safely to the trappers' side. Once darkness fell, the Blackfeet slipped away.

The next morning, trapper Tom Fitzpatrick tried to remove the arrows from Bridger's back. The first one dislodged in a gush of blood. The second was not so cooperative. Fitzpatrick finally snapped off the shaft. The arrow remained in Bridger's back for the next three years until a Protestant missionary doctor, Marcus Whitman, removed it in 1835 at the Green River Rendezvous.[34]

Frontier surgery wasn't the only colorful event occurring at these wild affairs. These gatherings, in the words of trapper James Beckwourth, were the scene of "mirth, songs, dancing, shouting, trading, running, jumping, singing, racing, target shooting, yarns, frolic, with all sorts of extravagance that whites or Indians could invent."[35] In 1837 Osborne Russell described

"Louis, Rocky Mountain Trapper" by Alfred Jacob Miller, 1837. Courtesy of Buffalo Bill Historical Center, Cody, Wyoming. Gift of Coe Foundation.

the attendees of the yearly spectacle as a "mixed multitude: the whites were chiefly Americans and French Canadian with some Dutch, Scotch, Irish, English, half-breed, and full blood Indians, of nearly every tribe in the Rocky Mountains."[36] He reported that while some gambled or played Indian stick games, others engaged in horse races or simply congregated to reconstruct the year's events.

The trappers selected the location for these wild affairs a year in advance—a central location with large valleys, ample grass, and water for the animals. But although the trappers relished these reunions, the events could easily turn deadly. Trapper Joe Meek recalled seeing a man seize a bottle of whiskey and pour it over the head of a tall, lank, redheaded fellow, while repeating a baptismal ceremony. No sooner had he concluded than another man with a lighted stick touched the soaked trapper. In an instant he was enveloped in flames. "Luckily, some of the company had sense enough left to perceive his danger, and began beating him with pack-saddles to put out the blaze. But between the burning and the beating, the unhappy wretch nearly lost his life."[37]

"Setting Traps for Beaver" by Alfred Jacob Miller, 1837. Courtesy of Joslyn Art Museum, Omaha, Nebraska.

In 1837 William Stewart commissioned Baltimore artist Alfred Jacob Miller to accompany the rendezvous supply train from St. Louis and capture this raucous event. Miller drew the only firsthand accounts that exist today. Although western artists such as George Catlin and Karl Bodmer preceded him into the region, they did not go as far west as Miller, nor did they document the fur trade or the events surrounding it.

By the late 1830s the fur trade was in decline. Silk had replaced beaver in European hat styles. The increasing availability of cloth from China, new technologies for felting hats, and the whims of fashion combined to diminish the market. The last rendezvous was held in 1840 at Green River. In that year mountain man "Doc" Newell wrote to Joe Meek, "Come, we are done with this life in the mountains, done with the wading in beaver-dams, and freezing or starving alternately, done with Indian trading and Indian fighting. The fur trade is dead in the Rocky Mountains, and it is no place for us now, if ever it was."[38]

In the 1840s the British closed Flathead Post and moved their trade center to the Flathead Valley, twenty miles east of Camas

Prairie. There they established Hudson Bay's last trading post south of the forty-ninth parallel. The company assigned Finan McDonald's cousin Angus to build the post. After its completion, Angus named it "Connen" after a river in his native Scotland. For twenty-four years in the American Rockies, it was known as Fort Connah and flew the British flag. With the beaver trade depressed and trade in buffalo robes centered on the eastern plains, the trade at Fort Connah centered around selling general merchandise to Indians, incoming settlers, and American explorers.

Angus McDonald was born in Ross Shire, Scotland, in 1816. After a sound education, he became a local business clerk. The profession bored the restless adventurer, so in 1838, like many of his relatives, he sailed to Canada to enter the fur trade. Initially, the Hudson's Bay Company sent him to Fort Colville, near Spokane, to serve under his uncle Archibald McDonald, then south to Fort Hall, near Boise.

While at Fort Hall, McDonald fell in love with a pretty Nez Perce girl named Catherine. Catherine was a cousin to celebrated war chiefs Looking Glass and White Bird. In 1842 Angus and Catherine were married in a civil ceremony at Fort Hall. Several years later the couple journeyed to Montana to finish construction on Fort Connah.

Over the next fifty years, McDonald became a trusted friend of the Salish. The tribe respected him as a sage, welcoming him on their hunts and tribal council and adopting the couple. McDonald embraced life as a nomad and preferred to live in a tent rather than the log house he and Catherine built.

The restless wanderer was also a scholar, widely read in the classics and philosophy. He spoke Salish,

"The Belle of the Rendezvous" is what Alfred Jacob Miller called this beautiful Salish girl who attended the 1837 gathering. Courtesy of the Walters Art Gallery, Baltimore, Maryland.

ANGUS MacDONALD 1816-1889
HUDSON'S BAY COMPANY.

Angus McDonald in 1848. Courtesy of the Montana Historical Society.

Nez Perce, Kootenai, Blackfeet, Okanogan, and Crow, as well as French, Gaelic, and English. He recorded memoranda on Indian history, legends, wars, and life on the frontier. In a ledger he carried in his saddlebag, he wrote notes and composed poems and songs. McDonald frequently played his bagpipe at tribal campfires. The Salish loved these performances and affectionately called the instrument "the bag that whistles."

Like his cousin Finan, Angus was tall and striking. In 1855 Edward Huggins described him:

> *I had heard a great deal about "MacDonald," and was anxious to see him. . . . He was a rather good looking man, about six feet in height, straight and slim, but wiry and strong. He had a dark complexion, with long jet black hair, reaching to the*

shoulders, and a thick long and very black beard and mustache.
He wore a dressed deer skin shirt and pants, and had a black
silk handkerchief tied loosely around his neck. He had a black
piercing eye, and a deep sonorous, rather musical voice, and a
slow manner of speaking. He was fond of telling Indian stories
and legends, and would sometimes keep an audience spellbound,
when walking to and fro in the large Nisqually reception room,
telling some blood curdling Indian story, in which he had borne
a conspicuous part.[39]

From 1846 to 1889, Angus McDonald watched the land and its
people undergo vast transformation. Trapping and hunting had depleted the country of bison and beaver. The migrant bison culture,
which had evolved with the horse's introduction, was dying. Many in
government understood the changes that the extinction of the bison
would foster. Early on they ignored the Trade and Intercourse Act of
1802, which specifically outlawed entering Indian country to "hunt,
or in any wise destroy the game."[40] Some even encouraged the slaughter as an answer to the "Indian problem," reasoning that once there
were no bison to follow, native people would become agriculturists.
This solution would also leave vast acres of prairie land free for incoming settlers.

After 1849 and the opening of the Oregon Trail, westward migration increased dramatically. With bison scarce, and the Salish and
Kootenai confined to the Flathead Indian Reservation, the tribes no
longer migrated to the plains to hunt and fight the Blackfeet. In his
memoir, "A Few Items of the West," Angus McDonald lamented the
changes to Camas Prairie:

In this plain of the Kamas, we hear no more the voice of
hundreds of men and women, keeping time to the wild pathetic
strain of the San-ka-ha, the red man's farewell before he leaves
for battle. To hear it sung by five or six hundred voices in a
calm, starry night is a rare thing, never perhaps to be heard
again. The Mothers and Sisters, always the most tender, could
not for a moment stand its thrilling notes, and they wept loud

Fort Connah, Montana's oldest building. Courtesy of George Knapp.

and deep for those that were and were not. In 1850, at a great gathering of Indians to dance this stolid, insisting strain, I stripped with the leading men, painted with vermilion the groves of my upper body, mounted my black buffalo charger with my full eagle feather cap and cantered round and round with them, keeping time to the song.[41]

McDonald and his fellow trappers mourned the passing of this ancient way of life even though they had unwittingly played a part in its alteration. But unlike the whites who followed, these mountain men did not consciously set out to alter Indian culture but adapted themselves to it. Trappers had an interest in sustaining traditional native society, which helped make their way of life possible. Many of them married Salish women and raised large mixed-race families.[42] In the end they lived more like Native Americans than whites.

The people who followed did not hold such stake in Indian society. Instead, their way of life determined its disruption. Like most trappers, Angus McDonald ascribed responsibility for the extinction of nomadic ways to those who came after his kind. Fur traders blamed the priests, the army, and the farmers.

Chapter 4

They Overran the Land

*A*ngus McDonald had a point: Catholic priests were the first to arrive with a conscious agenda to change Salish culture. In turn, the priests argued that the Indians had invited them.

Early in the 1800s, Iroquois trappers introduced the Salish to Catholicism. Many of them had received their religious training at the Caughnawaga Mission near Montreal. Because whites possessed powerful weapons, the Iroquois assumed white religion would be potent as well and, hoping to enhance their own spiritual strength, adopted these new beliefs. An old Iroquois named Ignace told the Salish all he knew of the white faith, but he also told them they must seek the "Black Robes" themselves. He refused to teach Christian prayers because he was "afraid of changing the Word of God."[1]

Salish legend foretold of the priests. Long before the tribe knew of Europeans, a Kalispel shaman named Shining Shirt prophesied their coming. In his vision, pale-faced holy men wearing black robes arrived, gave the people new names, and taught them how to survive after the game disappeared. Shining Shirt announced that once the Black Robes came, Indian wars would cease but that others would follow and overrun the land. The shaman told his people that to avoid bloodshed they must listen to the priests.[2]

Anticipating the missionaries' entry into their country, in 1831

Fathers Adrian Hoecken (left) and Pierre-Jean De Smet. In 1844 Father De Smet directed Father Hoecken to begin the St. Ignatius Mission north of Pend d'Oreille Lake. In 1852 the mission was moved thirty miles east of Camas Prairie to the base of the Mission Mountains. Courtesy of Jesuit Missouri Province Archives.

two Salish and two Nez Perce journeyed to St. Louis to find the holy men. They visited Captain William Clark, the only white contact they had, and requested his assistance. However, Clark could not help them and they left the city disappointed. Then in 1835, while attending the trapping rendezvous at Green River, Ignace and his sons implored the Protestant minister Marcus Whitman to send a missionary to the Salish. Still no one came. Again in 1837, Ignace, three Salish, and one Nez Perce set out for St. Louis. At the summer rendezvous, a small group of trappers joined them on their journey east. Once they reached Ash Hollow on the North Platte River, Sioux warriors surrounded them and killed Ignace and the other natives.

Even this tragedy did not dissuade the Salish. Finally, in 1839 a fourth delegation reached the St. Joseph Mission at Council Bluffs and implored Father Pierre-Jean De Smet to return with them. Finally, the seekers had found their priest.

Eighteen years earlier at the age of twenty, Father De Smet had sailed from Belgium to America. During his Jesuit training in Flanders, he'd learned of his church's work among the natives of

America. Understanding De Smet's adventurous spirit, his superior, Father Nerinckx, encouraged the young priest to consider such a calling. De Smet's incurable wanderlust and longing to see an untamed new country moved him to accept.

However, after arriving in Philadelphia in 1821, he found the city disappointingly civilized. So in 1823 he and six Flemish novices set out for Missouri. The dedicated young zealots constructed an Indian school and helped build the Jesuit novitiate at Florissant.

By the time the Salish reached De Smet, he had worked at the school for more than ten years and was ready for a new adventure. With the blessing of Joseph Rosati, bishop of St. Louis, De Smet promised the Indians he would leave for their land the next spring.

In May 1840, De Smet departed with Andrew Drips—leader of the last American Fur Company rendezvous brigade. At the Wyoming rendezvous, a Salish escort waited for the priest. They led De Smet to Pierre's Hole in Montana, where fifteen hundred Indians had gathered to see him. There, the priest preached to the Salish and Nez Perce, baptizing six hundred of them. That winter De Smet returned to St. Louis to raise money for his wilderness mission. After collecting $1,100, he returned with more missionaries and supplies.

This time, De Smet brought Brothers Gregory Mengarini and Nicholas Point to assist in spiritual instruction, and Brothers Claessens, Specht, and Huet to act as blacksmith, tinner, and carpenter. As soon as the priests arrived in the Bitterroot Valley, they began to construct St. Mary's Mission, near present-day Missoula.

Upon the priests' arrival, the Indians announced that Christian prayer had already served them well. In a recent battle, in which they were sorely outnumbered, the Salish had killed seventy Blackfeet and lost only one man. They believed their success resulted from the new Catholic rituals. De Smet wrote that the tribe regarded "the sign of the cross as a sign of victory" and believed that baptism gave them power to "conquer any enemy whatsoever." The Salish sought white religion to enhance their military prowess and believed that with it came "all other imaginable blessings, not only courage to fight, but also corporeal health."[3] Instead of seeing Christianity as a means of forgiveness, the tribe embraced the new religion to achieve victory in battle and to preserve health. The concept of humanity's separation from God or need for reconciliation was alien to them.

De Smet did not resent the Indians' motives. In *Across the Wide Missouri,* Bernard De Voto wrote that the Salish had at last found their messenger: "He was the famous Jesuit Pierre-Jean de Smet: he did not ask much of the Flatheads except that they should assign his supernaturals a more powerful medicine than their own, and beyond that he loved them."[4]

De Smet's open-mindedness derived from his view of evangelism. To a large extent, he believed the tribe should be given the same freedom the apostle Paul bestowed in Corinthians when he opened Christianity to non-Jews. Just as Paul declared gentile Christians free from the Levitical law of Judaism, De Smet believed the Indians of America should be freed from most European dictums.

Although many priests objected to De Smet's liberal approach, such tolerant ecclesiology had worked for the Catholics before. At the close of the sixteenth century, Jesuit missionary Matteo Ricci requested that Rome recognize Chinese converts as distinctly Chinese and not European. During the seventeenth century, Jesuit Roberto de Nobili called for similar religious universality in acceptance of native Malabar rites in India. During the eighteenth century in Paraguay, the church successfully established its missionary outreach by allowing the native culture to remain largely intact and to serve as the context for a new expression of Christianity. De Smet extended this freedom toward American Indians and believed U.S. gains would be even more impressive than those experienced in Paraguay.

For a year De Smet lived at St. Mary's and traveled among the Salish. He described them as "a tribe of chiefs [and] a chosen people. . . . They are characterized by the greatest simplicity, docility, and uprightness, and yet to this simplicity is joined the courage of heroes."

In the fall of 1841, accompanied by several Salish guides, the priest journeyed north. On November 1, the party arrived at Camas Prairie. De Smet's diary testifies to his impressions of the valley: "We proceeded to cross a smiling little plain, called the Camas Prairie, where the Flatheads come every spring to dig up that nourishing root, which, together, with the game they are able to procure, forms their chief nourishment." De Smet described the animals in the hills surrounding the valley:

> *The hills abound in sheep, whose wool is as white as snow and
> as fine as silk; also in all kinds of bears, wolves, panthers and
> carcajoux (an animal with short paws, some four feet long and
> remarkably powerful; when he has killed his prey, deer, antelope
> or bighorn, he tears off a piece of skin big enough to stick his
> head through after the fashion of a hood, and thus drags it off
> whole to his den). There are also found tiger cats, wild cats and
> whistlers, a species of mountain rat. The moose is found here,
> but is very seldom caught, on account of its extraordinary
> vigilance, for on the slightest rustling of a branch it leaves off
> eating, and will not return to its food for a long time afterward.*

De Smet also commented on the nightly devotional given by the chief. "I cannot pass over in silence a beautiful custom that is observed by these good people: every evening, after prayers, the chief instructs his people, or gives them some salutary advice, to which they all listen with most profound attention, respect, and modesty." In the midst of such beauty De Smet also noted the dangers on Camas Prairie: "Wolves are very numerous and very ferocious here; last spring they carried off and devoured more than forty of the Kalispel's horses." While setting up camp, he discovered a Blackfeet warrior hiding among the tents. To avoid a bloody confrontation, De Smet did not tell his companions; however, he insisted an extra watch be posted that evening.

From Camas Prairie the party moved across Wild Horse Plains and on to the Clark Fork River. They ascended the waterway and spent the autumn in villages along its banks. The trip was a great success for De Smet. He rejoiced that the Indians "came from all parts and from great distances, to meet me on my way, and presented all their young and dying relatives for baptism. Many followed me for whole days, with the sole desire of receiving instructions." His Salish guides took painstaking care of him. About them he commented, "With pleasure I bear testimony to their devotedness, politeness, complaisance and rare hilarity. . . . These good Flatheads endeavored in every manner to anticipate all my wants." Up and down the Clark Fork, De Smet taught the tribe prayers and instructed them in doctrine. During the journey, which lasted forty-two days, he preached to more than two thousand, baptizing 190. In December the small party arrived back at St. Mary's.

The next spring the priest journeyed to the Willamette Valley in Oregon to meet with Fathers Demer and Blanchet. During the meeting they agreed that De Smet should began a new ministry, raising money and securing religious workers in Europe and America. After De Smet began recruiting, he seldom returned to the Salish. For the rest of his life he traveled between both continents collecting funds and serving as an emissary of the U.S. government encouraging tribal peace.

With De Smet's departure, the Paraguayan approach vanished as well. Fathers Mengarini and Point saw little in Salish culture or religion that they approved of. Mengarini especially resented the buffalo hunt because it interfered with the daily lessons he taught. Once hunting began, all efforts centered on guarding the horses and killing buffalo. Mengarini complained that the activity "keeps them barbarous and takes their attention from the faith."[5] The priest also insisted that whenever the hunters captured a Blackfeet warrior, they release him unharmed. Although the men obeyed the request, they resented the priest's interference. After one such confrontation they threatened to abandon Mengarini on the plains.

To wean the Salish from hunting, the priests encouraged them to raise crops and adopt a sedentary life. They obtained seeds from Fort Colville, in present-day Idaho, and taught the Indians how to plant and harvest wheat, oats, and potatoes and to raise cattle, hogs, and chickens. In 1845 the priests set up a flour mill to process wheat and a sawmill to cut lumber for homes. However, even Mengarini admitted, "The soil is naturally dry and filled with large rocks . . . and we cannot find arable spots. In addition the large rocks frequently break the plows."[6]

Father Point crusaded to eliminate the spirit quest. During the rite, he wrote, "Satanic power is firmly established; human dignity is degraded, divine majesty is eradicated, and an untold number of souls are eternally lost. Such are the fruits of the perfidious work called 'medicine.' Those who undertake the journey are 'wretched, ignorant, worthy of pity, I almost added good for nothing.'"[7] He sarcastically described the Indian experience:

> *The sky is to him nonexistent; he thinks only of the earth and wants only the earth, since it is the earth that gives existence to everything anyone knows. Thus it is to the earth that he addresses his first prayers. If she remains deaf to them, he turns to a nearby tree moved by a need to pray to a being more powerful than himself. Embracing the trunk wildly, he cries, "O you who are the most beautiful, the greatest, the strongest of all the children of the forest, take pity on an unfortunate one who has recourse to you."*

Father Point insisted that when youths told their spirit quest stories, "You can be sure that his genius for invention will be able to make up for deficiencies." In contrast, Father De Smet insisted that the Salish were "scrupulously honest . . . lying is hateful to them beyond anything else."

Resenting the priest's hard line, the Salish began to avoid the mission. Mengarini and Point blamed De Smet for the Indians' rebellion. They wrote to Father Roothram, Rome's appointment to oversee the missions, and complained that De Smet had given the Salish false hopes by telling them the church would establish villages and provide plows and animals. "We are expecting other distressing things to occur very soon by reason of the lavish promises which Father De Smet scattered about him everywhere in his journey." The priests also complained that De Smet misrepresented the extent of the physical hardship they would experience in the rugged mountain missions.

De Smet's vision of a Paraguayan community gave way to Christianizing through immersion in white culture. In general, the church was not prepared to take a liberal approach to converting the natives of America. Most church officials recognized that Salish animism differed radically from Roman Catholic theology. For the Salish, animal, human, and earth were interconnected—life breathed through all. Catholicism, as is true of most European religious thought, separated spirit and matter. The roots of Black Robe theology were firmly planted in European soil.

This world view evolved during the sixth century B.C. when Greek philosopher Parmenides proposed that a divine principle directed the world from afar. This essence was objective, static, and distinct from the earth and humanity. From this dualistic separation much of the religious intellectual thinking of Western civilization developed.

In contrast to Parmenides, Heraclitus, his peer, taught that the world was alive. The Greek hylozoists, who ascribed to his teachings, believed spirit and matter coexisted. Endowed with *pneuma* or cosmic air, the earth breathed like a human body. This organic view paralleled that of ancient Indian philosophy already flourishing in the East and the Americas.

In western Europe, Parmenides' view stuck. In 500 B.C. Aristotle systematized and organized it with his heavenly realm juxtaposed against the carnal earth. Plato reinforced it with his notions of forms and ideas, and after the death of Christ the apostle Paul christened it. Paul wrote that all of creation was completely separated from God. Because of Adam and Eve's sin, humanity would toil against the thorns of a fallen planet (Genesis 3). Humanity's instincts, essence, and goodness were filth in the sight of a holy creator (Romans 3). According to Paul, Christ's sacrifice paid for human sin, but creation would be forever tainted with its stain.

The church's preoccupation with human wickedness became more obvious in the Middle Ages. In an attempt to bridge the gap between God and human, monastic orders arose. Saint Anthony (A.D. 251–356), regarded as the founder of monasticism, sold all of his possessions, gave the money to the poor, and lived in a cave. To achieve holiness and win God's approval, Saint Simeon (A.D. 390–459) buried himself up to his neck for three months, then climbed a sixty-foot pole near Antioch and spent the next thirty-five years atop it. Other Catholic monks lived in fields like cattle, eating grass, or burned their fingers off to dispel the temptation of women.

This view of the fallen nature of man and earth was completely foreign to the Salish. Their myths reflect a belief in basic (although sometimes confused) human goodness and connectedness to the earth and its creatures. Coyote was both animal and human. He had the face, hands, and feet of a man, and the body of an animal. In the beginning, the Sun created the heavens and earth and commissioned Coyote to prepare the land for humans. The fortunate creature took beautiful Indian maidens, and from these unions the various tribes emerged. He also transformed wicked monsters into mountains and valleys.

South of Camas Prairie existed an evil creature who swallowed innocent passersby. After a battle of wits, Coyote defeated the monster and turned him into Corican Canyon. Coyote also gave the Salish the gift of fire and taught them to make utensils and weapons. Still, the Trickster was far from perfect. Alongside his benevolence lay cunning and greed. He loved to play tricks, mock, and imitate others. Unlike the perfect Christ, in native religion God's representative wore a human face, possessed an animal's body, and had a human's strengths and weaknesses.

The Salish also viewed the earth differently. To them it provided more than sustenance. From it evolved their traditions, power, and religion. Instead of considering it alien and fallen, they embraced it as god, mother, and tutor. The world possessed a life force to unite with, as the ancient Yokuts chant describes:

> *My words are tied in one*
> *with the great mountains,*
> *with the great rocks,*
> *with the great trees,*
> *in one with my body*
> *and my heart. . . .*
> *And you, day,*
> *and you, night!*
> *All of you see me*
> *one with the world.*

Mengarini and Point preached a different point of view. When the Salish began to reject their dogma, the priests warned of God's judgment. When game became scarce Point declared the following:

> *As for the results of hunting and fishing, if they have not been what they used to be, blame no one but yourself . . . you know what God's punishment is; you may well tremble lest you be so punished. Search your hearts and your lodges to see whether there does not remain something of the old superstitions. And if something does still remain of them make haste to bring it to me that I may burn it to remove the cause of the misfortunes threatening you.*

Rebukes like this caused the Salish to avoid the mission, remaining longer on their fall buffalo hunts. They left the priests without food or protection from Blackfeet attacks. Fearing for their lives, the priests appealed to De Smet.

De Smet's solution, however, alienated the Salish even further. In an attempt to establish peace, he traveled to the Blackfeet and offered them Christianity. Delighted to have access to enhanced power, the tribe embraced the Christian message. For years they had witnessed the Salish praying before battle and then, even though greatly outnumbered, triumphing. Happy to embrace this potent medicine, the Blackfeet added Catholic rituals to their own.

The Salish interpreted De Smet's missionizing as bestowing their aggressors with protective power and, therefore, as a betrayal. Although the priest assured his original converts that Catholicism would unite the tribes in peace, the Salish believed differently, and their suspicion of Blackfeet pacifism proved valid. Within months the eastern tribe began attacking again. By now the Salish had almost completely abandoned St. Mary's. The priests continued to rebuke them, citing apostasy as the reason for a smallpox outbreak that claimed eighty-seven lives.

After Cayuse Indians killed the Protestant missionaries Marcus and Narcissa Whitman in 1847, the priests grew even more concerned.[8] Finally, in 1850 the church sold St. Mary's to trapper John Owen, who promptly converted it into a trading post that served incoming settlers. Mengarini declared that its closure was intended to "punish the Indians and bring them to a sense of duty."[9] The priests hoped that the Salish would repent and request to return. However,

St. Mary's remained a trading post until the Catholics reopened it sixteen years later to minister to a small group of followers.

Once Owen took charge, he placed a whiskey keg in the same location that Mengarini had offered mass. Trader Richard Grant wrote, "I am inclined to the opinion that religion and the fur trade in these parts are hand in hand declining as civilization is increasing."[10]

Politicians

The U.S. government set out to see that "civilization" did indeed increase. Although most politicians did not carry the banner of Christ, their view of nature often mirrored the church's. Many saw the earth as separate and disposable, and the West as a wilderness to be tamed. Like Catholicism, this secular dualism also sprang from Europe.

European intellectual heritage, established during the Enlightenment, declared matter to be dead. Sir Isaac Newton explained this view in his *Philosophiae Naturalis Principia Mathematica*. Classical physics proclaimed that immovable "natural laws" drove everything. In this steady-state model of the universe, the earth, objective and distinct from humans, marched to unchangeable rules. Both Darwinism and the Industrial Revolution bolstered this mechanistic outlook, helping form the underpinnings of much American thought. Many in the United States, especially the political elite, built their world view on this positivist, static notion of life and applied it to the land.

Although naturalists did exist, by and large most Americans viewed the West merely in terms of settlement. The government encouraged this objective, systematic cultivation of the soil, calling it the great Manifest Destiny of the nation. Thus, westward expansion became the rallying cry of politicians who believed such a movement to be an inevitable and necessary component of America's promising future.

However, Jefferson's ideal of yeoman farmers methodically cultivating wilderness into farmland would only be possible if they had access to it. The government took seriously its self-appointed task of getting Americans onto open land, believing the most efficient way of accomplishing this was over railroad tracks. Many declared that

Gustavus Sohon's 1853 sketch of Camas Prairie.

once rail lines existed, people and goods could be transported across the continent and the foundation for America's greatness would be complete. To establish tracks, in 1853 Congress authorized the War Department "to ascertain the most practicable and economical route for a railroad from the Mississippi River to the Pacific Ocean." Next, it commissioned three surveying expeditions to explore a northern, a central, and a southern route.

It appointed Isaac Stevens, governor of the newly established Washington Territory, as head of the northern route between the forty-seventh and forty-ninth parallels from the Mississippi River to Puget Sound.[11] Stevens left St. Paul in early June 1853 and headed west. He ordered Lieutenant Rufus Saxton to leave Fort Dalles on the Columbia River and to meet him at Owen's post in Montana. With eighteen soldiers, including Lieutenant John Mullan and German-born enlisted officer and artist Gustavus Sohon, the party journeyed east via the Columbia River and up the Clark Fork. They moved overland at Wild Horse Plains, crossing Camas Prairie and reentering the river at Perma, then south to the post. En route, the force met Owen himself. The trader told them he was tired of defending himself against Blackfeet attack and was abandoning the trading store. Saxton reassured Owen that the U.S. Army would remedy such aggression and convinced him to return to the fort with them.

Stevens reached Fort Owen soon after Saxton arrived. The governor declared the railroad's biggest challenge would be blazing a trail through the Rocky Mountains. To obtain adequate information to construct such a route, he ordered Mullan to conduct extensive surveys of the intermountain region. Sohon, who had become quite fluent in Salish, was assigned duties as linguist and artist of the expedition. Stevens continued west for Olympia.

Mullan moved fifteen miles south and on the Bitterroot River constructed fourteen log huts to serve as headquarters, naming the settlement Cantonment Stevens. During 1853 and 1854, the party crossed the Continental Divide six times, making extensive observations of landmarks, weather, flora, and geography while Sohon sketched the landscape. In 1853 from its northwest entrance, he sketched Camas Prairie.

In the spring of 1854, Sohon drew a remarkable series of portraits.[12] Chief Victor of the Flatheads was a boy when Lewis and Clark passed through the Bitterroot Valley. His father, then head chief, welcomed the explorers. Victor's Salish name was Mitt to', or Plenty of Horses. As a child he embraced traditional Salish religion and received the powerful spirit of the rabbit, which saved him from death when he fell from a horse during a raid on the Crows. He lay concealed in the brush just outside the Crow camp for an entire day while the tribe searched around him.

Victor accepted Christianity immediately after De Smet arrived. He became the priest's devoted friend and mourned the loss of St. Mary's. Victor tried to convince his people to remain faithful to the church. However, when an enemy struck Victor and, in an attempt to respond in Christian humility, he did

Victor, head chief of the Flathead. Sketch by Gustavus Sohon.

Moise, second chief of the Flathead.
Sketch by Gustavus Sohon.

not defend himself, he lost much standing with the tribe. Nonetheless, he remained chief and became a major player in the 1855 Hellgate Treaty. It was at Victor's request in 1864 that the priests returned to St. Mary's. Victor also remained a dedicated friend to fur trader Angus McDonald. On his deathbed he requested that after his death his prized horse be given to McDonald.

As a boy, Moise of the Flathead also met Lewis and Clark during their visit to the Bitterroot Valley. His Salish name was Stet-ish-lutse-so, or Crawling Mountain. As a man, he headed the delegation that welcomed Father De Smet. Moise sent his finest horse ahead as a gift for the priest. De Smet named Moise (French for "Moses") upon his Christian baptism. The priest surnamed him "Bravest of the Brave" because of his incredible valor in battle. He also claimed that Moise was "one of the greatest chieftains of the tribe, in whom real piety and true valor at war were united."

Moise wore a long red scarf after the manner of the marshals of France and was acknowledged for his superior skill as a horseman and war leader. Sohon commented that Moise "possessed a keen and realistic insight into the military problems of the region." Although Moise embraced white religion, he refused to give up his native customs. When Victor did not return the blow of his rival, Moise declared the act cowardice.

The shaman Bear Track received great power from the white buffalo calf. His medicine allowed him to foresee the outcome of battle and the approach of the enemy. Although the priests baptized Bear Track and gave him a Christian name, he was never mentioned in their voluminous correspondence. His great magical powers influenced the people and infuriated the priests. For instance, during the hunt one year, the tribe could not find buffalo, so Bear Track erected a long tent, entered it, and called to the white buffalo calf. After his prayers, he emerged and said to his people, "The buffalo are coming, and the white calf will lead them." The next day a large herd of bison appeared, led by an albino calf.

Bear Track could also locate missing people. After a woman requested his help in finding her husband, he described the location of the man's horse but told her sadly that her husband was gone. The tribe found the horse in the exact location specified. The hunter's body lay some distance

Bear Track, Flathead chief and medicine man. Sketch by Gustavus Sohon.

away. A few nights before, the hunter had built a fire and after he fell asleep a burning log rolled off and killed him.

Along with the Flathead portraits, Sohon added the Pend d'Oreille and Kalispel Indians, claiming that they were the same people. By 1850 whites often grouped the two tribes, simply calling them Pend d'Oreille.

Alexander, head chief of the Pend d'Oreille, had the Indian name Tum-cle-hot-cut-se, which translated as No Horses. When the Blackfeet stole his horses at Fort Benton in north-central Montana, he formed a party of five men to retrieve them. Once he'd gathered the steeds, he returned directly through the camp of his deadly enemies. Even as a boy Alexander displayed great courage. At age thirteen, he volunteered to ride alone through hostile Crow country and obtain badly needed ammunition. As a man he made a similar trip to Fort Benton for bullets. He and two companions passed through the heart of Blackfeet country,

Alexander, head chief of the Pend d'Oreille. Sketch by Gustavus Sohon.

Big Canoe, second chief of the Pend d'Oreille. Sketch by Gustavus Sohon.

where they stopped to kill nine buffalo before returning home safely. Sohon recorded that Alexander was known for his "high-toned, sterling and noble traits of character. He was a brave man."

Big Canoe was born in 1799 and was nearly sixty years old during Sohon's visit. Big Canoe's Indian name was In-er-cult-say, which translated as Rotten Under the Belt, in honor of the enemy scalps he kept tied to his belt. Indian agent Peter Ronan claimed that he was "considered one of the greatest warriors the Pend d'Oreille ever had" and that "stories of battles led by him would fill a volume." However, although Big Canoe was a war leader, he worked diligently to achieve peace until his death in 1882.

Several months after Sohon sketched these Salish chiefs, he returned with Lieutenant Mullan to Fort Dalles on the Columbia River.

American Indian Policy

In the early 1800s, the U.S. government treated native tribes as miniature sovereign nations. It recognized that Indian peoples had long interacted with one another under this political structure. Each tribe was unique and had a firm set of enemies and alliances. But as the white population increased, along with its desire for Indian land, politicians ruled that tribes would now be treated as domestic, dependent nations and, in order to retain any of their sovereign status, they had to agree to relocation on land west of the Mississippi. Moving these Indians resulted in such tragedies as the Trail of Tears, during which one in eight Cherokees died on their way to their new "homeland."

Soon, however, American expansionists' dreams intervened again. As whites crossed the plains, they killed game and destroyed crops on this new Indian land. Unwilling to control white settlers, the government improvised with another plan, the creation of reserves. The program moved tribes onto smaller tracts of land, thus opening more soil to white settlers and enforcing a separation of the races. The government viewed these sites as training grounds to prepare Indian peoples for ultimate integration into white society. By temporarily separating them onto reservations, it set out to teach farming and language skills to Native Americans.

A great proponent of this system was Governor Stevens. Soon after arriving in Olympia in 1854, Stevens began plans to annex Northwest natives onto reserves. He wrote to the commissioner of Indian affairs, stating, "There is much valuable land and an inexhaustible supply of timber east of the Cascades. I consider its speedy settlement so desirable that all impediments should be removed." Stevens also bemoaned, "Under the land law of Congress it is impossible [for settlers] to secure titles to land, and thus the growth of towns and villages are obscured."[13]

The series of councils began in late May 1855. The first was held in eastern Washington and included the Walla Walla, Cayuse, Umatilla, Yakima, and Nez Perce. The governor, accompanied by Sohon as interpreter-artist and twenty-two soldiers, met the Indians at Mill Creek, six miles above the site of the ill-fated Whitman Mission.

Stevens wrote his treaties beforehand, arriving at the councils merely to obtain Indian signatures. As he would with all tribal negotiations he performed, he started by promising much and then, when the chiefs hesitated, used threats and humiliation to force their compliance. Not long into the meetings, the angry Cayuse talked of ambushing the governor. With that, the Nez Perce intervened and protected Stevens by pitching their tepees around his. The uneasy negotiations finally resulted in cession of more than sixty thousand square miles of native land to the U.S. government. In return Stevens promised the five tribes three reservation sites. Once he received the necessary signatures he departed, leaving many of the Indians feeling angry and cheated.

From Walla Walla, Stevens moved eastward into present-day Montana. On the banks of the Missoula River, seven miles northwest of today's city of Missoula, Stevens met with Sohon's old friends. The governor insisted that one chief represent each of the tribes.

This form of arbitration was foreign to the Salish, who made tribal decisions in full councils of chiefs, subchiefs, and warriors. However, Stevens appointed as spokesmen Victor for the Bitterroot Salish or Flathead, Alexander for the Pend d'Oreille and Kalispel, and Michele for the Kootenai. Subchiefs present included Moise, Bear Track, and Big Canoe.

The council opened on July 9, 1855. Counting on the legendary friendship the Salish extended to the whites, Stevens believed the proceedings would take but a day. He also assumed Victor would be lethargic and easily led. He felt the old chief appeared simple-minded, and rather wanting in energy. The old chief was about to surprise him.

Before Stevens arrived, Lieutenant Mullan told the Salish that the purpose of the council was to establish a peace treaty between them and the Blackfeet. Instead, immediately upon convening, the governor informed the tribes of his desire for them to inhabit a single reservation, comprising a small portion of the land they had traditionally held. When the chiefs objected, Stevens listed the benefits they would receive: $120,000 over the following fifteen years to construct homes and fences and to purchase food and clothing; an agricultural and industrial school open to Indian children and stocked with books and supplies; a blacksmith shop; a tin and gun shop; a carpenter's shop; a wagon and plowmaker's shop; a sawmill and a flour mill; a hospital stocked with medicine and furniture; and a physician. All facilities would be kept in repair and fully supplied by the U.S. government. And because the head chiefs provided leadership for the people, each would be given a comfortable, furnished house, with ten acres of plowed and fenced land and $500 a year.[14]

Stevens adjourned the meeting without having achieved consensus. The governor felt that given a day to discuss the benefits, the chiefs would surely compromise. When Stevens opened the council the next day, Big Canoe spoke. With pride he pointed out that the Salish had not spilled a drop of white blood, so why was there need for a treaty? In light of the tribe's concept of hospitality, he believed everyone could live together peaceably. Stevens ignored Big Canoe and turned to Victor, Alexander, and Michele and asked if they had made a decision. The chiefs told him of their willingness to live on one reservation but added they could not decide on a location. No one wanted to leave any tribe's traditional homeland.

Frustrated, Stevens adjourned the meeting. He blamed Angus McDonald for the Indians' stubbornness. Several years earlier the government had demanded that the Hudson's Bay Company cease trading at Fort Connah. The Canadians had continued a vigorous business, and Stevens believed McDonald plotted to sabotage U.S. dealings with the Salish. To turn the negotiations around, he proclaimed the next day one of feasting and supplied meat, sugar, flour, and other goods.

During the festivities Alexander approached Victor to discuss the treaty. He told the chief that the Pend d'Oreille would move to the Bitterroot Valley. At that, Pend d'Oreille headsman Red Wolf laughed and told Alexander that no one would follow him. Bear Track declared he would never leave the Bitterroot Valley, and Moise added that he objected to any land cession whatsoever. When Victor refused to respond to Alexander's offer, the Pend d'Oreille chief withdrew.

The next day Stevens anxiously reconvened the council. Anticipating rapid acquiescence, he asked for a verdict. Subchief Ambrose revealed that Alexander had approached Victor but nothing was agreed upon. At that, Stevens went into a rage. He turned to Victor and called him an old woman and a dog. The aged chief stood up and walked out of the meeting. Alexander retorted that Stevens was twice as dumb as a dog.

Victor kept Stevens waiting for three days. On Monday, July 12, he informed the governor he would not move his people until the president of the United States came to Montana to survey the area. The old chief trusted only the "Great White Father" to make a fair decision. Until then he would not budge. Anxious for an agreement, Stevens had the compromise written into Article 11 of the treaty.

Everyone but Moise signed the Hellgate Treaty of 1855. When presented with it, Moise bitterly denounced the contract, declaring that the Salish would never have come if Lieutenant Mullan had not promised them there would be "no talk of land" and that the purpose of the council was to establish a peace treaty with the Blackfeet. He added that he had no faith in Governor Stevens's promises.

Unaffected by the comments, Stevens wrote to Indian agent Colonel Simmons in Olympia, reporting things had "proceeded grandly" and he would soon journey east to confront the Blackfeet. Victor, Alexander, Moise, Bear Track, Big Canoe, and ten other Salish warriors accompanied Stevens east.

Once the Blackfeet assembled, Stevens revealed his plan of intertribal peace and his desire that both tribes share a limited hunting ground east of the Rockies, west of Crow territory, and south of the Musselshell River. All other buffalo land would be Blackfeet territory and closed to the Salish. The land off-limits to them included the ancient hunting ground over Marias Pass.

Stevens's treaty was signed intact and he immediately made preparations to return to Idaho and convene his last council with the Spokane, Colville, and Coeur d'Alene tribes. However, on October 29, the day after his party left, a mounted courier brought alarming news. War had broken out between the Columbia Plateau Indians and whites. A war party had defeated Major George Haller, and a large force of Yakima warriors who had attended the Walla Walla council waited to intercept Stevens and kill him. Acting governor Charles Mason urged Stevens to return to Olympia, Washington, by traveling east and boarding a ship from New York that would travel around the continent. Instead, the governor purchased additional guns and ammunition from Fort Benton and quietly crossed the Northern Rockies.

After Stevens arrived home in Washington, he sent Dr. Richard Lansdale, a Puget Sound physician, to Salish country to survey the land and determine the best location for the reservation. While hunting buffalo on the Musselshell, Victor's band were oblivious to the fact that, instead of a U.S. president, a physician would soon forecast their future. It was only the first of many promises Stevens and the government would break.

Landsdale declared in favor of the northern location around the newly established St. Ignatius Mission. Several years after the closure of St. Mary's, Father Adrian Hoecken had moved his struggling St. Ignatius Mission from north of Lake Pend d'Oreille to the base of a beautiful mountain range thirty miles east of Camas Prairie.

Boundary of the Flathead Indian Reservation compiled for the General Land Office under the direction of Captain William Ludlow, U.S. Corps of Engineers, and published in May 1875. Courtesy of National Archives.

Landsdale felt the mission would be an asset in teaching the Indians farming skills. However, although the land to the north was officially declared the territory of the Flathead Indian Reservation, the Bitter-root Salish (or Flathead) refused to move and remained in the valley, waiting for a president to arrive.

A U.S. president was never sent to fulfill the terms of Article 11. The government did not ratify the Hellgate Treaty until 1859 and, even after that, did not carry out its physical or monetary commitments to the Salish and Kootenai. Instead of the needed physical aid, the government sent the Indians a series of disreputable Indian agents, men who either stole the meager goods that did arrive or stayed too drunk to care about unsatisfied promises. One such character was John Wells. Intoxicated most of the time, he imagined wolves constantly prepared to attack the agency. He kept the entire staff on watch to dispel the phantom beasts. Wells's son fled after he was caught in a liaison with the cook, after which Wells decided his elderly workman Charles Schafft was in fact his son.

Wells called a conference in which Victor, Alexander, Angus McDonald, John Owen, and Father Giorda—newly appointed to the St. Ignatius Mission—attended. When the chiefs tried to address the Hellgate Treaty, Wells immediately ended the meeting, commenting that he was glad to see the Salish looking "well, strong, fat and not sick."[15] The hungry Salish returned home.

With each passing year, game was becoming scarcer. To compound the problem, Stevens forbade the sale of ammunition to any Native American in the territory. Even after Victor reiterated the Salish's commitment of friendship, Stevens refused. The governor's heavy-handedness and deceit had helped spur the Northwest Indian Wars. Stevens was knee-deep in trouble and couldn't take any chances.

The Army

Plains tribes to the east and the Columbia Plateau Indians to the west attacked white settlers. White encroachment from the gold rush and broken promises, like those of the governor, ignited smoldering resentment. In response, the U.S. Army established Forts Kearny, Laramie, and Walla Walla to protect whites from Indian reprisal.

In 1876 Lieutenant Colonel Wesley Merrit visited the Bitterroot Valley and concluded that it also needed a military presence to protect settlers from "outlaws" and "half-breeds" who carried on contraband trade with the Salish. In February 1877, President Grant authorized the building of Fort Missoula.

Conflict between whites and Indians ignited battles across the West. The Oregon Volunteers marched against the peaceable Walla Walla Indians. When the distinguished Walla Walla leader Peu-peu-mox-mox proffered a white flag while approaching the white soldiers, they seized and murdered him. In the words of a witness, "They skinned him from head to foot, and made razor straps of his skin."[16] The officers reportedly drank toasts from glasses containing his ears. After the mutilation, the Walla Wallas took up arms against the whites.

When gold was discovered in the Black Hills in 1874, white miners demanded that the Lakota Sioux relinquish the land. When the Indians refused, the government dispatched troops to protect miners in the hills. Angry Sioux warriors gathered at the camps of Sitting Bull and Crazy Horse to discuss the miners' trespassing. U.S. Army troops closed in on the camps. At the Battle of the Rosebud in eastern Montana, the Sioux defeated their attackers. Then in June, under command of General George Armstrong Custer, six hundred U.S. soldiers launched another assault. This time, two thousand allied warriors waited for them. At the Little Big Horn, when Custer arrogantly divided his battalion and attacked, the Indians converged and annihilated the white soldiers. The next year, the Nez Perce made their astonishing flight through Montana toward asylum in Canada.

The Nez Perce had always been friendly to whites. In 1805 they saved the Lewis and Clark Expedition from starvation. They traveled with the Salish to seek Catholic missionaries and welcomed settlers into their territory. At the Walla Walla council, they protected Isaac Stevens and then peacefully ceded much of their homeland to the government. Even after other Columbia Plateau tribes went to war in protest of the treaty, the Nez Perce remained pacific.

In the Walla Walla treaty, the United States promised the Nez Perce specific tracts of land, one of which was the Wallowa Valley of northeastern Oregon. However, in 1863 gold was discovered in its foothills and whites soon began encroaching on the land in violation of the 1855 Stevens Treaty that stated, "Nor shall any white man be permitted to reside upon the reservation without the permission of the Indian tribe." The government ignored the trespass and eventually found a Nez Perce subchief named Lawyer, who did not live in the Wallowa Mountains, to sign a new treaty relinquishing the valley—along with other Nez Perce lands. The agreement cut the tribe's holdings to one-tenth the size agreed upon in the 1855 treaty. An ecstatic superintendent of Indian affairs, Calvin H. Hale, wrote to the Washington Territory Indian commissioner that nearly seven million acres had been obtained at "a cost not exceeding eight cents per acre."[17] Chief Joseph, along with war leaders Looking Glass and White Bird, refused to acknowledge the new contract.

Joseph had received his name, Hin-mah-too-yah-lat-kekt, "Thunder Rolling in the Mountains," during his spirit quest in the Wallowas. When his father, Tuekakas, died in 1871, leaving Joseph chief at age thirty-two, the old warrior warned his son that the whites would soon come for the land. Tuekakas told Joseph, "My son, never forget my words. This country holds your father's body. Never sell the bones of your father and mother." Joseph replied that he "would protect his grave with my life. I buried him in that beautiful valley of windy waters. I love that land more than all the rest of the world."[18]

On May 21, 1877, Tuekakas's warning came true. General O. O. Howard informed Joseph that he had thirty days to gather his people and stock and move to the Lapwai Reservation in Idaho. Joseph insisted that the Snake River was too high at the time and fording it would be extremely dangerous. Howard told Joseph if he did not move his people, the U.S. Army would—with bullets and bayonets. If he stayed the military would attack the tribe.

By June 8, Joseph and his people had crossed the Snake, leaving most of their stock behind. Once on the other side, Joseph and the other Nez Perce leaders gathered for a council. Joseph advised against war, but on June 14, after three warriors killed four white settlers in anger about the treaty, he knew conflict was inevitable. Joseph told his people that whites seldom distinguished between the actions of individual Indians and those of an entire tribe.

The young chief was correct. Although the Nez Perce raised a flag of truce over their camp at White Bird Canyon, U.S. troops attacked. After a bloody battle, the army retreated and the Nez Perce began their remarkable flight toward Canada. Once General Howard heard of the skirmish, he began his own pursuit of the Indians. However, when he engaged the Indians at the Salmon River, the Nez Perce outsmarted the general and the people escaped eastward. When Howard caught up with them at South Fork, the Nez Perce defeated the general once again and fled.

On July 21 the Nez Perce entered Montana. They made their way down Lolo Pass and entered its hot springs to bathe and care for their wounded. Settlers in Montana feared that the Salish would join the Nez Perce and wage war on the whites. Montana governor Benjamin Potts contacted the new Flathead agent, Peter Ronan, asking him to talk to the Salish and to counsel alliance with the whites.

Montanans feared that Charlot, Victor's son and chief since his death, would willingly join Joseph. They knew he had reason to. A year earlier, in 1871, many of the same settlers had petitioned the government to evict the Salish from the Bitterroot Valley. Charlot and his people remained, citing the fact that no president had come to the Bitterroot to fulfill the stipulations of 1855. Now whites numbered in the thousands and insisted the Salish be moved north onto the reservation. President Ulysses S. Grant sent James Garfield to persuade Charlot to go. In council, Garfield promised Charlot and two subchiefs, Arlee and Adolph, that once they relocated to the reserve the government would build them comfortable homes. Both Arlee and Adolph signed the contract, but Charlot refused. Garfield claimed, however, that he believed Charlot would eventually sign, and when the treaty was published an "X" appeared next to Charlot's name. Garfield admitted he had decided to "proceed with the work in the same manner as though Charlot had signed the contract."[19] Victor's son was furious and reiterated his refusal to move. In an attempt to force his compliance, a property tax was imposed on the tribe. Charlot again bitterly denounced the tactics by stating that the whites wanted money "for things he never owned and never gave us."[20] With the incident so fresh at hand, the settlers feared an alliance between the Salish and their Nez Perce friends.

Nonetheless, when Ronan visited with Charlot, the chief responded with these words:

> *It was my father's boast that the blood of a white man never reddened the hands of a single Indian of the Flathead tribe. My father died with that boast on his lips. I am my father's son and will leave that same boast to my children.*[21]

111

Chief Joseph, Hin-mah-too-yah-lat-kekt, or Thunder Rolling in the Mountain in 1877. Courtesy of the Montana Historical Society.

Instead of joining the Nez Perce, Charlot maintained strict neutrality. He would not fight the whites, but he also would not fight against the Nez Perce. Charlot advised Joseph, Looking Glass, and White Bird to travel north, where few whites lived, through the reservation and into Canada. With the news of Charlot's advice, a pony express rider fled through Camas Prairie and to Wild Horse Plains, warning settlers to flee.

However, the settlers had little to fear. The Nez Perce had not come to Montana to fight. They believed they'd left the conflict behind. As Duncan McDonald (son of Angus and Catherine) would later report, "Looking Glass said he did not want any trouble on this side of the Lolo. . . . He did not want to fight either soldiers or citizens east of the Lolo because they were not the ones [he] had fought in Idaho."[22] The Nez Perce believed that the people of Montana did not identify with the people of Idaho and that they were entirely distinct, having nothing to do with each other. They entered Lolo

Chief Charlot, Stemxaike', or Little Claw of the Grizzly Bear, circa 1870. Courtesy of the Montana Historical Society.

Pass, where Captain Charles C. Rawn, who had recently arrived in Montana to begin construction of Fort Missoula, met them. Initially, Rawn, two dozen soldiers, and a number of civilian volunteers had set out from Missoula to force a Nez Perce surrender. However, Rawn soon realized the futility of such a plan and allegedly made a peace pact with the Indians. After talks on July 26 and 27, the Nez Perce genuinely believed that if they did no harm to the Bitterroot settlers, the Bitterroot settlers would do no harm to them. The Nez Perce crossed Lolo Pass and traveled south to Stevensville, where they traded with merchants.

Angus McDonald's wife, Catherine, herself Nez Perce and a cousin of both Looking Glass and White Bird, advised the tribe to travel east through Montana, where they could hunt buffalo before reaching Canada. After the chiefs held a council, they decided indeed to move southeast.

Meanwhile, however, the army had continued its pursuit. During the evening of August 8, at Big Hole Basin, General John Gibbon's squadron surrounded the encampment of men, women, and children. The Nez Perce, convinced their war was over, had neither sent out scouts nor posted sentries. To compound their disadvantage, they'd spent the evening in celebration and dancing and were in a deep sleep when, on Thursday morning, the soldiers attacked. As Duncan McDonald reported, "The camp was awakened to find their enemies plunging through it, dealing death and destruction in every direction." Within twenty minutes the soldiers had complete possession of the camp and were following orders to destroy everyone in it. A warrior named Wounded Head would later recall awaking to the horrible realization that his wife and baby both had been shot. Women and children were massacred while getting out of bed. One soldier entered a tepee and killed the five children who slept there.

Miraculously, the Nez Perce rallied amid the slaughter. Sharpshooters took to the hills and began picking off the soldiers. Warriors stormed the camp and captured the army's howitzer and two thousand rounds of ammunition. The Indians then set fire to the grass and the frightened army retreated. Both sides lost nearly thirty men. Along with soldiers and warriors, however, more than fifty Nez Perce women and children were killed. After viewing the dead bodies, Major John Mason wrote to his wife, "It was a dreadful sight, dead men, women, and children. More squaws were killed than men were. I have never been in a fight where women were killed, and I hope never again to be." Corporal Charles Loyne recalled seeing a young Nez Perce woman "lying dead with the baby on her breast crying as it swung its little arm back and forth—the lifeless hand flapping at the wrist which had been broken by a bullet." General Gibbon later called the action "unavoidable" but also admitted that it "marked the culminating point of the maltreatment of the Indians in this country."

Observing the battlefield two years later, fur trader Andrew Garcia wrote, "Human bones were scattered through the long grass and among the willows . . . and leering skulls were scattered around us as though they had never been buried. . . . This ghastly display of Indian dead made me doubtful for the first time in my life if there is a Jesus or a God."

From the Big Hole Battlefield, the surviving Nez Perce fled southwest, crisscrossing Idaho and Montana. For three months they brilliantly evaded thousands of U.S. troops as they made their elusive northern advance. On September 13, Colonel Samuel Sturgis attacked at Canyon Creek. Again the tribe frustrated the military and escaped. Despite the army's investment of $1 million to capture them, the Nez Perce were still at liberty. News of the Indians' ability to baffle the military reached the eastern press. To make matters worse for the army, settlers began to sympathize with the tribe. After Elizabeth Fisk, a settler in southwestern Montana, encountered the tribe she wrote, "The Nez Perce warriors seem civilized and, like the gentlemen of the South in the days of the Rebellion, only ask to be let alone."

The tribe moved into Crow country, where they hoped to find refuge. However, they discovered Crow warriors had hired on as U.S. scouts, and so the weary Indians continued their push north. Finally, forty miles south of Canada and sanctuary with the self-exiled Sioux and Chief Sitting Bull, the Nez Perce rested before the final leg of their journey. They realized that Howard, whom they had evaded for months, was now far behind them. What they did not know, however, was that the general had sent a message to Fort Keogh, near present-day Miles City, Montana, instructing General Nelson Miles to wage an attack from the east. Miles and his mounted force sped northwestward across the plains.

On the morning of September 30, along the rain-drenched Snake Creek under the Bear Paw Mountains, 350 soldiers attacked the exhausted tribe. Even then, the warriors made a valiant defense. They dug into the steep riverbank, taking advantage of their expert marksmanship and forcing the army to charge repeatedly, while hundreds of their women and children escaped into Canada. Miles called it the hardest battle he'd ever waged.

After six days of bloody fighting, Chief Joseph and General Miles met to negotiate. Miles feared Sitting Bull was on his way to help the Nez Perce, so he promised Joseph that if the tribe surrendered he would return them unharmed to the reservation in Idaho. With this, Joseph relinquished, speaking these famous words:

I am tired of fighting. Our chiefs are killed. Looking Glass is dead. Toohulhulsate is dead. The old men are all dead. It is cold

115

and we have no blankets. The little children are freezing to death. My people, some of them, have run away to the hills and have no blankets, no food. No one knows where they are, perhaps freezing to death. I want to have time to look for my children and see how many of them I can find. Maybe I shall find them among the dead. Hear me, my chiefs. I am tired; my heart is sick and sad. From where the sun now stands I will fight no more, forever.[23]

In more than twenty pitched battles, this was the Nez Perce's only defeat. Joseph, Looking Glass, and White Bird had mastered a flight of eighteen hundred miles in seventy-five days with women, children, and the elderly. With never more than 250 warriors, they had engaged two thousand U.S. troops. General Howard arrived to claim victory, and West Point graduate Thomas Woodruff wrote to his mother, "We have Joseph and all his people, about 380 souls. It is the greatest victory over the Indians in our history."

When General William Tecumseh Sherman heard of Miles's promise to return the Nez Perce to Idaho, he overruled it. Sherman confessed that the Nez Perce "displayed a courage and skill that elicited universal praise; they abstained from scalping, let captive women go free, did not commit indiscriminate murder of peaceful families, and fought with almost scientific skill." Still, he intended to make an example of the tribe. The decorated general remained committed to his belief that all Indians must be "killed or maintained as a species of paupers."[24] In exchange for humbling the U.S. Army, Sherman made sure that Joseph was never allowed to return to his beloved Wallowa.

Instead, the general transported the tribe to Leavenworth, Kansas, then shifted them from place to place for years. During the next eight years, almost half of the Nez Perce captured at Snake Creek died from starvation or disease. Finally, in 1885, Joseph and 150 of his people were relocated to the Colville Reservation in western Washington. For the remainder of his life, the chief requested relocation to the Nez Perce homeland. However, both government officials and the valley's white homesteaders continually thwarted his efforts.

In November 1903, Joseph made his final public appeal in Seattle, Washington. He asked that, because he was an old man, he be allowed to return home to die. Once again he traveled back to Colville with no answers. Ten months later one of Joseph's wives found him slumped next to a pole inside his tepee. He had died of a heart attack. The agency doctor wrote that a broken heart had killed him. Officials refused Joseph's final request to be buried in the Wallowa Valley next to his father.

The Salish received little reward for their loyalty to the whites during the Nez Perce War. Because of its determination to keep ammunition out of the hands of all Native Americans, the U.S. government continued to withhold bullets from the tribe, leaving them with little means of providing meat for their families. Father D'Aste, a priest at the St. Ignatius Mission, questioned the future of the Salish: "I am afraid that plenty of suffering is in it for them. They are now very poor, and if the government fails to come to their help. . . . I am afraid that starvation will get the lot of them."[25]

In 1880 an aggressive assault on the Montana bison herd commenced to take advantage of the newly constructed railroads that provided a perfect means of transporting bison robes to eastern tanneries. By 1882, five thousand white hunters and skinners roamed the grasslands, annihilating the animals. By 1883 the plains bison had all but disappeared. That winter, the main source of meat for the Salish was nearly extinct and half of the Blackfeet tribe starved to death.

Meanwhile, miners poured into northwestern Montana in search of gold. Its discovery in the Coeur d'Alene Mountains brought thousands, exerting a greater demand on the land and its byways. Whites turned the Indian trail that passed through Camas Prairie into a wagon road, naming it the Clark Fork Trail.

During the 1860s Senator W. A. Clark bought a mail contract and began a pony express over the route beginning at Fort Missoula and ending at Fort Walla Walla. Clark built small cabins along the way and a post office at Wild Horse Plains. Heavily armed riders traveled day and night, stopping only at log huts to water their horses and to eat. The first leg ended at the St. Ignatius Mission. There

A Flathead Reservation Pony Express in Ravalli, circa 1880. Courtesy of Paul Fugleberg.

the mail was relayed to another rider, who completed the second leg following the Flathead River to Perma, across Camas Prairie, and over the low pass at Dog Lake to Wild Horse Plains. The mail carrier then traveled down the Clark Fork River and on to Idaho and Washington.

Clark's pony express was a vigorous business until he sold it to the Northern Pacific Railroad in 1883. A new means of postal service and transportation had arrived in Montana. The transcontinental "iron horse" would make even the remotest parts of the West accessible and the government's dream a reality.

Chapter 5

Dividing the Claim

fter funding extensive railroad surveys, the U.S. government
bestowed land grants toward laying tracks. For western railroads alone, Congress extended more than 125 million acres, along
with loans ranging from $16,000 to $48,000 per mile, depending
upon the nature of the terrain the lines crossed.

Congress calculated that these land grants would benefit the government, the small farmer, and the railroads. It divided the acreage
along the tracks in checkerboard fashion, granting one section to the
railroads and selling the next to settlers. Because the land adjoining
the line was more valuable, the government limited farm sections to
80 acres, in theory making the land twice as expensive as the traditional 160-acre homestead sites, and thus generating as much revenue as if the grants had never been given.

The farmer also gained. Railroads provided an inexpensive means
of receiving goods and transporting crops. Most farmers preferred to
settle along railroad routes or to attract the lines to areas that had
already been homesteaded. The railroads profited as well when farmers
lived nearby. By selling excess land-grant acreage to farmers, the rail
owners obtained funds to defer construction costs and the number of
paying customers increased. In fact, when the railroads or government
could not coax homesteaders into an area, companies went bankrupt.

This symbiotic relationship benefited all three parties. The government encouraged westward movement into untouched territory, the railroads built lines and clientele, and the farmers accessed an important key to their success—efficient transportation. It also created the infrastructure for the West's modern extractive economy. By providing transcontinental transportation for grain, timber, and minerals, as well as enlarging the markets for these goods, the east and Europe now had access to the region's great natural wealth.

The Northern Pacific, which pushed through the Flathead Reservation in 1883, would be the first transcontinental railroad to cross the northern United States. Financed by eastern investors and bolstered by land grants, the Northern Pacific carried Montana resources to both coasts: copper from Butte, lumber from the Rockies, and wheat from the prairies.

In 1882 the Northern Pacific petitioned the Salish for the right to cross their reservation. At first the tribe refused, regarding the tracks as "fatal to their interest, and the sure precursor of abandonment of their homes and lands to the whites."[1] Assistant attorney general Joseph McCammon met with the Salish chiefs and promised that if they negotiated with the Northern Pacific, he would propose adjusting the reservation boundary north to the Canadian border, thus giving the tribe adequate land for hunting and fishing. On September 2, 1882, the tribe agreed to sell a strip of land two hundred feet wide and fifty-three miles long. The railroad paid the tribe $16,000 for the property. McCammon never made good on his new boundary proposal.

As the railroad lines moved south from Lake Pend d'Oreille and approached the reservation, the Salish and Kootenai ejected Northern Pacific employees who had come to survey reservation land. Failed promises weren't the only thing the tribe worried about. Agent Peter Ronan wrote to the Indian commissioner:

> *An immense crew of railroad constructors is now at work west of the reservation, consisting of 7,400 with camp followers, gamblers, ex-convicts, and lewd women. They are rapidly advancing to the borders of the reservation, accompanied by*

> *portable saloons, gambling houses, etc. Merchants and traders of*
> *all descriptions also advance with the construction party.*[2]

Ronan and the Salish had reason to be concerned. Ten miles north of Wild Horse Plains the town of Weeksville had formed, attracting some of the country's most notorious outlaws.

Weeksville was named after I.S.P. Weeks, the Northern Pacific engineer in charge of the company's Missoula division. The town emerged after railroad builders stopped to blast a series of rock cliffs protruding from the Cabinet Mountains. To tear the granite apart, the crew ignited railroad cars filled with gunpowder. Hundreds died in the process—most were Chinese.

About six thousand Chinese laborers worked on the line from Spokane Falls to Helena. Along this distance of 380 miles, one thousand died. One explosion near Weeksville buried one hundred men under a hillside of flying debris. Another blast killed 150 after it hurled a rock cliff into their campsite. In unending mounds along the tracks, foot-deep graves appeared. In places, coffins emerged from the earth. Finally, in 1910 the Northern Pacific removed the graves to Missoula.

Chinese and American powdermen, merchants, saloon keepers, prostitutes, and criminals occupied Weeksville. By February 1882, twenty-two log houses and rows of tents existed. Four saloons thrived among the huts. Missoula merchant A. H. Hammond built a black-

Northern Pacific engine near Weeksville in 1890. Courtesy of Paul Fugleberg.

smith shop with stables, a bunkhouse, and a mess hall serving more than 125 meals a day. He also opened a department store and ran a sawmill that produced fifteen thousand feet of lumber each day, mostly for railroad ties. Helena resident Charles Zimmer moved in and built a hotel, and several Chinese washhouses opened for business.

The railroad paid its employees in silver and gold, and the merchants made sure workers had plenty to buy. This form of wage also attracted those who offered nothing in return. Within months, robbery became rampant and the citizens of Weeksville appointed Lew Wyghant as town marshal. Wyghant told the troublemakers to leave town.

Men like "Dick the Diver" had arrived from Arizona. Contemporaries described him as a "thief and a skull-breaker," an "ugly, stocky man who was a former associate of the Earp boys." Diver fronted as a night watchman and during the day robbed railmen and merchants. After a warehouse heist, he murdered the owner.

Other gunmen did not pretend to hold respectable jobs—bragging that robbery was their only means of support. Bandits named "Ohio Dan," "The Barber," "Sweeney," and "Billy the Kid" (not the infamous gunman who was killed a year earlier by Pat Garrett) all occupied this category.[3] Ohio Dan and The Barber worked together robbing and looting Weeksville businesses. Billy the Kid entered saloons and demanded that the gamblers hand over their gold pieces. Sweeney, usually drunk and drugged with opium, shot anybody naive enough to beat him at stud poker.

The townspeople feared helping one another lest they themselves be murdered. A Missoula businessman opened a saloon and left after he witnessed a killing and the assailants threatened to shoot him if he testified against them. Crime became so rampant that in December the citizens of Weeksville decided to replace Wyghant with a vigilante committee.

After Dick the Diver wore the hat of one of his murder victims to the man's funeral, he became the vigilantes' target. As he played blackjack in a saloon, the vigilantes surrounded the bar and called him to the door. Once he appeared they lassoed and gagged him, then dragged him onto the high back porch of the Weeksville Hotel.

The committee strung him up—slackening the rope just long enough to let him name his crimes, then tightening it and pushing him over the edge.

When Sweeney entered Curley Campbell's saloon and began harassing an old man who huddled near the stove, Campbell warned the intruder to get out. Completely intoxicated, Sweeney shot at the barkeep. When the bullets missed, Campbell, himself a gunman of notable talent, immediately put a bullet through Sweeney's chest. The vigilantes conducted a hurried inquiry in which Campbell was declared innocent, then they hid him in a barn until he could be smuggled out of the territory.

Ohio Dan and The Barber came next. The committee overtook them less than a mile west of Weeksville. The Barber had accidentally shot himself in the foot during a recent Wells Fargo heist and was on crutches. When the men saw the vigilantes riding toward them, Ohio Dan refused to abandon his friend, and they were both easily apprehended. After listing the crimes against their prisoners, the committee pronounced the men guilty and hanged them. They left the bodies dangling for several days, then cut them down and buried them near the railroad tracks. From The Barber's grave they protruded his crutches, which, oral history recounts, remained there for twenty years.

After the vigilantes warned Billy the Kid to leave Weeksville, and he sent word back for them to go to hell, three men pulled him out of a saloon into the street. Instead of hanging him, they ordered the boy to run for his life toward the Clark Fork River. He wasted no time in doing so, but before he reached the water they shot him to death.

Within months the committee had killed more than fifteen men. *The Missoulian* reported on January 26, 1883, that in Weeksville "everything is quiet and peaceful . . . no deprecations committed since the vigilant committee cleaned out the ruffians and cut-throats." The article also stated that the railroad was now "a stone's throw from the Flathead Indian Reservation."

It took the Northern Pacific most of a year to lay tracks through the reservation. The railroad line ran along the Clark Fork and Flathead Rivers through Perma—bypassing Camas Prairie—on to Ravalli, then south to Arlee and Missoula. Although some anticipated trouble, after the line had crossed the reserve, Peter Ronan observed a different outcome:

> *As proof that the [Salish] while undoubtedly brave, are also law-abiding, I refer with pride to the fact of the completion of the Northern Pacific Railroad through their lands, and against their strongest wishes, without any annoyance or opposition being offered to the Railroad Company.*[4]

By 1891 the Northern Pacific connected Seattle to Chicago. With the railroad complete, Salish fears proved prophetic.

Allotments

By this time, the legal groundwork for white settlement on the reservation was already in place. Five years earlier, Massachusetts senator Henry Dawes had proposed that Native Americans on reserves be assigned to individual tracts of land. The remaining land would then be declared "surplus" and made available to white settlers. The bill stipulated that these individual allotments could not be sold or taxed by the U.S. government for a term of twenty-five years. The bill, called the General Allotment or Dawes Act, passed without a hitch, pleasing both eastern reformers and western expansionists.

Eastern reformers, who dictated much of Indian policy, believed that property ownership and individual autonomy formed the cornerstones of civilization and that the nomadic, communal existence of native peoples prevented them from adapting this lifestyle. In 1889 the commissioner of Indian affairs praised the concept by stating, "Tribal relations should be broken up, socialism destroyed and the family and autonomy of the individual substituted. The allotment of land in severalty, the establishment of local courts and police and the development of a personal sense of independence and the universal adoption of the English language are means to this end."[5]

The western expansionists viewed the uncultivated acreage of reservation land as wasteful. Senator Dawes addressed this topic:

Inasmuch as the Indian refused to fade out, but multiplied under the sheltering care of reservation life, and the reservation itself was slipping away from him, there was but one alternative: either he must be endured as a lawless savage, a constant menace to civilized life, or he must be fitted to become part of that life and be absorbed into it.[6]

For the next thirty years, the Bureau of Indian Affairs applied the act with speed and lack of safeguards that surprised even Dawes himself. In 1881 Native Americans held approximately 156 million acres of land in the United States. By 1900 they held less than half of that.

Although in theory the act applied to all reservations, in fact a more specific bill was required to divide individual reserves. To protect the Salish and Kootenai, Agent Ronan fought its application, telling Congress that the tribe was bitterly opposed to land allotment. Ronan battled to keep whites off the reserve by impounding their stray cattle and taxing those he found. Ronan abated the encroachment until his death in 1893. Then, in 1895 state senator William H. Smead from Missoula introduced to the Montana legislature a measure to open the reservation to settlement. The legislature sent the recommendation on to Congress, and in 1897 Smead was appointed the new Flathead Indian agent.

While Montanans petitioned Congress to open reservation land, Smead took charge. He discouraged traditional ceremonies and forbid the Salish to hunt game in national forests. Smead also worked to fill government-funded schools with Indian children. Commissioner Hiram Price joined Smead's crusade. Price withheld rations and annuities from parents who refused to send their children to the school at the St. Ignatius Mission.

The Catholic Indian Bureau had obtained government funds for instruction at the mission school. Students were taught reading, writing, arithmetic, catechism, and household arts and provided with new clothing. They were taught popular ballads and Italian operas and provided with band instruments to replace native drums. They attended cultivation classes about the virtues of farming. The Catholic nuns cut the children's hair and forbade them to speak Salish and

The famous St. Ignatius Mission Boys' Band in Helena for a concert, circa 1900. Courtesy of the Montana Historical Society.

Kootenai. After visiting the school, a pleased supervisor of Indian education, William M. Moss, reported, "Very few . . . can speak Indian and have to talk to their parents through an interpreter."[7]

Even so, school supervisor R. C. Bauer worried that only 160 of the 500 Indian children on the reservation attended the mission school. To keep their children out, many Salish left the reservation before the beginning of the school year and did not return until late fall. To stop the truancy, Smead demanded that any Indian leaving the reservation obtain a pass.

To further assimilate the tribe, Smead crusaded to rid the reservation of "worthless" ponies. Each season, the Salish sold nearly nine thousand horses to eastern brokers who then retailed them to wealthy families. The agent believed this practice kept the Indians from becoming farmers. In 1903 he levied a tax on the herds. Each man could own a hundred and paid a dollar-per-head tariff for more than that.

The Salish on Camas Prairie, who for centuries had raised thousands of beautiful horses, would not pay Smead's tax. Because the valley was an adequate distance from the mission and was now bypassed by the railroad and most white travelers, Native Americans who chose to live a traditional lifestyle migrated to the secluded valley. Soon the name "Camas Prairie Indian" became synonymous with those who rejected government authority and the English language. Even into the 1930s, Catholic priests complained that they could not serve the Camas Prairie Indians because only twenty-five of the ninety elderly understood the priests' language.

Instead of paying the tax, warriors captured settlers' cattle that had roamed into the valley from Wild Horse Plains and then told Smead they would collect a tax of their own. Although the Indians eventually released the cattle, Smead wrote to the district attorney, asking him to punish the Camas Prairie Salish, "a bad lot of Indians that have been defying the government long enough."[8]

Chief Charlot also protested the tax. In 1891 he and his band moved onto the reservation. For twenty years after the forgery incident in 1872, Charlot refused to budge. By the 1890s thousands of settlers had moved into the Bitterroot Valley. Game was scarce, and because the Bitterroot Salish had always refused government assistance, the tribe was now completely destitute. Facing starvation, Charlot finally agreed to negotiate with General Henry Carrington and relocate.

Even after the move, however, Charlot continued to fight for Indian rights. When Smead proposed his pony tax, the chief made a trip to Washington, D.C., to talk to the secretary of the interior. Angus and Catherine McDonald's son Duncan accompanied him as interpreter. Charlot complained to the secretary that the tax penalized Indians who demonstrated wealth in the old way—by raising quality horses. Charlot questioned why ownership of their forty-five thousand head did not constitute success in the eyes of whites as well. The secretary would not answer and refused to rescind the tax.

By 1903 the pony tax was overshadowed by a bigger threat. Re-addressing the allotment issue, Missoula attorney and U.S. senator Joseph Dixon argued in Congress that Article 6 of the 1855 Hellgate Treaty allowed for dividing Salish land. The article declared, "The President may from time to time, at his discretion, cause the whole or such portion of such reservation as he may think proper to be surveyed into lots, and assign the same to such individuals or families of the said confederated tribes as are willing to avail themselves of the

The Northern Pacific Railroad had advertisements of its own.

privilege and will locate on the same as a permanent home." When senate discussion arose over the stipulation that the Salish must agree to the allotments, Senator Henry Teller of Colorado declared that he had made "inquiry as to the condition of the Indians and the needs of the people up there, and I find that there are no Indians objecting to the bill." In reality the only inquiry Teller made was to Montana legislators. Teller's comments, along with Dixon's untiring work and hundreds of letters from Montana businesspeople, helped to see the bill enacted into law in April 1904.

A Montana harvest pictured in William H. Smead's Land of the Flatheads, *circa 1910.*

Dixon and his friends had much to gain by the opening of the reserve. Dixon's brother-in-law Frank Worden owned and operated a general store in Ravalli. C. H. McLeod, his close friend and business confidant, was vice president of the Missoula Mercantile, which operated stores in Ronan and St. Ignatius and ranged cattle on the reserve. J. H. Ryman, a friend and vocal advocate of white settlement to stimulate reservation business, arranged the loan that enabled Dixon to buy *The Missoulian.* Dixon himself owned the Island Realty Company as well as the newspaper, which both stood to profit much from white development of native land. As McLeod stated in a brief pamphlet encouraging Montana homesteading, "This opening of the Flathead Indian Reservation will do more to stimulate business in western Montana than anything else possibly can." Montana businesspeople immediately began advertising the opening of reservation land, and companies arose to help incoming settlers file for homestead rights.

Even Smead, who had been discharged as Indian agent in 1904 for illegally leasing reservation land to white cattle growers, created the Flathead Reservation Information Agency to assist homestead clients. His pamphlet *Land of the Flatheads* coaxed people into the area by optimistically stating, "There is little snow save in the mountains. . . . Severe storms are almost unknown. Seldom are there over three consecutive days when the thermometer averages below zero." About summertime he wrote, "June brings the rains . . . during this month the crops are thoroughly watered. . . . God's promise verified that, Seed time and harvest shall not fail."

Although most of the tribe continued to protest allotments and the opening of their land to white settlement, the government sent Agent Charles McNichols to conduct a census of the plots. By 1905 he had 2,133 names recorded. The 111 Camas Prairie Indians refused to be registered.

Charlot made yet another trip to Washington. This time he spoke directly to President Theodore Roosevelt. He protested that the U.S. government was trying to "create white men out of the Indians." He received no comfort from Roosevelt, who had earlier praised the Dawes Act, stating it was a "mighty pulverizing engine to break up the tribal mass."[9] Realizing the inevitable, Charlot then pleaded for a forest reserve to serve as a source of firewood and logs for cabins and a guarantee of Indian water rights for irrigation. Roosevelt still made no promises.

Embittered, the old chief returned home. About his trip, on March 18, 1905, *The Missoulian* stated, "Chief Charlot of the Flatheads is irreconcilable. He is a grand and pathetic figure in Montana. He has no use for the whites. . . . He is a crownless monarch on a seatless throne. Though we may feel sorry for the old man, a grand old man, we also feel that he must bow to the inevitable."

On January 10, 1910, Charlot died. Two weeks later the government announced that the Flathead Indian Reservation would be open to white settlement on April 1 of that year. A series of amendments to the Dixon Act reserved additional acreage for an Indian agency, power installations, and a national bison range. However, the federal government failed on its Dawes Act promise to protect the sale of allotted land for twenty-five years.

Within months President Taft signed another Dixon bill allowing the Salish to sell 140 acres of their 160-acre allotments. On March 13, 1910, *The Missoulian* editorialized, "The permission granted the Indians to sell their lands down to 20 acres will place much of the most desirable land in the reserve upon the open market and add

*Chief Eneas of the Kootenai, circa 1880. Courtesy of
Cheney Cowles Museum/Eastern Washington State
Historical Society, Spokane, Washington.*

materially to the available land for the homeseekers who are coming
this spring."

The terms of the Homestead Act, which had been implemented
across the United States for years, provided designated plots to settlers who paid a small filing fee and resided on and improved the
land for five years. Once settlers had paid for or remained on the land
for the allotted time, they had "proven up" on their claims and owned
them. Irrigated homesteads of 40 to 120 acres—1,800 of them—and
nonirrigated homesteads of 160 acres—600 of them—were to be
awarded to those chosen in a lottery. From across the country, entries
began flooding into the Missoula land office.

As frustration and dislocation increased among the Salish and
Kootenai, so did the alcoholism rate. Chiefs and Indian judges attempted to punish offenders. However, the death toll from liquor
abuse only increased. Chief Eneas of the Kootenai stated that "the
beginning of all Indian trouble is whiskey . . . [my people] have acquired

The Vanishing Race, *an Edward Curtis photo that introduced his depictions of the North American Indian, 1904. Courtesy of the Special Collections Division, University of Washington Library.*

the habit and love the influence of it. In the old times I would take my whip and chastise any of my Indians that broke the law either by getting drunk or committing adultery, or any other crime, and they feared me and my authority . . . I could control my children then."[10]

Whites were even more pessimistic about the condition of Native Americans. Many had already deemed them a dying race. Edward Curtis, a premier society photographer from Seattle, dedicated his life to documenting an Indian culture that he was convinced would become extinct. In 1906 he relinquished his business to his assistant so he could travel full time and capture the traditions of these "vanishing people." Curtis set out to create an ethnographic record of native customs and traditions so future generations would not forget the native way of life before the arrival of the whites. Curtis believed that the American Indian was only authentic when living in this untouched state, and Curtis refused to capture any other kind of image. Ironically, railroad magnate J. P. Morgan, whom Northern Pacific had helped end the Indian's ancient lifestyle, agreed to finance Curtis's Herculean project.

Children of the Leaves. *From Eleanor Whitfeld,*
"Opening of the Flathead Indian Reservation," Overland
Monthly, *June 1908. Courtesy of the Special Collections*
Division, University of Washington Library.

With Morgan's backing, over the next twenty-six years Curtis
took more than forty thousand photographs, collected more than 350
traditional tales, produced a full-length feature film, and created more
than ten thousand recordings of Indian speeches and music and seven
hundred copperplate photogravures. In 1930 he completed the final
edition of his forty-volume *The North American Indian.* For nearly
three decades Curtis's life had centered around preserving the image
of America's "noble savages." His view of their future, however, was
far from romantic.

In 1910 Edward Curtis arrived on the Flathead Indian Reservation to record Salish and Kootenai culture. Eastern journalists such
as Eleanor Whitfeld also traveled west to write about the opening of
the reservation and what she interpreted as the inevitable loss of
Indian culture.

Chapter 6

This Century

B y the twentieth century, not only did politicians, journalists, and
artists believe that Indian culture would disappear, but historians did as well. In 1893 historian Frederick Jackson Turner declared
the nation's frontier closed. He based his assertions partly on the U.S.
census. Because most land west of the Mississippi then held a population of more than two persons per square mile, he claimed America
was settled and its Manifest Destiny complete. With this demise of
open soil, Turner believed native tribes would die out. Even the eastern reformers or "friends of the Indians" expected this extinction—
unless, of course, the Indian could be turned into a white.

For a time, the nation's pessimism about native culture seemed
warranted. Unwilling to become farmers like whites and unable to
return to a familiar existence, many Indians sold their land and wan-
dered their reservations in poverty. By 1933, forty-nine percent of
Indians on U.S. reservations were landless—forced to rent or live
with relatives. The rest held property amounting to an average value
of $800. American Indians experienced twice the infant mortality
rate of whites and the deepest and most widespread poverty of any
group in the United States. During the same period they also endured intrusive government interference in their family lives and
religious practices. In 1921 Commissioner of the U.S. Department

of the Interior Chas H. Burke wrote the following document to reservation superintendents:

> *The latest reports of Superintendents on the subject of Indian dances reveals encouraging conditions, indicating they are growing less frequent, are of shorter duration, and interfere less with the Indian's domestic affairs, and have fewer barbaric features . . . native dance still has enough evil tendencies to furnish a retarding influence and a troublesome situation . . . the dance is apt to be harmful and we should control it by educational processes as far as possible, but if necessary by punitive measures. I regard such restriction as applicable to any dance which brings Indians together from remote points to the neglect of their crops, livestock and homes interests.*

Yet, even in the midst of this assault and upheaval, Indian culture clung to its traditions. Ceremonies such as the Sun Dance continued.

In the summer months, allied tribes gathered and a renowned shaman or "lodge maker" oversaw the Sun Dance. In a special tent, the shaman helped prepare individual Sun Dance pledges for the intense undertaking. Following the shaman's guidance, other members of the tribe collected items needed for construction of the Sun Dance Lodge, a consecrated meeting place built to represent the entire earth. A forked tree stood as a sacred central pole. Stationed north, south, east, and west, four smaller trees symbolized the four corners of the world. Offerings of precious animal skins, medicine pouches, and buffalo-hide effigies were placed on the central pole. The finished bundle was called an Eagle's or Thunderbird's Nest.

Once the lodge was constructed, Sun Dance pledges entered it for spiritual testing. In tribes such as the Blackfeet, Lakota, and Crow, participants were skewered through the skin of the breast or back and attached by thongs to the top of the center pole. While dancing and chanting, they stared at the Eagle's Nest until they tore themselves loose or were released by the dance leader. The Lakota taught that by suffering at the pole of the Sun Dance Lodge, dancers took on the agony of their people. Such physical sacrifice also proved their

Salish and Kootenai raising a Sun Dance Lodge near Camas Prairie in 1908. The shaman who called the dance also selected the sacred pine used for its central pole and stood on top of it while supervising the construction. Courtesy of the Montana Historical Society.

deep humility and strength. Crow warriors believed their pain was an offering of thanksgiving for the many blessings given by the Creator.

The Salish, Kootenai, Ute, Shoshone, Arapaho, and Kiowa also conducted the Sun Dance, but without such physical tortures. However, they did undergo great bodily testing. Dancers fasted from four to eight days while dancing and staring at the sacred bundle at the top of the center pole and giving thanks and praying for power. In all tribes, the participants blew eagle-bone whistles. They believed its sound convinced the Eagle Spirit to bless them and give them endurance.

This endurance came in various forms. In addition to enabling them to complete the ceremony, it also helped the culture to stay strong. The Sun Dance survives today. Many aspects of it have changed while others remain the same. The Sun Dance Lodge is constructed in similar fashion and a Sun Dance Maker still sponsors the ceremony.

In modern times participants hang colored cloth at the crook of the foundation pole and fast while praying for the good of all people.

Like the Sun Dance, other contemporary Indian dance is both ancestral and dynamic. In traditional dancing, participants use exaggerated upper-body and active head movements. They throw their chests out while rocking and twisting their shoulders. They peer from side to side as if searching for the enemy. Dancers retain a proud, almost haughty demeanor. The style emulates that of ancient warriors.

Other symbolism also endures. Round drums continue to represent the universe—their steady beat, the pulsating heart of God. The Creator still uses it to stir humankind into awareness of the mystery and power of life. Outfit designs are communicated to individuals in visions and dreams. Hide leggings, geometric beadwork patterns, and eagle and hawk feather headdresses are still popular. As always, the dancers' feet stay close to the ground, keeping them mindful of their ultimate connection to the earth.

Other aspects have changed. In early times, men performed most public dancing while women stood to the side and participated by singing. In the 1950s, females began to enter the dance circle. Today women are a strong element of every powwow. They usually dress in ankle-length white or buckskin dresses with long fringes extending from the arms, ornamented shawls, high-top beaded moccasins or leggings, brass tack or concho belts, and otter braid wraps. Each year women's dancing evolves with new words, melodies, steps, and dress designs. The fancy-shawl and jingle-dress competitions constantly feature innovations, particularly in the freedom of movement.

Men's dancing has also evolved. During the 1950s more intricate footwork became popular. As songs increased in tempo, participants began to spin and use their bodies more. Today even greater emphasis is placed on fancy footwork, energetic body work, and strong head motions.

Modern outfits are more vibrant and ornate. At times bright Day-Glo colors replace the primary hues of old. Plastic frames lighten the wooden bustle. Tin-can leg rattles substitute for turtle shells, and metal saltshakers replace hollow-gourd rattles. Sequins, trade beads, plastic bones, and other mass-manufactured items blend modernity with antiquity.

Dance celebrations help recall and reinforce a nucleus of pride and participation. While Indian dance constantly modifies and regenerates itself, it also binds its people to an extraordinary past. In the end, powwows are, as Salish dancer Phillip Paul states, "A celebration of life. We dance, sing, and gather to be happy that we are alive. This is a time to celebrate our survival." In such festivity and thanksgiving, Indian people stay strong and pass their heritage on to the next generations. This reinforcement and selective melding ensures that they will endure for centuries to come.

While clinging to ancient rituals, the tribes also became politically astute. This phenomenon began around 1934, when a white commissioner of Indian affairs named John Collier began a movement to establish Indian rights through strong tribal government. With his Indian Reorganization Act (IRA), Collier attempted to end forced assimilation and to set up tribal structure with internal sovereignty. Any tribe that ratified the IRA elected a tribal council to govern itself and promote economic development.

In 1935 the Salish and Kootenai adopted the program and their newly elected council began exploring the reservation's tourist, hydroelectric power, agricultural, and timber potential. It then offered loans to members for farming and commercial enterprise.

Tribes throughout the United States also adopted Collier's Reorganization Act. By 1940, instead of whites running the Bureau of Indian Affairs (BIA) and reservation government, Native Americans started to take control. In 1933 only a few hundred Indian employees worked for the BIA, but by 1940 the number had increased to 4,600. Collier's plan to reestablish tribes as semisovereign nations was solidifying.

In 1946 a national organization called the Indian Claims Commission sought financial restitution for lands illegally obtained through agreements such as the Hellgate Treaty of 1855. In 1959 the Confederated Salish and Kootenai Tribes received $5,626,451 in compensation for the 14,062,000 acres that Governor Stevens had illegally confiscated. The payment gave the tribe additional money to rebuild.

Then in the 1960s the U.S. Supreme Court issued a series of decisions asserting further Indian sovereignty. It elevated a tribe's legal status above that of a state, thus limiting state authority on reservations. Since then, the Salish and Kootenai have established their own governmental departments: Cultural Preservation to guard tribal relics; Natural Resources, Land, Water, and Environmental Protection to preserve the environment; and Wildlife, Recreation, and Conservation to safeguard its plant and animal population.

This political clout has helped protect the entire reservation from environmental exploitation. In 1993 Camas Prairie's mail carrier Gene Stone smelled diesel oil as he drove past Camas Creek. In the meantime Morland Neiman's cattle began to abort their calves and Chuck Hunter became so ill he could not get out of bed. When Stone investigated, he discovered gas bubbling out of the ground near the creek. There was no doubt the Yellowstone Pipeline had burst again. This time it was seeping into the underground aquifer and contaminating the wells of both Neiman and Hunter.

The Yellowstone Pipeline extends 532 miles across Montana into Washington; fifty-five miles of it crosses the Flathead Indian Reservation. Constructed in 1954, the 10.75-inch single-walled pipe had been buried three feet below ground along the Flathead River, crossing over at Perma and up through Camas Prairie and Wild Horse Plains. Until the pipeline's closure in 1996, fuel originating at Billings constituted an average of 29,358 barrels or 1,233,036 gallons of petroleum per day through the reservation and on to Moses Lake.

With minimal transportation costs, the pipeline yielded huge profits to its owner companies: Conoco, Exxon, and Union Oil. Because Yellowstone Pipeline Corporation (YPC) was structured as a limited liability corporation, in case of a spill board members were shielded from financial threat. This loophole must have given them great comfort. The thin pipe, laid decades before U.S. Department of Transportation regulations, failed three tribal-sponsored hydrotests conducted in 1994 alone.

The test results came as no surprise to local residents. The pipeline had a notorious record. In September 1986, a spill near Perma had resulted in 4,494 gallons of jet fuel spewing onto the ground. On July 3, 1987, another rupture east of Camas Prairie, near Magpie Creek, dumped 162,204 gallons of diesel into the soil. Both spills were not detected by the company but acknowledged only after passing motorists reported them.

Under pressure from the tribe, Yellowstone Pipeline drilled wells to determine the general extent of the contamination, burned off what fuel it could, and removed soil. Later it acknowledged that a large quantity of diesel remained trapped in a clay layer below the surface of each site.

The new spill discovered by Gene Stone near Camas Creek had been leaking for six weeks. Hunter immediately contacted YPC. Days later YPC hydrologists arrived to test the area. In the meantime, Neiman shut off his well and Hunter moved from his contaminated land. Several weeks later, YPC promised the break was fixed. Within six months, however, two more leaks, resulting in another eighty-four-gallon spill, occurred in the same spot. Before YPC succeeded in sealing the crack, it poured ten thousand gallons of diesel, jet fuel, and unleaded gas into Camas Prairie's soil and underground water system, destroying native roots and medicinal plants that may never be restored. A year later, YPC official David Vanderpol estimated that two hundred to five hundred gallons of fuel remained locked in the valley's soil.

Hunter began a suit against the company. The Confederated Salish and Kootenai Tribes supported his action and took some of their own. They informed YPC that renewal of their upcoming twenty-year lease would be under review. Several months later, upon the easement's reissue date, the tribe began negotiating an environmentally responsible contract consisting of double-walled pipe lining, more sophisticated monitoring systems, and an adequate cleanup process. Pipeline officials responded that even with the best equipment, they could expect to cut the spills only in half. Council chair Micky Pablo replied, "No spill is acceptable."

The tribe also objected to the fact that during negotiations representatives from Exxon, Conoco, and Union Oil declined to sit at the bargaining table. Council members charged that YPC alone was merely a "shell" company and, in the event of a major spill, could quickly claim bankruptcy and avoid responsibility.

Instead of addressing environmental concerns, YPC offered the tribe money—between \$25 and \$30 million in return for the easement. The council warned YPC that money was not the issue and that until its environmental concerns were addressed there would be no deal. YPC issued another offer, which was almost the exact duplicate of the original, and then ran a public relations campaign asserting that if the pipeline were closed thousands of workers at the Billings refinery could lose their jobs.

Consequently, in what seemed to shock YPC, on July 14, 1994, the Confederated Salish and Kootenai Tribes refused the $30 million and demanded the line's closure. The council also turned down a short-term proposal of $1.5 million that would keep the pipeline open while a new one bypassing the reservation was constructed.

Pipeline officials began pleading for another chance to negotiate and ran apologies in local newspapers that read, "We've done serious damage to the land at the Camas, Magpie, and Perma leak sites. For this we are truly sorry. We're continuing our work to clean up these sites, but we know the land may never be the same. . . . Equally important, we've been bad neighbors. We've not communicated with tribal leaders and tribal public. For this, we're paying a severe penalty." Vice president Jim Taylor told tribal leaders, "We've begun to realize the priceless value you put on your land."[1]

However, the tribe would not repeal the decision and informed the company to take the appropriate steps to dismantle and remove the pipeline in an environmentally safe manner. The tribe notified pipeline officials that after October 27, 1995, the company would be billed $3,561 per day for trespassing and would continue to be held responsible for complete cleanup and remediation of existing spills on reservation land.

After the closure, YPC began hauling gas via truck across the reservation and exploring new routes. Taylor announced that the alternate site would probably be Ninemile Valley, located west of the city of Missoula. Although the route had been considered briefly as part of the Environmental Impact Statement (EIS) prepared previously, the land was deemed too fragile. In fact, the final EIS revealed that a Ninemile route would cross 21.4 miles of alluvial soil that could liquefy in an earthquake, parallel the Ninemile fault for several miles, and cross ninety-one streams and the habitats of twenty threatened, endangered, or sensitive animals and plants. Outraged by the plan,

Ninemile residents added their concern about potential damage of the Missoula aquifer, irreplaceable land in the Ninemile Valley and Siegel Pass, and sensitive wolf, bald eagle, and elk habitats.

Nonetheless, YPC vice president David Winans stated that "unlike the reservation, the Ninemile is not a sovereign nation and land can be taken by way of eminent domain. . . . if a landowner is unreasonable, if he is blocking our line, eminent domain is a tool that pipelines and other regulated utilities can use." President Bill Hicks added, "We will prevail. We are in business to provide a product."[2]

Although the Confederated Salish and Kootenai Tribes had already succeeded in protecting their own land, they stayed involved, stating their intent to protect aboriginal lands off the reservation—including those near Helena, Lolo Pass, and the Panhandle National Forest. The tribe also began working with the U.S. Forest Service and Missoula, Lake, Mineral, and Sanders Counties on pipeline issues affecting the environment.

Tribal officials also joined with the Ninemile Valley Preservation Council (landowners in the Ninemile and Frenchtown area) to fight the pipeline's construction. Ninemile resident Bob Latham told *The Missoulian*, "We intend to continue our relationship with the tribe. We will present a coherent and unified front." The debate continues today.

In addition to successfully protecting the land from environmental degradation like that perpetrated by YPC, the tribe also manages two large conservation areas in the hills east and west of Camas Prairie. Early in the 1980s the tribe created these game reserves to introduce bighorn sheep and rejuvenate a dwindling elk population. Because sheep and elk from the reserves wander off onto federal land, the agency also works in conjunction with the Montana Fish, Wildlife, and Parks Department. Together they manage the entire area of the Ferry Basin and Cabinet Mountains.

In the Ferry Basin, the tribe oversees its elk reserve, which prior to 1980 numbered only twenty or thirty animals. To build the herd for tribal hunting, it closed the area to the public. By 1997 the elk numbered between 250 and 275 in the summer and as many as 500 in the winter. Today the land is open to fall tribal hunting and then closed after the first of December, giving the animals a safe haven throughout the winter. The herd also serves as a means of providing meat for funerals and wakes. When needed, a tribal warden harvests an elk for such gatherings. Through managed hunting, fencing, and controlled burning, the Ferry Basin has now become one of Montana's best grazing lands. As it continues to improve, mule deer and Chinese pheasants repopulate the area as well.

In 1980 the tribe also transplanted seventeen bighorn sheep from Flathead Lake's Wild Horse Island into the Cabinet Mountains west of Camas Prairie. The area provided an ideal habitat of grassland, timber, and rocky cliffs—keeping the sheep and their lambs safe from predators.

Adjoining the reserve on federal property, the Montana Fish, Wildlife, and Parks Department created its own bighorn sheep district. Today 482 sheep roam the area, allowing both tribal and nontribal members premium hunting opportunities. Both government and Indian officials claim their cooperative management of the area has benefited animal and human alike.

While cooperating with federal officials, the tribe also works to encourage communication with those inside its membership. When legal decisions are made, the spiritual elders are consulted. While younger council members are considered experts on government, law, and politics, Salish elders work to preserve native culture and traditions. An intermediary group, the Culture Committee, acts as a liaison, facilitating interaction between the parties.

During the Yellowstone Pipeline controversy, the elders recommended pipeline closure—a course of action they believed would best preserve the land, traditional values, and culture. Elder John Peter Paul told the council that the pipeline "wasn't any good for us. Nobody wants 'em."

John Peter Paul advises the council and also serves as tribal name giver. His own Salish name, Tsnuprno, comes from warrior days and means "He Got Hold of an Enemy and Held Him Tight." Paul remembers when, in 1918, his family took him to the mission at St. Ignatius and left him there. It wasn't long before the priest "started givin' us names like Frank and George." Now John Peter Paul gives

Salish children back their traditional names—names given in honor of the deeds their ancestors performed. To a family with a heritage of healing, Paul bestows the name Grizzly Bear.

Another elder, 101-year-old Joe Enas, was born at the Catholic mission in St. Ignatius. Once he began school there, he was not allowed to speak Salish and was forced to abandon his Indian name, Susep. The priests renamed him Enas, a form of Ignatius. After leaving the school, he joined the 32nd Red Arrow Division and served in World War I, where he was wounded in the line of duty. After he came home he worked on ranches and in sawmills. Each year he hunted and fished with fellow Indians, feeding his family and sharing the meat with others.

Today, Enas teaches Salish to his people and tells them stories of the past, tales about hunting, early traditions, and changes. He claims that during the twentieth century transformation has been the norm. About the land he claims, "It used to be free. You could go anyplace. No fences. But after a while, you had to stay on the road."

The Culture Committee records the stories of Enas and Paul and encourages elder participation in tribal decisions. It also takes an active role in providing language classes to the tribe. This commitment to the language is also evident in people such as Frances Vanderburg. For thirty years, Frances has been teaching the Salish language to both natives and whites on the reservation. She has held classes in schools across the reservation and in her own home. Today she teaches kindergarten through sixth grade at Arlee Elementary. In one week, she sees more than 270 students. At the beginning of the school year, each child chooses a Salish name. Most pick the name of a flower or bird. Frances loves the process until, she says, "Someone wants the name Tyrannosaurus Rex."

This dedication to Indian culture and education is evident at Salish Kootenai College, which was established in 1977. Angus and Catherine McDonald's great-great-grandson Joe McDonald is its president. About 850 students attend the accredited institution of higher education. Classes provide tools for "survival in a rapidly-changing and technological world, while maintaining the cultural integrity of the Salish and Kootenai people."

It's unfortunate that Frederick Jackson Turner and his contemporaries did not factor in this kind of flexibility before prophesying extinction. Turner was a historian and should have recognized the historical pattern of adaptation in Indian culture—a pattern that survives today. Durability was a time-tested skill that Native Americans had perfected long before the turn of the century.

For example, in 1820 northwestern Chinooks greeted fur traders with the phrase "Clak-hon-ah-yah," which apparently originated in their having "heard a gentleman named (William) Clark frequently addressed by his friends, 'Clark, how are you?'"[3] The Chinook added this greeting to their vocabulary and used it to address whites twenty years later. For millennia, sovereign native nations had engaged in a dance of cultural synthesis with one another. When whites arrived, the Indians simply added their traditions as well. Among the tribes most skilled at this eclectic adaptation was the Interior Salish.

Camas Prairie's Farmers

At the beginning of the century, Frederick Jackson Turner's pessimism also extended to the whites. His story of the westward movement dealt mainly with white males forging civilization out of empty wilderness. He lamented the passing of this westward conquest because, he claimed, it built American character and turned frail Europeans into robust U.S. citizens. Now, the Jeffersonian ideal of hearty yeomen having room to move and grow no longer existed. Because this rugged journey had forged strength into its citizens, acting as "the line of most rapid and effective Americanization," Turner worried that hard-earned grit and integrity would erode.

Other than a slip in national disposition, Turner also feared that the nation's ecological abundance was giving way to scarcity. Once the land had been eaten up, its natural resources would in turn disappear. Turner and his contemporaries thought these changes ended the pioneer era and signaled a great loss for the nation. They declared that a vital stage in American history had come to an end.

Turner's view left the West with no positive place to evolve. With its tough, individualistic pioneers becoming lazy and lethargic, its

A 1918 postcard produced by the Great Northern Railway depicting the potential of homestead land. Courtesy of Lon Johnson.

resources devoured, and its "noble savage" extinct, the region's future seemed colorless. Turner's popular theory led Americans to mourn the loss of the "true" West. Buffalo Bill's turn-of-the-century Wild West Show presented the last "real" cowboy, the last "true" Indian, and the last "real" buffalo herd. The "significant" West was dying, and Americans grieved its passing. In an attempt to hold onto a legacy of strength, they simply retold the old story in different versions.

Through art, Charlie Russell, a contemporary of Turner, also lamented the passing of what he considered the true West. He wrote about this to a cowboy friend:

> *You need no book to help you remember the West you knew and loved. She was a sweetheart of yours and mine, a wild maid with maney lovers The West we knew is an old woman now . . . but we still love her. The reformers will bury her without flowers but her name will live in . . . [our] harts.*[4]

Like Turner, Russell believed the only way to preserve the West was to retell its pioneer story.

For the early part of the twentieth century, Turner's version of the West seemed to dominate historical narrative. Other than the

Government promotional literature.
Courtesy of the Montana Historical
Society.

fact that it ignored much of
the region's history (that of
Asians, Blacks, Hispanics,
Indians, and women), it also
failed to anticipate the resil-
ience and vitality of the West
and its people. For a time,
however, Turner's cynicism
seemed justified.

By the mid-1930s, many
of Camas Prairie's original
homesteaders had declared bankruptcy and moved on. The situation
repeated itself across Montana. Writing about the exodus, M. L.
Wilson, a turn-of-the-century specialist in farm economics at the
Montana Extension Service, wrote, "Today the enthusiasm of 1916
is replaced by a depression that spread fast through years that brought
drought, weed, pests, and visitations of crop destroying insects." Of
the 234,024 homestead applications filed in Montana, 151,600 had
been forsaken by 1940. Settlers deserted almost two-thirds of the
claims staked in the state. It's no wonder, once reality hit that the

*Actual homesteads looked more like this: "Rat" Ratcliff shack on the
Flathead Reservation, 1910; and below, Roy Bras in front of his
homestead shack in Lonepine Valley, 1914.*

railroads and government had stretched the truth concerning the fertility of the land.

Another federal promise that didn't materialize in time to save many was an irrigation system. In 1904 Congress amended the Homestead Act to set aside money to build such networks on reservation land. It hoped this incentive would coax people to come west. One who was convinced was my mother's grandfather.

In 1909, from his Missouri dry-goods store, Roy Bras read the promotions of fertile, irrigated homestead sites for sale in Montana. With only booster pictures and promises for incentive, he sold his

business, packed his family, and headed west. The Bras family arrived in Kalispel in 1910 and entered the homestead lottery. Once their number was drawn, Roy explored the reserve and picked his land in Lone-pine. He built his meager shack, plowed his land, and hoped the irrigation system would soon reach them.

Two years before he'd arrived, Congress had appropriated

Barren Montana homestead land with eroded soil blown to the top of the fence posts, circa 1910. Courtesy of the Montana Historical Society.

$50,000 to survey for the Flathead Irrigation Project. In 1910 another $250,000 was granted and construction began. The Department of the Interior transferred mules and horses from the Shoshone Project in Wyoming and supplied plows, scrapers, dump wagons, picks, shovels, hammers, and bars to build waterways. Many of the original structures were built of wood and later replaced with hand-mixed concrete.

It wasn't long before the undertaking was fraught with trouble. The Pablo Dam had to be sealed off because it leaked through the mountain into Polson. The Newell Tunnel was also abandoned. After two years of blasting and digging rock, for a distance of seventeen hundred feet at the cost of $101,685, surveyors discovered the area could be irrigated with strategically planned ditches. Meanwhile, most homesteaders still had no water.

In 1916 appropriations from Congress began to dry up—just in time for the droughts of 1916, 1917, 1918, and 1919. Homesteaders formed the Polson Chamber of Commerce and sent James Harbert to Washington to beg for completion of the system. Unfortunately, the United States was embroiled in World War I and no money was left for the project. After Harbert returned with the bad news, the first major exodus began.

It was not until 1925 that more money was allocated and ten years later before the Flathead Irrigation Project was finished. During those irrigationless years, many moved on. However, like their Native American counterparts, farmers survived and learned their own lessons in durability.

The mistakes of predecessors in other parts of the country had demonstrated the dangers of poor farming techniques. By carelessly exposing topsoil, early homesteading pioneers had created a dust bowl and ruined some of the nation's most fertile land. By overplanting, they had depleted large sections of what remained. My father's generation was forced to rethink the process.

In 1941 Dad purchased land from his grandmother and began exploring different techniques. He and his compatriots gathered to discuss the benefits of soil protection. Like their parents, they congregated at the community hall to dance, play cards, and tell stories, but at these social events they also debated new agricultural methods.

These dialogues led to crop rotation. For eight years they cycled wheat, planting it one year, then letting the land lie fallow the next. After the wheat's harvest, they harrowed the stubble into the ground with a spade drill that resembled a large Indian arrowhead. This hilly composite protected topsoil by trapping water. The moisture then rotted the straw, creating a natural fertilizer that replenished the land with humus and nitrogen. After eight years of this rejuvenation process, they planted alfalfa. When the quality of the alfalfa began to decline, the land went back into wheat. They did this to avoid soil erosion and the fate of those before them who lost everything.

In 1953 my father married my mother, who had grown up on the homestead in Lonepine. Together they built a home over the ashes of John and Anna's shack, where they still live today, and over the years worked hard, adding to their cattle herd and acreage. Unlike the communities of Lonepine and Arlee, however, Camas Prairie didn't have an open water source to receive the same irrigation benefits that were available to the rest of the reservation. Consequently, my parents planted crops and prayed for rain—an age-old dry-land farm custom.

In the 1960s the U.S. Soil Conservation Service proposed using border dikes to water the soil. The dikes were narrow mounds of dirt

The family farm in 1954.

three feet high and six feet apart and ran in rows for the length of a field. The plan was to flood each section from an underground well for twelve hours and then to turn off the water. Instead of properly irrigating the land, however, the process washed away topsoil and turned the remaining dirt into gumbo clay. The plan wasn't a well-funded government subsidy program either—just an idea the department convinced farmers to try.

Over the years Camas Prairie farmers have received very little in subsidies or grants, contrary to growing belief that most in the occupation enjoy such perks. In fact, the family farmer's yield isn't large enough to greatly benefit from such assistance. Much of this government aid goes to corporations, joint ventures, and industrial-scale farming operations ($29 billion since 1985). These "venture farmers" are the top 2 percent of farm subsidy recipients and haul in 27 percent of the federal assistance paid out. In 1995 the Environmental Working Group analyzed 112 million farm payment records obtained through the Freedom of Information Act. The group found that "Farm subsidies are always defended on the grounds that they help struggling family farms. Our study shows that over the past 10 years, most of the subsidies went to a very few, large farming interests and absentee owners."[5] Many of these "agriculturalists" don't even live on the land but in America's largest cities. Over the past decade, taxpayers wrote 1.6 million agriculture subsidy checks worth more than $1.3 billion to people whose permanent mailing addresses were in New York, Los Angeles, Chicago, and Detroit. Over the years, though, the family farmer hasn't benefited a great deal from this aid. Although government programs, like those of the Soil Conservation Service, have helped small farmers, they mostly have had to figure out what works on their own—by sweat, trial, and error.

Once Dad realized how border dikes affected the land, he leveled them. However, the problem of how to get moisture into the soil remained. Then he heard of sprinkler pipes. Sprinklers were new to Montanans and many viewed them with skepticism. Nonetheless, he gave the scheme a try by starting out with one line and then each year, after he sold the calves, adding another. The lines were each a quarter mile long and consisted of about forty individual pipes. These lines had to be changed or moved forward in the field twice a day, so after he'd purchased five, the whole family participated in the three-hour process.

Every lovely summer evening we'd pile into the back of the pickup and head for the field. After Dad turned off the clattering diesel pump that sucked the open well like a thirsty hedgehog, he'd move a red flag down the fence line twenty-five steps, and we'd used the landmark to keep the row straight—ensuring that every stem of alfalfa received water.

My father took the first pipe, my mother and brother the next, and my little sister and I the third. The navigator would "eye the pipe up" by straddling it, grabbing the long sprinkler stem, and, in a squatting position, lining up the metal spout with the flapping flag at the end of the field. Once the pipe was down, we watched carefully that snakes or mice didn't crawl up the exposed end. If such a creature did sneak through before the water was turned on, another thirty minutes would be lost shutting the system down, cleaning out the sprinkler head, and recoaxing the temperamental old machine back into action. After each sprinkler spurted convincingly, we'd move on to the next field.

As I trudged through the heavy, soppy muck, my little sister's golden hair, almost lost in the height of the alfalfa, bobbed happily at the other end. She didn't mind keeping up with me, and I figured she was simply too young and naive to recognize the hell we were in. During those adolescent summers, while my unfashionable rubber boots made a distressing suction slurp—something similar to the noise at the bottom of the last milkshake you'd ever get—I dreamed of how to escape this heritage of toil. One thing would be absolutely vital— never marry a farm boy. Such vows couldn't help my existing condition, however. To my chagrin, the process increased our yield threefold and, consequently, became an entrenched ritual.

Another chore I refused to appreciate was the cattle drive. Meticulously careful not to overgraze, my father divided our herd into small groups and rotated them from field to field. If the grassland looked slightly eaten down, we immediately moved them to the Parks', Shortys', Egans', Kennedys', Argos', or Cheeneys': old homestead sites that respectfully retained the original settlers' names. The cattle did not return to a pasture until it had fully recovered. Today I realize such maneuvering was necessary to keep the grassland healthy. Unfortunately, at sixteen proper land management didn't mean much. As the cows bawled and pooped all over the road, the only thing I thought about was the horrifying possibility of someone from town driving by. With the amount of time we spent moving cattle, I knew my luck would eventually run out.

One chilly evening it happened, as I realized with terror that our handsome high school honor-student quarterback and his family were slowly approaching. Sporting a tattered, oversized coat and gumboed rubber boots, accessorized by a multicolored stocking hat pulled low over my pigtails, I prayerfully thought, They could mistake me for the TV clown J. P. Patches and speed right on through. The situation was exacerbated by the fact that the rest of my family had gone ahead to cover gates and I was the only cowpoke behind the sloppy beasts. If they hesitated, I couldn't even masquerade as my sister. The Morgieus not only halted, but the family did the unimaginable—they insisted I get into the car and warm up while they followed the herd. Declining such kindness constituted a snub no farm kid would ever consider, so in my mismatched, worn-down getup, I crawled in back, next to their sweet-smelling son, and embarked on the longest three-mile ride of my life.

My father conducted these musical-chair cow drives to avoid the consequences of winters like 1887. For years on the eastern Montana plains, cattlemen had allowed their animals to eat the range bare. Once the cows became hungry enough, they even pulled up plants' roots. By 1886 overgrazing and drought had severely depleted the area. Once the raging winter hit, deep snow coupled with barren land underneath left little possibility of survival. During the twentieth century, Camas Prairie's farmers have worked hard to avoid such scenarios, contending that well-managed rangeland would remain perfectly healthy.

A recent Oregon State University and Agricultural Research Center study reveals such optimism is possible. The fifty-year survey compared vegetation growth and soil measurements taken in 1936 from both grazed and ungrazed areas with those taken throughout the 1990s. The research scientists used two indicators of rangeland health: the abundance of plant cover and nutrient content in the soil. Rangeland expert Tony Svejcar reported, "In grazed areas, the plants are smaller, but there are more of them. In ungrazed plots, there are fewer, larger plants, and the soil isn't broken up as much, but both seem to be healthy, functioning rangeland."[6]

Over the past decade, however, keeping the land healthy hasn't been the farmers' only concern. During the 1990s, farmers struggle to maintain their very economic viability. As operation costs have skyrocketed, the price of grain and cattle haven't kept up. In 1946, after my father received $2.56 per bushel for his summer wheat, he bought a new Massey-Harris combine for $13,000. Today wheat goes for $2 per bushel, and a new Massey-Harris combine costs more than $100,000.

And although the U.S. food and beverage industry is one of the most profitable sectors of the economy, many of America's food providers are going bankrupt. In the past ten years, 250,000 farmers have sold their land. The U.S. Department of Agriculture reports that one-third of the nation's farm families live below the poverty level. Partly, this statistic results from the profit disparity between the Kellogg

Company and the wheat growers, John Morrell and Company and the cattle producers, and Minute Maid and the orange growers. A box of Wheaties, which primarily consists of winter wheat, sells for $3.50. The American farmer receives four cents for the grain used in each package. Twenty ounces of Cheerios sells for $3.99—the oat farmer receives five cents. In a $3 box of Corn Flakes, three cents goes for the corn.

Farmers also claim that the large meat packers are making undue profit while each year more cattle growers face foreclosure. IBP, the king of the meat packers, doubled its income in 1994 alone. ConAgra has experienced a fivefold increase in profits over the past decade. Another corporate packer, Cargill, experienced a revenue jump of 30 percent in 1994.[7] Although a special investigation authorized by the Senate Governmental Affairs Committee declared these companies innocent of monopoly, many farmers point to statistics that indicate that while raising a cow, the cattle grower receives 97 cents per day, the feeder 143 cents per day, the packer 7,350 cents per day, and the retailer 32,250 cents per day.[8]

So far the North American Free Trade Agreement (NAFTA) and the General Agreement on Tariff and Trade (GATT) have only added to the ranchers' struggles, creating a trade imbalance between the United States and Canada. In 1996 Canada shipped 26 percent more slaughter cattle into the United States than during the same period in 1995.[9] While the U.S. consumer pays nearly the same price for beef as two years ago, the farmer receives fifteen cents less per pound. Some politicians say the situation will soon change. However, many farmers won't survive this temporary condition.

Analysts predict that because of this squeeze, only large ranches will move into the twenty-first century. As profit margins decline, cattle growers must increase their output to stay solvent. Researchers at Kansas State University (KSU) reported that the bigger the herd size, the lower the average unit cost of producing the stock is.[10] Huge ranches can weather downswings in the market because their operating costs are lower and profit margins don't have to be as high. KSU researchers claim that to survive this 1990s "liquidation phase," ranches will have to be large and lean.

While this makes life difficult for the small farmer, many also worry about the condition of this incoming beef. Foreign meat does not undergo the same rigid inspection U.S. beef does. Many in addition to cattle growers declare that this process is sorely inadequate. In July 1995, NBC's *Dateline* interviewed U.S. Department of Agriculture meat inspector Bill Lehman, who reported that on July 22 and 23, 1994, of the approximately one million pounds of Canadian beef crossing the border at Sweetgrass, Montana, only four hundred pounds were inspected. Meat inspector Les Wagner also reported a similar story from his post in Blaine, Washington. As Americans wisely worry about *E. coli*, they should remember that 47 percent of the hamburger sold in the United States is imported.

To survive, farmers are getting creative. In hopes of receiving a better price for their cattle, some are selling them by satellite video. It's a process in which a camera crew tapes the herd and then runs a continuous telemarket of them on a Texas cable station. So far this new approach seems promising.

Another option is to sign a conservation easement. Since 1970 a half million acres of Montana farmland have gone into this program, which pays the farmer not to subdivide or alter the land in any way. In *The Missoulian*, rancher Jim Coleman stated that new alliances are forming, "some that once would have been heresy before . . . including working with, instead of fighting, environmentalists." Programs that encourage ranchers to keep the land intact are being offered by private organizations such as the Nature Conservancy and the Rocky Mountain Elk Foundation, as well as federal agencies such as the Department of Natural Resources and Conservation and state agencies such as the Montana Department of Fish, Wildlife, and Parks Department. Although these incentives don't solve the problem of low cattle prices, they help to generate needed income and preserve the land for future generations.

Some ranchers, however, refuse to explore such options. Some cling to uninformed stubbornness, distrusting all government programs and tagging environmentalists as "radical Earth First!ers." In a recent farm journal article, the author encourages his readers to vote against the Montana Clean Water and Public Health Protection Act, which targets excessive mining pollution. The author reasons, "If the ability to conduct mining is lost in the state of Montana, which industry will the environmentalists come after next?" Such alarmist thinking is neither good for the rancher or Montana.

Recently, I attended a seminar in Missoula where a noted environmentalist stood up and very eloquently extended a hand of cooperation to the farm community. She suggested that the two work together to protect the land. After her talk, a rancher—about twice her size—cornered her and began accusing her of trying to end his way of life, one he and his family had enjoyed for generations. Unless he'd heard something I hadn't, she had not advocated anything of the sort. This kind of paranoia stifles any real progress.

There are environmentalists, as well, who would prefer to battle than to collaborate. Several years ago I submitted a paper on the West to a conference being held in Colorado Springs. When I arrived, the organizer introduced me to a woman he identified as "the environmentalist you will be debating." He told her I was the "rancher's daughter" she'd be pitted against. He added that he couldn't wait for the lively session we'd be treating them to. The environmentalist immediately told me that she believed ranchers had the instincts of rapists, and that Sharman Apt Russell, who wrote *Kill the Cowboy*, had been far too easy on the despicable group.

For the next thirty minutes I attempted to find some common ground with her. However, I excused myself after she informed me that her ancestors had also been farmers but she refused to defend them—instead she'd decided to tell the truth. As I walked back to my room, the sickening realization that I'd cut into the food budget to fly myself into a mud-wrestling match hit me.

The premonition wasn't far from reality. The following day she started the session with a gut-wrenching slide show of the devastation of the Gila National Forest. Ranchers had leased large sections of this federal land and then let their cattle forage creekbeds and overgraze the grassland. Her slides incited the group—mainly friends who had come to hear her speak—into a frenzy.

I certainly didn't object to her slides or her thesis. I agreed that the cattle growers responsible for this mess should have been thrown off the land long ago. It was her narrative that made me nervous. If the word "rancher" had been replaced with any conceivable minority group, she could have been arrested for hate speech. My talk followed. She sat next to me emitting grunts of disgust as I described farm life. During the question-and-answer session, she completely dominated the floor with one anecdote after another about the depravity of the ranching community. To her, any person involved in raising cattle was a cruel opportunist, dependent on government programs.

I was furious. Despite the fact that I'm politically liberal, like Bruce Babbitt, and donate to the Nature Conservancy, at that point I couldn't have cared less about common ground. All I wanted to do was tell this "environmentalist" she was in dire need of some personal therapy. The intensity of the anger on both sides made me guess that such discussion isn't worth much. Rather than making progress toward land stewardship, it's about as valuable as the *Jerry Springer Show*. Apparently, it had been that effective in the Gila.

Sometime later, a young man sneaked up to me and said he had recently come from the Gila National Forest. He'd gone there to do research on the land-lease question and to write a graduate paper. He claimed that my environmentalist "friend" had stirred up so much anger and resentment that she and a local rancher had almost come to blows. Since then, both sides had retreated into entrenched corners. He doubted whether any real progress would be possible for quite some time.

Because they infuriate people, such dogfights rarely promote any understanding of the issues. An interesting irony of the land-lease question is that plenty of cattle growers are as opposed to it as environmentalists are. They are equally incensed when they hear that 59 percent of our public rangeland is in poor condition because cows have eaten it down to the dirt. And they most certainly resent being lumped together with these poor managers. Besides, much of this leased land goes to corporate agribusiness or large beef producers. The U.S. General Accounting Office found that ninety million acres of federal grazing land are controlled by the five hundred largest cattle and sheep operations and 6 percent of these ranchers control 32 percent of this land. Some of them even subdivide it and rent it out, using public property as a cash cow. Such abuse doesn't make much sense. Low rent on federal land also puts small farmers like Chuck Stipe at a distinct disadvantage.

Today, Chuck rents pasture from my family and pays a monthly rate of $18 a head per acre for it. It's a puzzle to me how he can compete with those who pick up federal lease land for $1.86 a head. I've never heard ranchers talk much about this inequity—probably because they don't usually criticize their own in public. However, when Americans see barrel-hatted cowboys hollering at Bruce Babbitt for attempting to negotiate land-lease compromise, it doesn't represent the entire culture.

These images make good news copy, though. They also promote distinct polarization—a situation some ranchers and environmentalists thrive on. It allows some cattle growers to retain their lack of accountability and stranglehold on public land—land that no longer belongs to the citizenry but remains at the mercy of the ranchers' own special interest. For certain environmentalist groups, it's a lot easier to raise money when they can whip the public into a fervor over the vilified cattle grower. However, this winner-take-all attitude squelches any progress and will never protect the open spaces that both groups cherish.

Admittedly, it can be difficult to set aside our own opinions and see another position. When I protest the use of weed spray on sections of our land—killing not only cinquefoil, knap weed, and toad flax but bitterroot as well—I must remind myself before I get too indignant that suburbanites dump five times the herbicides on their coiffured lawns as farmers use. I am also forced to consider the alternatives. If a farmer doesn't do some spraying, the entire area will be overtaken with weeds and, as my father might say, "The land won't be worth taxes." If that happens, the only thing left is to subdivide and sell to developers. The environmental degradation that "civilization" brings dwarfs what is happening now.

At one time the Bitterroot Valley of Missoula, the traditional digging ground of the Bitterroot Salish, was covered with its beautiful namesake. The town of Missoula arose and paved over every bitterroot plant. Today the only wild bitterroot that remain are on farmland. In the Yellowstone area, "ranchettes" and housing developments have so encroached on riparian areas that much of it can no longer sustain wildlife. Large tracts of feeding range are completely lost. The bumper sticker that reads "Pavement Lasts Forever" captures the permanency of this change.

Squeezing the farmer off the land will only encourage such urban sprawl. If ranchers can't make it, developers will move in and both rancher and environmentalist will lose. That is why many suggest that a goal more important than raising lease prices is enforcement of better stewardship on federal grazing lands. Darrell Knuffke of The Wilderness Society states, "If a fee increase has the effect of driving ranching families off the land on a wholesale basis, we will lose a critical and irreplaceable piece of the Western land mosaic: private, agricultural open space."[11] Knuffke suggests a tax break for ranchers who are willing to comply with grazing regulations and conservation easements.

This middle-ground compromise will make more headway than all the shouting in the world. When environmentalists and ranchers begin working together and emphasizing common goals, much can be accomplished. In his book *Beyond the Rangeland Conflict: Toward a West That Works*, Dan Dagget writes about the victories of such conservation-ranching partnerships.

For two decades Dagget worked as a tireless environmental crusader. He was the conservation chair of the Northern Arizona Sierra Club and wrote for numerous environmentalist publications. He opposed the ranching community over the killing of mountain lions and bears and the depletion of grassland. Dagget circulated petitions and used the political process whenever he could. Then, several years ago, he and five of his environmentalist friends began to meet with six ranchers. What transpired surprised them all. They found not only that they communicated well but that they actually agreed on a number of things such as "a love for open spaces, a hitch in our chests when we saw wildlife, and a concern over population growth and the inexorable march of suburbs."[12] Before long, the group stopped demonizing one another and began emphasizing what they held in common. Once they did, they made more progress than Dagget imagined possible. Today, his perspective has changed.

He has abandoned the political process because, he claims, with each new administration a mere majority can wipe out a generation's worth of hard-fought environmental gains. Dagget states, "The political process is too fickle, too unreliable, too reversible to solve long-term problems such as the extinction crisis, global warming, and destabilization of the worldwide ecosystem." Rather than focusing on petitions, lawsuits, and politics, Dagget now spends his time working in the world of trees and grass, bugs and streams. His fellow laborers are ranchers, vegetarians, wise-users, and Earth First!ers. This patchwork group celebrates success by healing riparian areas and increasing their biodiversity. Dagget has abandoned showdown tactics for teamwork. He claims that such collaborations have yielded more fruit than all his years in the environmentalist–rancher war zone, where the goal often became defeating the enemy rather than improving, restoring, and reviving our damaged ecosystems.

Dagget's book explores ten cases in which rancher and environmentalist have successfully joined together and, through managed grazing, improved the land. In one instance, Ivan Aguirre and his partners now herd three thousand cattle over the dessert grassland of northern Mexico. Rather than letting them feed on one patch too long, however, they are driven in a fashion similar to the way ancient bison moved across the prairie. As a result, they are moved through the area before overgrazing occurs. The effect has been to promote healthy grassland and cattle.

S. J. McNaughton, a research biologist at Syracuse University, studied the way grassland responds to grazing around the world. His research revealed that dense "movement" herding allows grazers to crop the grasslands in a way that increases forage and encourages the productivity of many different grasses. This kind of grazing disperses seeds, fertilizes soil, and removes dead stocks. Once these stocks are eaten off, plants and soil are exposed to the sun's warming rays and will rejuvenate during a rest period. These are the "favors" large grazers performed for plants on the Pleistocene savannas and, if managed properly, can perform for grasslands today.

Dagget's approach and success are being played out across the West. In central Nevada, an association of ranchers, environmentalists, and citizens called the Toiyabe Wetlands and Watersheds Management team has helped reverse the effects of more than a century of overgrazing. In the past few years, more than seventy western coalitions have been organized around the issue of watersheds alone. In Arizona and New Mexico, rural citizens have joined the Nature Conservancy, government bureaucrats, and scientists to form the Malpai Borderlands Group. Their collaboration has managed the use of wildfire to see that it once again performs its natural function of keeping the grasslands free of invading species. They have also helped stop the dividing and selling off of private farmland. In Colorado, the Western Slope Environmental Resource Council, a collaborative advisory group, works to improve elk habitat, cattle forage, and riparian health in the West Elk Wilderness. In Montana, organizations such as the Blackfoot Challenge, Trout Unlimited, Ducks Unlimited, and Defenders of Wildlife are demonstrating that federal and state government, private landowners, and environmentalists can collaborate to revive damaged lands and protect fragile ecosystems. These are only some of the successful efforts unfolding across the West.

Even academic institutions are getting involved. Five western universities now teach natural-resource conflict resolution. One such effort is the University of Nevada's Reaching Sustainable Agreements (RSA) Program. Through RSA, Professor Hudson Glimp and his colleagues have helped reintroduce elk to the 4,725-acre Howard Ranch in northeastern Nevada. And western publications, such as *High Country News* and the *International Journal of Wilderness,* also encourage both rancher and environmentalist to join forces, while giving them important news and tackling current issues that effect the West.

I believe this trend will continue to grow. Cooperation seems necessary to protect the land and its culture. Wallace Stegner once said that the West is characterized and preserved most by cooperation, not rugged individualism. This cooperation has been a vital part of the region from the beginning. Even in the midst of stubbornness and independence, the West's harsh way of life has taught its people the necessity of alliance for survival.

This summer, as Butch Horton ran the swather over our hayfield, a spark caught the wind and started a fire. Butch grabbed the extinguisher, but it was too late. In minutes the prairie was ablaze. The dry wind, accelerated by the flame's combustion, impelled the inferno across the open grassland. Ranchers from around the valley saw the smoke, jumped off their own machinery, and headed toward our field. Carol Heath (Phil Pelley's daughter) called my parents and warned them to come quickly. She then called other families, who made phone calls to their neighbors before jumping in their vehicles and rushing to help.

By the time my folks arrived, their neighbors were fighting wildly to control the blaze. Ranchers, their wives, and their children, armed with gunnysacks and buckets of water, fought against the raging heat. Farmers, who could recall homestead days, fought alongside children on summer vacation. Brian Webber rushed over with his water truck and the volunteer fire departments of Dixon and Hot Springs were summoned. The fire was extinguished just before it would have jumped the county road and devoured another 160 acres. Without the concerted effort of our neighbors, the flames would have also consumed my sister's house, along with several tons of hay stacked next to it.

There are still people on Camas Prairie with whom my father does not see eye to eye. They arrived immediately and fought alongside everyone else. This is the legacy of the West. On the surface these folks might appear inflexible or headstrong, but compromise and humility control their instincts. They are seasoned in the art of adaptation, common sense, and pragmatism.

This cultural norm is clear in Ivan Doig's beautiful memoir *This House of Sky*. After his mother's death, Doig's father and maternal grandmother formed an uneasy partnership to raise the boy. Although the alliance between the two adults "had problems that showed no sign of easing," Ivan's well-being took precedence over their disagreements. When Ivan's father landed a new job herding sheep in northern Montana, he knew the boy's grandmother wouldn't be happy about leaving her family, friends, and home of forty years in White Sulphur Springs to start over. In the end, however, she acted quintessentially western. Doig writes:

> *Whatever the ties of affection between her and me, I couldn't believe she could be talked into this total uprooting toward the*

north. We'll just have to see about her, Dad said. He rehearsed to
me a dozen arguments he would put to her, and when the
moment came simply fired out: This damn valley has never got
us much of anywhere, Lady. All either of us has to show for our
lives here is a helluva pile of hard work. I say we ought to try
out new country. Will ye come?

She was silent for a long while—but a thinking silence, not
a perturbed one. At last: All right then. When can we be gone
and get it over and done with? [13]

This kind of flexibility motivates those in the West. In the future,
I believe it will trigger an alliance between ranchers and environmentalists. They will use their hard-earned wisdom to adapt once more.
In this middle ground, ranchers will be able to preserve the magic of
the wide-open spaces and unique way of life they love. They will
endure to create new stories to tell to their children—an art as old as
the West itself.

Chapter 7

History as Story

*I*n much of the West, history exists as story—colorful and unwritten—narrative academic historians tend to mistrust. As unpredictable as these tales are, it's how the place keeps track of itself. Native Americans have transferred their history in this way since before the time of Odysseus. In *Powwow Country*, Salish-Oneida-Sioux Tony Brown states, "Our ways were never written down. They were passed on by our elders. Non-Indians feel if it ain't proven on paper it isn't so, and if it is on paper it is. Paper burns, gets old, crumples into dust."[1] In modern times, this reliance on oral tradition is rare. One of the few non-Indian cultures left that still relies on it is the farm community.

During the snowy winter evenings of my childhood, Camas Prairie's best storytellers sat around our kitchen table. Our household was usually quite subdued, so I loved Saturday nights when boisterous, high-spirited characters congregated there. Our hat rack filled with interesting variations on the western lifestyle. Men who drove four-wheel-drive pickups usually wore big cowboy hats. Most of the time they spoke louder and had more to say. Regular dirt farmers, like my dad, wore stained caps and didn't talk as much. When they did speak, they were usually done before too much attention had been drawn to them. Hats, I figured, said a lot about people.

Hats and syntax. The western dialect cuts all fat off the language bone. It's direct, with no grammatical fanfare, as though descriptive words were noxious weeds. A rancher will say "They went broke" rather than "They experienced financial difficulty and filed for bankruptcy." Metaphor saves even more energy. If some unfortunate soul has a habit of bad luck, a westerner will announce he's always "suckin' the hind tit"—which, of course, draws a parallel to a piglet runt who repeatedly gets shoved to the back of the feeding line. It's earthy, straightforward talk—like the lifestyle ranchers lead, devoid of frills and ambiguities.

In the midst of this common dialogue, the smell of strong coffee and huckleberry pie permeated the air. Children of every size and shape ran throughout the house. No one cared about spills or dirty hands. The only room off-limits was where the babies lay. After they fell asleep, their mothers lined them up on the bed, one tucked next to the other, like multicolored sardines.

Around the table, the stories unfolded. Once I had introduced the other girls to my dolls, I'd sneak back and wedge myself into the dark corner. Yarns about the hard-drinking, rattlesnake-carting characters these cowboys knew made me wonder if the civilized world carried on so.

My favorite storyteller was Arthur Argo. His father had been one of the valley's first homesteaders. Cecil Argo had passed on some amazing anecdotes to his son, who was happy to continue the legacy. In a loud voice, seasoned with a booming laugh, he would repeat them. I liked Arthur, whose heart was the size of his voice.

Arthur told about the time his father came to blows with his best friend, Charlie Neiman. Both men were bachelors when they homesteaded together on Camas Prairie in 1910. One Saturday afternoon Charlie came over to Cecil's to get ready for the evening dance. He took a $5 bill out of his pocket and set it on the table, then went in to get cleaned up. When he came out, he asked Cecil to give him his money back. Cecil said he hadn't taken it. Each man knew he was right and, as Arthur claimed, "Neither one was gonna back up." Before long, they were outside wrestling in the dirt. Eventually they looked up and saw an old sow watching them—with a $5 bill hanging from her mouth. The brawl ended immediately and they began chasing the pig around the homestead till they caught her and retrieved the money.

Arthur claimed that 1915 was the best year the homesteaders ever saw. It rained all spring and by summer the crops were so plentiful the farmers didn't know what to do. The entire valley worked together to get the tons of grain harvested. They didn't have adequate means of cutting, hauling, or storing it and ended up filling to the brim every empty shack on the prairie. They packed sheds so full of wheat the sides burst—in which case they simply built new walls around the grain. It was the only time such a boon happened. On its heels came the droughts of 1916 through 1919. Arthur contended that in the following years the sodbusters had to go back "to goin' on hope."

Arthur also told stories about his brother Johnny—who was tall, blond, and very good-looking. I had seen him several times and even as a little girl was impressed with his attractiveness. However, alongside Johnny's charm ran a hearty wild streak. He also had two interesting habits: He stuttered quite profoundly and loved to carry rattlesnakes around in his coat. Once Johnny walked into the Montana Bar, sat next to Henry Baker, and, asking him if he'd ever seen one up close, laid a rattler on the counter. From that day on, Henry never spoke to him.

Johnny caught these serpents with a long forked stick. After he'd pin their bodies underneath, they couldn't strike. Holding them behind the head just right, he could safely pick them up. He didn't hurt them, just liked their company. He did get bitten a few times. One day, while he was trying to open a gate, he loosened his grip and the snake struck him on the arm. He also took several bites on the leg. No wonder the handsome wild man stuttered, I thought.

In colorful western lingo, Arthur told these stories—those he had heard from his dad or antics his brother had performed. As early as 1774, German philosopher Gottfried von Herder claimed that such content and use of language embodied the distinctiveness of a people. Unique dialect revealed inner character and transmitted traditions across the generations. In Herder's conception, culture found its highest and truest expression in the unusual poetry, songs, and stories of its people.

Arthur acted as this idiosyncratic transmitter of our way of life. His stories also connected us to this arid valley—told us we belonged here. They suggested that if our ancestors could survive on this land, when so many had starved out, we would continue to hold on. Our struggle, however, would be waged together. In *The Healing Power of Stories*, Daniel Taylor claims that tales are universal in serving this purpose for cultures. "Like ritual, stories create and bond a community. They draw us together to share in the ritual of telling. . . . Stories not only help us to make sense of our present and past experience, they also allow us to imagine possibilities for ourselves in the future."[2] The entire communal campfire of Arthur's telling created a deep sense of assurance. Even though I no longer live in the midst of this farm fraternity, I know I will always be part of it.

After I left Montana years ago, I decided to polish myself up. I didn't tell people where I came from. I guarded my colloquialisms like a bad reputation. I ruthlessly eradicated phrases like "plug nickel" and "two bits" from my vocabulary. I always made sure my mascara was on and learned quickly never to call dinner "supper"—a dead giveaway for the lack of savoir faire. I was mortified when, in moments of spontaneity, something slipped out like "He's crazier than a pet coon"—which compares a person's common sense with that of a domesticated wild raccoon, stating, in other words, that they've been confused right out of any.

However, once I turned about thirty or so, I decided it was time to make peace with my heritage. I began to realize that this earthy ranch society had given me much. My instincts would be forever theirs. We are at the core, whether we like it or not, what we're nursed on. At forty, like Albert Rios, I am thankful for a "language-rich, story-fat upbringing."

This sonorous, fertile tale-telling has cohered Indian culture as well. Because Native Americans kept no written records, the maintenance of their history depended entirely on oral tradition. Each tribe had its own historians who considered it their sacred duty to instruct selected young people in the customs of the nation. The pupils gathered in a lodge, where the elders carefully repeated in words and actions these captivating tales. They retold each one until the hearers had committed them perfectly to memory. This process ensured that the sacred stories, elaborate rituals, and tribal history stayed alive. These aged teachers took immense pride in their knowledge of the tribe's past and traditions and had a consuming desire to pass them on in the precise form they had received them. If they found a child who manifested a special interest and ability with memory, they doubled their effort in his apprenticeship.

In *Roots of Survival*, Abenaki storyteller Joseph Bruchac describes the magic in this process. One early autumn, Bruchac was helping Mdawelasis, his elder and teacher, carve a basswood log into an effigy, or totem pole. His friend was teaching him not only the skill of carving but "to feel how this is done, to learn in the old way by both watching and doing." Suddenly they spotted a loon flying overhead. Mdawelasis began to rub his hand over the half-carved log that was taking the shape of a turtle. He declared, "There's thirteen squares on Turtle's shell—always thirteen—one for each of the moons, twenty-eight smaller plates around the outside—one for each of the days in the moon—always twenty-eight. The thirteen plates also stand for the thirteen Abenaki nations: Sokoki, Cowasuck, Penacoc, Pigwacket. . . ." Bruchac wrote about the incident:

> *And as he speaks the names of our old nations, I know that I will remember. I, too, will feel the tribes and seasons beneath my palm as I touch old Turtle's back. Everything in this moment, the smell of wood smoke in the air, the feel of cool earth beneath our bare feet, the sound of his dog Awasos scratching the floor as it stretches on the nearby back porch, will be as clear in my memory as the whistling of the loon's wings which told the old man that the time was right to share this story. So, too, my own mind was open to accept the story. And that was as important, for a story is truly told only when someone listens.[3]*

This tale did more than instruct Bruchac about the lunar calendar and names of the Abenaki nations. It connected him to Mdawelasis, his culture, the animal world, and the earth as a whole. This kind of affiliation gives people strength to face life at its most difficult.

In her novel *Ceremony,* Leslie Marmon Silko explores how culture and people are kept vital through these stories. Her preface quotes an aged Pueblo storyteller:

I will tell you something about stories [. . .]
They aren't just entertainment.
Don't be fooled.
They are all we have, you see
all we have to fight off
illness and death. [. . .]

He rubbed his belly,
I keep them here [. . .]
Here, put your hand on it
See, it is moving
There is life here
for the people.

And in the belly of this story
the rituals and the ceremony
are still growing.[4]

The elderly, like Mdawelasis and this old Pueblo elder, have had time to collect experiences and ruminate on them. Moving through decades of life shapes sagacity and patience. Oral cultures realize this and honor those who have accumulated these irreplaceable storehouses of knowledge. They appoint such well-lived members as the rightful guardians of this truth. It was one of these aged legend keepers who gave me stories about Camas Prairie prior to the homestead era.

Before the Whites

His name was Jim Grinder and he was a full-blooded Nez Perce who had arrived on the Flathead Indian Reservation in 1905, at age thirty-seven. When I knew him, in 1975 at age 107, he described the events of his life with accuracy. Jim resided in Hot Springs at the convalescent center where I had hired on to care for him and his tired western companions. It was my rare and lucky privilege that he began reminiscing to me.

It didn't happen at first. Jim was a quiet man who kept to himself. He would rise early and make his bed carefully, tucking the corners into perfect edges. Then he would climb on top and, pulling his long legs up to his chest, sit staring into the darkness—silent and still. Jim was tall and handsome, with the exquisitely defined cheekbones the Nez Perce possess. A ragged scar edged its way down his beautiful features, and around the pupil of his eyes swirled a smoky ring—the same you'd find in an old mountain lion—intense, patient, and aware. When he looked at you, solid and steady-like, you knew he saw deeper than most. In his calm he could feel your soul's breath.

The nurses liked Jim because he never asked for anything or caused any trouble. Well, almost never. Once in a while, after weeks of solitude, he'd walk down to the Pioneer Bar, and after sitting up at the counter, roll a Bull Durham cigarette, order a drink, and chat with the locals.

Eventually the bartender would call the old folks' home and ask that someone come to pick him up. Jim never made a fuss but silently followed the attendant back to the stuffy place. Inevitably, however, he'd try to smuggle a flask of whiskey inside his sock. Because he was so quiet and unassuming, even this offense didn't rile the nurses. When they found it, they'd simply scold him and pour its contents down the sink.

Jim's roommate was a small Asian man named George. No one knew where George came from, or why he came to Montana, maybe to work on the Northern Pacific Railroad or in the copper mines at Butte. Whatever he'd done, it had cost him his mind. George never spoke but simply shuffled back and forth, wringing his hands and moaning in lonesome singsong gibberish. Jim didn't complain about George's madness. I figured it's why they roomed them together. No one else would have put up with the noise. You had to keep an eye on George; he liked to reach out and touch a woman's soft parts. I took refuge in the fact I had little yet in the way of soft parts.

Each day I delivered the bachelors a snack. Jim watched as I chatted at George, bemused at my determination to keep an eye on his roommate's hands. After the one-sided conversation, I'd turn to Jim and ask how he was doing. At first he merely nodded, figuring, I'm sure, that my question was rhetorical. One day he decided it wasn't.

He asked me who I was. I told him I was Sid Cross's daughter. It's the country's way of introduction: It attaches some history to you—gives the asker something to size you up by—especially if you're a young woman. He smiled, which probably meant he liked my father or the land associated with him, or possibly both, and began telling me about Camas Prairie and his adventures spanning almost a century.

For the rest of the summer I rushed through my work, returning breathless to sit on the tattered chair beside his bed. I took his weathered hand, its skin like parchment worn desperately thin with age, and listened to tales of buried gold, wild broncs, and a West that died ages ago. He started with his early years in the area—also his best he claimed—cowpunching and buffalo herding for Pablo and Allard. Pablo and Allard, as Jim called them, were an interesting pair.

Michel Pablo, who was of Spanish descent, was born at Fort Benton in 1846. Michel and his brother Laurette were the only survivors of a Blackfeet raid on their white settlement outside the fort. Michel's only recollection of the incident was feeling the Blackfeet wrap him in a buffalo robe. At age twenty-two, he moved to the Flathead Reservation to work as a cowhand. Indian agent Peter Ronan hired Michel as an interpreter because he was fluent in English and several native languages. Around 1870, Michel married a Kootenai woman named Agette Finley and began the Pablo Cattle Ranch. Their stock flourished and soon numbered more than ten thousand head.

His partner, Charles Allard, came to Montana from Idaho in 1862. When Charles was ten years old, he and his father, Louis, drove a herd of horses over Lolo Pass to sell to miners in Superior. The deal went so well that Louis went back to Idaho to get more. Fortunately, he left young Charles with friends. Louis was en route during the Northwest Indian Wars, and on the return journey a warrior mistook him for another man and killed him.

To survive, young Charles went to work in the mines. After reaching adulthood, he married a Crow woman and they moved together onto the Flathead Reservation and started a cattle ranch north of the St. Ignatius Mission. In 1882 and 1883 Allard furnished beef to crews building the Northern Pacific. He drove the cattle to these railroad camps, where the animals were slaughtered immediately.

In 1884 Pablo and Allard went into business together, not to enlarge their cow herds but to buy thirteen buffalo from a Pend d'Oreille named Walking Coyote. In 1873 Walking Coyote had captured four baby bison on the eastern plains. After he trained them to follow him, he led them across the mountains, eventually arriving in the Mission Valley. Ten years later Hudson's Bay fur trader Angus McDonald inquired about buying the animals. However, when Pablo and Allard offered Walking Coyote $2,000 for the bison, he accepted their proposition. Taking his modest fortune to Missoula, Walking Coyote began a celebration that lasted a week. By the end of the party, all of his money was gone and, within days, he was found dead under the Higgins Avenue bridge.

For the next twenty years the Pablo-Allard herd grew. In 1893 the partners exhibited several at the Chicago World's Fair. At the expedition, Allard met Buffalo Jones and negotiated to buy another twenty-six purebreds, along with eighteen hybrids. The hybrids—called "cattalo"—were a fifty-fifty cross between a cow and a buffalo. Jones shipped the bison on railroad cattle cars from his ranch in Nebraska to Butte. From there, Pablo and several hired hands drove them north to the Mission Valley. To keep the cattalo from mixing with the pure breeds, they transported them to Wild Horse Island in the middle of Flathead Lake.

Finally, in 1904, after Congress passed the Allotment Bill and the reservation prepared itself for homesteaders, Pablo, now sole owner of the herd, decided to sell. He offered the bison to the U.S. government, but because the feds showed no interest he approached the Canadian Park Service. Pablo negotiated to deliver the buffalo on railroad cars from Ravalli, Montana, to Wainwright, Alberta, twelve hundred miles away. Once the animals had arrived safely, the Canadians were to pay him $250 apiece.

In the spring of 1907, Pablo built a sturdy set of corrals at his ranch (four miles south of the present-day town of Pablo) and hired

Bison herding the cowboys (top). Hauling the bulls to Ravalli (bottom). Photos circa 1910. Photos courtesy of Paul Fugleberg.

Cowboys corralling bison into a Northern Pacific boxcar on its way to Canada, circa 1910. Courtesy of Paul Fugleberg.

twenty-five of the country's best cowboys to start the roundup. At age forty, Jim Grinder numbered among the wild bunch. The wranglers crossed the Little Bitterroot Valley, a range of more than fifty miles, looking for the beasts. Once they'd locate a small group, the hard work began.

Corralling bison was like herding enraged cats, give or take two thousand pounds. The fast, agile creatures dispersed in every direction. If they didn't scatter, they charged their captors, gored horses, and treed photographers. One bison knocked a cowboy and his horse down and, even after being shot twelve times, broke through the corrals and escaped. Another bull carried a man and his pony three hundred yards on his horns before stumbling and dropping the passengers.

To avoid as much chaos as possible, the cowboys separated the cows and calves from the bulls. They drove the cow and calf pairs south to the railway stockyards in Ravalli. Then they ran the bulls into large mobile carts with sturdy ten-foot sides and hauled them to Wainwright. After an entire summer's work only a hundred were in captivity.

Pablo abandoned the roundup until the next spring when he put Charles Allard Jr. in charge. Young Charley, a good friend of Jim,

Sketch from a letter from Charlie Russell to Phillip Goodwin describing the great buffalo round-up, January 1909. Courtesy of the Stark Museum of Art.

tried another approach. He and his hired hands built a ten-mile fence line along the ridge of a hill that led diagonally down to a narrow point in the Flathead River. On the other side of the river they built corrals with chutes that opened into stock wagons. The bison were driven down the hill into the water and made to ford the river. Once the exhausted animals emerged, they walked into the pens, up the chutes, and onto the wagons.

Although this new strategy worked better, it still took five years to gather all of the stock. The final headcount reached seven hundred and became the largest transfer of Old Man Buffalo ever recorded. The "Great Buffalo Round-Up" attracted journalists, photographers, and artists from the United States and Canada.

In 1908 and 1909 Charles Russell rode with the cowboys and sketched the colorful spectacle. Russell participated firsthand in the event. He roped a calf and then, deciding the little fellow needed a ride, picked him up, slung him over his saddle, and carried him to the holding corral. At one point when he and Pablo attempted to head off a large bull, the bison charged him. To keep the animal from harming the painter, Pablo shot it. Russell's excitement over the Pablo roundup is evident in the unusually long letters he wrote to friends

Phil Goodwin and Norman Forsyth.

While the artists painted and the photographers snapped pictures, Jim and his cowboy associates brought in the bison. The last shipment of bison arrived at Canada's Woods Buffalo Park in 1912. When Jim wasn't a cowhand or buffalo herder, he followed the rodeo circuit. In 1915 he participated in the Missoula Stampede.

Jim Grinder falling from a bison in the 1915 Missoula Stampede rodeo. Photo courtesy of the Folson-Flathead Historical Museum.

In addition to money and fame, Jim's prowess as a rider also won him pardon from the Montana State Penitentiary at Deer Lodge. During the early part of the century, it was not uncommon for a man to "borrow" a few cattle from oversized herds. Jim and his horse cajoled some of these adoptees to swim across Flathead Lake onto Wild Horse Island. Even though success of the operation was next to impossible, they all arrived safely—not before the local sheriff received a tip-off, however. For the caper, Jim was sent to Deer Lodge. His stay would have been quite extended if the warden hadn't possessed a sense of humor.

On the prison grounds lived an infamous, unrideable horse named "The Ghost." Hearing of Jim's reputation, the warden made him a deal. If he could ride the white devil he'd grant him pardon. True to his word, after Jim broke The Ghost, the astonished warden paroled him.

Jim made his last ride in 1937 at the Hamilton Rodeo when he and his horse Scarface careened into the stands. Jim emerged blood-soaked with a deep gash down his face and neck. At sixty-seven, his rodeo days were over.

Jim never told me about his life over the three decades before 1900—only that he had come from John Day, Oregon—near the Wallowa Mountains. Had he, at age ten, been with those who escaped into Canada when the Nez Perce were expelled from Oregon? Or did he travel perhaps with Chief Joseph through Montana, escaping north during their last battle near the Bear Paws? At seventeen, I didn't know enough to ask, only to listen.

Jim also talked about Camas Prairie, the Indians who lived there, and the gold he buried in its foothills. He instructed me to go find the stash. More than once I left his room with the coordinates of buried treasure scratched on the napkin of his afternoon snack.

Before I knew it, the summer had passed. I left for college in September 1975, and in the early winter, when, as in centuries past, the Nez Perce began their storytelling, Jim died. Although his body has returned to the land, his voice remains with me.

Several years ago, I decided to look for Jim's gold after I mentioned the story to my uncle at a family reunion, and he encouraged me to do so. My uncle's wife is Salish and Nez Perce, and he has collected much history about both tribes over the years. When I told him the tale, he speculated that it was the stolen wealth of Chief Michele, the last chosen Kalispel chief on Camas Prairie. As in ancient days, Michele served as both leader and spiritual guide to his people.

Early in the century, the Kalispel in the valley had large herds of cattle and horses. Chief Michele sold this livestock to the local merchant in Wild Horse Plains, who usually paid in goods. The payment, my uncle asserts, went something like this: one cow for several blankets and pots. However, at times Michele also received gold coins for the animals as well as for beadwork the women of the tribe created. He kept this cache in a compartment hidden in the floor of his flatbed wagon. The chief traveled from the valley to Wild Horse Plains via Cottonwood Road, a narrow pass that wound around the mountain. Sometime around 1910, he was held up and, lore claims, robbed of a significant amount of gold. The stolen coins were never recovered, nor was anyone ever charged with the crime. Because the period corresponds with Jim's cattle-rustling days, my uncle was convinced he might have been the culprit.

My cousin, who is a friend of the aged Kalispel Indian who owns the land Jim claimed the gold was buried on, suggested she ask him for permission to conduct the expedition. If we found anything, we would give him half. The landowner agreed and said, "If Grinder claimed he buried gold up there, it's there." He had known Jim and the celebrated reputation that followed him. We set the date for the next summer.

In June we met, armed with a metal detector and directions that, if the heist story was correct, were eighty years old. Even in the excitement, I felt uneasy. I hadn't looked for the gold before out of the same hesitation. Whites have taken much from Native Americans. Digging on Indian ground for money, no matter who had sent me, seemed a different line from the same story. However, we'd been given a chance to travel through land rarely seen by whites, back into country on which, for centuries past, Salish youths had sought their spirit guides and rites such as the Sun Dance had been performed. The idea of it was irresistible.

We headed into the foothills that surround the valley. Not far into the journey we came onto an Indian graveyard near the tree line. The landowner's mother had been a shaman who possessed powerful medicine. She rested there alongside souls from the ancient past. I was glad the road veered off a considerable distance around the cemetery. Even as we circled it, I nonetheless had a feeling we were in over our heads.

There are mysteries of spirit and earth that, because they aren't visible, are sometimes easy to ignore. Those of us who live differently from people who readily acknowledge such truth can even convince ourselves such mysteries don't exist. Certain places on the earth, however, don't let us get away with such nonsense. We know when we come upon such places—centers where undefinable energy accumulates or resides. The wind speaks of it. It began warning us that this Indian burial ground stood as a portal into one such place.

We continued a short distance when suddenly the trail dropped off into a wide rolling meadow. A perfect grove of trees rested in the middle of it. In this country, such a tree formation means one of two things: Either an underground well has pushed its way to the surface and bubbled nearby or a stream is close at hand. Because the gold was buried near water, we took off down through the meadow. As we approached the grove, the wind's voice grew louder and I suddenly had an eerie sense that we were coming to something more meaningful than earthly treasure. We instinctively slowed to a cautious walk.

A pole fence weaved its way around the trees, alerting that the land had been set apart. Completely hidden inside was a long rectangular lean-to. Its boards were browned with age, wind, and erosion. Hanging from its sagging rafters, an ancient oil lantern swayed in the summer breeze. Next to it, affixed to a foundation pole, the rotting head of a six-point elk stared back at us. Its decaying skin hung by strips from its whitened bone. Now not only the wind called warning. Other animal skeletons ornamented the place, peering at us through the spaces of time. In the center of the dilapidated shelter was an Indian sweat house. We were on sacred ground.

The sweat house holds great significance to the American Indian. It plays a central role in native life and serves as a vital link to the Creator. Religiously, the sweat house rite ranks above all fasts and important ceremonies. In many native stories, the sweat house existed before the creation. There, in the core of the mist, long before the birth of water or earth, the "Giver" lived. As sweat beads dropped from the Giver's body, the land, sea, and human race were formed.

The ceremony of the sweat house also represents physical creation and birth. When Indians go into the ritual sanctuary, they do so as if entering a womb. If the lodge is covered with the skin of a bear or deer, the animal's strength occupies it. Bearskin houses are especially powerful. It is believed that during hibernation, Bear sleeps close to the spirit world. In similar fashion, those entering the body of a Bear lodge venture into the same realm. Inside, they are encased in the womb of the powerful spirit animal. Encircled in such darkness and strength, they pray for health and life. They emerge cleansed and reborn.

Native people believe each part of creation possesses special power. The sweat house ritual uses symbols from all these elements—earth, air, water, fire, animals, plants, and stones. While honoring these elements in the ceremony, participants pray to be blessed with their gifts.

The Salish use willow branches to mold the hut's skeleton into a half circle. Because willow bends with grace, it typifies vigor and resiliency. As a deciduous tree that dies and reawakens each year, it also illustrates resurrection. The theme of rebirth is evident in its very framework. Because the willow flourishes alongside flowing water, Indians believe it has special cleansing and healing potential. They use its bark to cure headaches and other pains. In modern times, its byproduct—salicylic acid—has been synthesized into salicin, an active ingredient in aspirin.

As in all sweat houses, the door to this one faced east. About ten feet from the entrance, stones lay in a perfect mound. This sacred fireplace is called the "fire of no end." To heat these rocks, the builders place sticks in bunches running north, south, east, and west—to honor the four directions of the earth. As the stones are heated, a prayer is given to thank the Creator for his protection and blessing.

Inside sweat houses, an altar designates the holy center where the Creator dwells. The earth taken from the opening is used to form a narrow trail leading to the rock pile outside. This pathway is called the "Sacred Path of Life." As participants walk along it, each step is a plea for guidance through this earthly voyage.

Stones are heated and carefully placed inside the lodge. Rocks, like animals and earth, are believed to contain life. Stones used in the sweat ceremony are never to be thrown or dropped. Like the mystic transubstantiation of a communion wafer, once heated the stones take on great spiritual significance. In the Lakota language they are called *tunka*, originating from the word "Tunkashila," meaning "Grandfather." Each stone is given the respect of a tribal elder. If a stone falls onto the ground during transportation, it is returned to the heating pile and another is chosen. Only stones that are round and about the size of a human head are used. Igneous lava rock is best because it holds heat the longest and doesn't crumble when water is poured on it.

Not far from the rock pile bubbled the source of water we looked for. It ran into a rectangular pool where the Indians immerse themselves after they sweat. This water is also poured over the heated rocks during the ceremony, making steam that cleanses the body and sends messages to the Creator.

Next to the lodge lay a fresh stack of pine branches. While relaxing in the sweat house, the Salish beat their skin with these boughs, claiming they bring great relief to muscle soreness. Native people also use pine-needle salves in poultices to pull infection from wounds and alleviate rheumatism.

With these symbols, all forms of life participate and are honored in the sweat ceremony. Creek Indians attribute the very creation of the lodge to the animals. Their story recounts that, long ago, the Indians had offended the wildlife by killing Deer, Bear, and Buffalo and using only part of them, leaving the rest to spoil. They caught Fish and threw its bones back into the stream or into the fire. They dishonored the very creatures who allowed themselves to be killed to provide food and clothing for the people.

The animals held a council to decide what to do. Some wanted to go to war with the humans. Bear, however, spoke up and said, "Because the people now have bows and arrows and can shoot us from great distances, we are no longer a match for them."

After much talking they came to the decision that sickness should be sent to the people to punish them. Deer sent swollen joints and arthritic pains and headaches. Bird sent stomach troubles. Before long, humans suffered greatly. The animals took pity on them and appeared in their dreams, telling the Indians what had caused such misery. They told them that because sickness had arrived it would always be with them. However, the animals also gave the people medicine songs and taught them how to use plants to cure these illnesses.

They also gave humans the sweat house. If humans crawled naked—like animals—into it and asked forgiveness, they would be purified and cured. If they remembered not to overhunt, their sicknesses would not return. Thus, herbal medicines, healing songs, and sweat houses were given to heal—but also as a reminder to treat the animals with respect.

This ceremony is a sacrament to native people. It encourages visions and healing and unifies them with one another and the earth. When early Europeans and priests observed its power and understood the intricate role it played in Indian society, many times they banned it.

Today, there are non-Indians who are charging money to lead such ceremonies. It is entirely understandable that the native community resents such profiteering. As Joseph Bruchac states, "If you are a Catholic and you take communion, it has meaning because it is done in a sacramental setting by a priest who is ordained. What if, however, 'Catholicism' became as interesting to popular culture as 'Indians' are? What would a devout Catholic think of businesses selling communion wafers and the vestments of priests to non-Christians so that at special 'authentic' ceremonies, for a price, they could learn to 'give communion' dressed in robes bought from the 'Catholic Arts and Crafts Store?'"[5]

As we walked back up the hill from this sacred site, the wind died down and I felt even stronger that whites, on a gold-digging expedition, did not belong in these hills. I was relieved when, once we found the spot that seemed to match Jim's description, the metal detector no longer worked. I won't go back. Some things are better left undisturbed.

Homestead Days

By 1910 the "Great Buffalo Round-Up" was drawing to a close and white settlers began moving in. Stories about the homestead era came to me from another great and aged storyteller I've known—my great-grandmother. Even in her nineties, she exuded the creative energy and good humor that hallmark the trade. Because Grandma immigrated to America at age thirty-four, she never lost her strong Czech accent or appreciation for the exotic—which also added to her tale-telling abilities.

Grandma's strong, childlike face would fill with joy as her ragamuffin great-grandchildren clambered into her cottage. The kitchen was our favorite place because it was so much like her. Amid the copper kettles swirled smells of simmering barley soup, rosemary, sage, and fresh rye bread—all things warm and Bohemian. Grandma's cooking, as well as her kitchen, mirrored her personality, Old World gourmet and pioneer utility: homemade pasta and gooseberry pie, mincemeat tarts and huckleberry dumplings. She stirred and sifted in the fragrant place, giggling amid the chaos. I loved to hear her bright laugh and to elicit it with requests for more of whatever she created.

After we ate, the family moved into a cluttered room of antiques, history books, legal papers, and beautiful linens she had tatted. She sat in her overstuffed chair and, holding herself steady with a cane, told us about her native land and an early Montana few had seen.

Anna Malleck was born in 1879, in Zahradka, Bohemia. She graduated from school at thirteen and ventured off to Prague to become a seamstress's apprentice. In 1899 she married John Svoboda and a year later, in Vienna, Austria, gave birth to my grandmother Marie. Two years later a son, Johnny, was born. In 1908 the family sailed to America aboard the *Kaiser Wilhelm the Great*.

Emigrating from Europe through Ellis Island in that year, the Svobodas became part of the nineteen million foreigners who flooded into America during the late nineteenth and early twentieth centuries. Like many, they settled in a tenement house in New Jersey. In 1910 crusading journalist Jacob Riis described such places as "scarcely fit to shelter brutes . . . merely dark, damp basements, outhouses and stables."[6] Among the filth, Grandma suffered several miscarriages.

The babies' deaths could have resulted from more than unsanitary conditions. When John Svoboda got drunk, he beat Grandma. Being a generous woman, she never told us about it, only that he was "mean." Years after her death in 1973, and only upon my sister's receipt from a Chicago archive of Anna's divorce decree, did we know the extent of her suffering. The document stated that he "beat, struck, choked and threatened her with a knife. On May 2, 1910, he tried to kill her with a hatchet."

Once the family moved to Chicago, Grandma made her escape. After the divorce, she and the children boarded the Union Pacific Railroad and headed west to stake a claim among the Nebraska sandhills. The railroad and the Homestead Act made such an audacious scheme possible for a single mother. Events that spelled tragedy for Indian culture provided hope for Anna.

Many of her countrymen were migrating to Nebraska as well. In 1913 the state contained the greatest percentage of Bohemians in

America—they probably congregated there because no one else wanted to. Homestead sites in the sandhills were sectioned off in 640-acre plots—instead of the usual 160—which in itself reveals a lot about the land.

Bohemians, like most immigrants, also grouped in communities because they provided protection and a common language. Many never got the hang of English. My great-grandmother didn't learn to speak it until her daughter taught it to her years after arriving in America. However, also like many immigrants, Grandma refused to teach Czech to her grandchildren—telling them that they were Americans and English should be the only language they spoke.

Grandma staked her claim on the bleak prairieland and, from strips of grass she and the children plowed up in the field, they built a sod house. The hut was dark and wet, and as one Nebraska girl described, "There was running water in our sod house . . . it ran through the roof."[7] These families hosted centipedes, mice, spiders, and snakes that crawled out of the walls.

To warm the hovel, Grandma and the children gathered the only heat-producing combustible available to them—dried cow chips. They borrowed a wagon and team of horses, drove out on the desolate prairie, and collected manure. One load went to the rancher who loaned the wagon; the other was theirs.

Anna also hired on as a cook at a cow camp that fed cowboys and drifters. The money she earned went for land payments and fed the family. For seven years they survived alone. Then in 1918 she agreed to help another Bohemian named John Lauerman. John held a temporary visa and would soon be forced to leave the country. His only reprieve was marriage.

Not long after they wed, John and Anna read of a homestead claim that was being deserted on Camas Prairie, Montana. Its owner, a man named Costeka, wanted to return to Chicago. His wife, Sylvia, had recently fallen from her horse and been dragged across the hillside to her death. Neighbors argued that Sylvia was an excellent equestrian and her husband an abusive man. Their interpretation of the event was that he had killed her himself and tied her body to the horse to cover his crime. Montana has never been a place for one weak in the stomach. John and Anna went anyway. Not long afterward, Marie and her new husband, Richard Cross, followed. They bought an abandoned homestead on the south side of the valley.

Like Anna, John, and Marie, many of the homesteaders on Camas Prairie were immigrants from various points around the world. Ed Muster came from Austria, Mike Marrinan from Ireland, and Erick Jorgenson from Sweden. They arrived with high hopes and broken English. Homesteader Billie Shaeffer described the eclectic group as a melting pot of "moonshiners, horse thieves, eccentric bachelors, buxom ladies, petite 'school marms', prospectors' widows, midwives, blacksmiths, harness makers, doctors and lawyers."

The Native Americans, who also spoke little English, took their allotments on the west end of the valley. The whites filled in on the east. At first, the Indians stayed to themselves and watched the newcomers with silent interest. It must have been a curious sight to behold.

Once their own shacks were built, the pioneers' first order of business was to construct a schoolhouse. Because many of these homesteaders were from the "old country," they felt an American education was vital for their children. Some of the Indian children attended school as well. Here my father made lifelong friends. One was Victor Pierre.

One day Victor brought dad and his brother Herb a beautiful full-quilled arrow each. His grandfather, Chief Michele, had given them to him. Victor was bestowing his young white friends with a very special gift.

Delighted with the beautiful arrows, they ran inside the schoolhouse to show their teacher. Miss Price, who was also quite taken with the exquisite relics, asked the boys if they would sell them to her. They hesitated. Victor, who had followed them inside, stood there in silence. Miss Price persisted. "Wouldn't you take ten cents?" "Ten cents apiece?" Victor finally spoke up. "If you sell them, you should split the money with me." They struck a bargain—for Miss Price at least. The boys divided the money three ways, ran to the store, and bought enough candy for a month.

The homesteaders also worked together to build a community hall, a blacksmith shop, and later a gymnasium. They formed basketball and baseball teams to challenge their counterparts in Lonepine and the Little Bitterroot Valley. On summer evenings, they swam in the muddy, cattailed Green Springs Pond or watched silent movies at the community hall.

Once a week Jim Carter from Wild Horse Plains brought a movie. During Charlie Chaplin, Hoot Gibson, and Rin Tin Tin shows, Mrs. Nick or Mrs. Walters played the piano while Carter kept the noisy gas-powered engine that ran the movie, and the only electric light, going. The community held box socials and dances. Settler Wavie Charleton described them as "joyous affairs with much stomping and do-si-do-ing to the screeching of fiddles and piano music." The musicians combined tunes from their native countries with improvisations of their own. Ed Muster played the Vienna accordion, Clifford Culligan the banjo, fiddle, and guitar, and Jim Podobinik the piano. Podobinik, who was an accomplished pianist, made his neighbor Joe Erchul a deal. If Joe milked his cows, he would perform evening concerts for him and his wife.

Summer brought the rodeo season. Each year Nip Lynch transported his bronc stock and racehorses from Wild Horse Plains. The valley's farmers and Indians added their own wild animals—horses they bet no one else could ride or the ones they simply wanted "broke." The bucking events and races took place near Green Springs so everyone could have a good swim afterward.

In the snowbound winter, the settlers braved the bitter cold to gather for card parties or hay rides up Cottonwood Road. They went as far as Dog Lake, where they cut and hauled back huge blocks of ice. They stored the cubes in root cellars filled with sawdust and brought them out in summer to make homemade ice cream during Sunday get-togethers.

Although they loved merrymaking, they were a tough, practical lot who had come to claim the American dream. Hardship was simply part of the bargain. When the settlers discovered extra money in the school fund, they hired a nurse from Missoula to come out and check their children's tonsils. As the students filed by, the stoical woman reached inside their throats with medical "pliers," pulled the organs out, and tossed them into a dishpan. My mother, who grew up fifteen miles away, had her tonsils removed by the same procedure.

Thrashing wheat on Camas Prairie in 1912.

The tonsil pull was a precursor of pain to come. The homesteaders soon discovered the foolhardy optimism of dry-land farming in the arid West. Even in fertile soil, crops suffered without consistent rainfall. Some years the valley produced nothing but a bumper yield of fan weed. And often, along with the drought, the grasshoppers came.

Each family attacked the bug problem in their own style. Some doused the creatures with a concoction of lemon juice, blackstrap molasses, salt, and arsenic. Others built grasshopper fences: tall, oilcloth barriers the low-flying insects couldn't navigate over. Others dug trenches and filled them with water to capture the invaders—as the hoppers jumped into the ditches, they were carried through a flume and dumped into sacks below. Great-grandma raised turkeys and geese—to eat them.

Instead of struggling against insects and drought, others found an easier way to make a living. Camas Prairie became a hotbed of

Casteel Blacksmith Shop, 1910.

First Camas Prairie School in 1910.

moonshine production. Deep ravines tucked inside the hills provided perfect camouflage for bootleg whiskey operations. The liquor business also flourished because federal agents feared entering the reservation to look for it. They came as far as the Flathead River at Perma and then refused to advance into the wild country. Indian and white distillers took great advantage of their freedom.

P. J. Bonner operated the most profitable enterprise. With his money, he sent his two sons to the University of Montana. John, the eldest, became an attorney and Montana's thirteenth governor. Another man, named Billy Phillips, had such a thriving business agents finally decided it was time to bring him in. West of the reservation they waited, and when he crossed the boundary they seized him and sent him to Deer Lodge for a year.

To avoid other arrests, the bootleggers traveled the back hills on a road that became known as the "Whiskey Trail." The rugged path crossed Camas Prairie west to Wild Horse Plains and east to Polson, running almost exclusively on reservation land and safe from detection.

When liquor exportation got so vigorous that glass containers became scarce, my adolescent father and his brother Herb started their own lucrative business collecting empty whiskey bottles and selling them back to the moonshiners for five cents apiece. Early one Sunday morning, the boys headed to the gymnasium. Saturday night's dance ensured fortune. Upon investigation, Herb found several

Boys in front of the Camas Prairie Gym in the early thirties. Left to right: Phil Croghan, Phil Pelley, Bill Holland, Sid Cross, Victor Pierre, Tom Holland, Jack Marrinan, Walter Mortson. Front: Gordon Cross.

fine quart jugs under a woodpile. There was only one problem—they were full. Because the boys couldn't sell their own product back to the moonshiners, they quickly solved the dilemma by dumping the premium whiskey on the ground. When Lou Burgess discovered his substantial unsold stash gone, he was furious. The young entrepreneurs made certain they hocked his quart bottles to another bootlegger.

Other homesteaders didn't farm either, but they made their living legally. One was Chub (some called him Shorty, others Stub) Collingsworth, whose homestead adjoined John and Great-grandma's. Chub outfitted a team of mules between Wild Horse Plains and Polson. He'd fill his wagon with goods at Wild Horse Plains and start across the hills. One soppy spring his brimming wagon got stuck. He walked to John McCoy's and requested assistance. When the two men approached the hopelessly bogged cart, Chub asked John to throw some posts under the wheel, after, of course, he lifted the thing. John laughed and said he figured the feat to be downright impossible. Chub simply smiled and heaved the wagon up from the mire. The shocked schoolmaster wedged the posts under the wheel, and Chub and his team of mules were on their way.

As a teenager, my father learned firsthand about Shorty's strength. One day Dad coaxed his younger brother, Gordon, into a boxing

*Anna and John Lauerman and Shorty, Chub, or Stub
Collingsworth, 1934.*

match. While Shorty mended Grandma's fence, he watched the cocky boxer take advantage of his smaller opponent. Finally, Shorty asked if he could go a few rounds himself. My agile father was delighted to have a chance to teach his rotund neighbor a few tricks about the sport. Within seconds the old mule skinner had served up enough blows to force his opponent's humble surrender. Dad later learned that Shorty had graduated from Kansas State University as a champion boxer and wrestler.

After the days of mule skinning and moonshining were over, and the drought and grasshoppers had discouraged even the most hardy, whites began moving out of the valley. In a turn-of-the-century pamphlet, the U.S. government's promise that in western Montana "all vegetation thrives to a high degree . . . no pestilential visitations are experienced and crop failure is absolutely unknown" had proven downright false, as did the government's 1905 prediction that "Within five years of the opening of the reservation, 25,000 people will live upon it, and within ten years it will support a population of 50,000 people." In reality, only one-fourth of the land offered to homesteaders was ever claimed and even less was "proven up."

In addition to failed crops, the economic depression, which had begun for the American farmer in the 1920s, raged on. Roosevelt's New Deal hadn't touched the Montana prairie and, as in most parts of the West, recovery was still years away. Hungry families started the long journey back east or on to Seattle.

The 1930s brought a different kind of pain to my family. In 1936, in front of my thirteen-year-old father, Richard fell dead of a heart attack. Dad pulled him onto the porch and tried to revive him, but his father never recovered.

Left behind on a rugged land, without the presence of this kind and gentle man, Marie and the boys began their struggle to survive. Heartbroken, she went to the bank in Wild Horse Plains to relinquish the farm. The loan officer informed her that the land was not worth what she owed against it and she couldn't even give it away. Great-grandma and John scraped $50 together to get them through the winter.

In the spring Marie approached a wealthy financier named Clifford Rittenaur. Rittenaur loaned money to people unable to get bank support. Financing an immigrant widow held a risk no institution cared to wager on. She and the boys bought milk cows, bum calves, lambs, and chickens. They scratched their way through the Depression, like many Americans, one step in front of disaster.

It was not long until John also was dead. One morning while Anna was gone, John couldn't get the wood in the stove to ignite, so he threw gasoline into it. The embers burst into an explosion that caught him and the entire house on fire. He ran outside but could not extinguish the flames. When John ran over the hill to the Egans', he was so badly burned that Mrs. Egan did not recognize him. She threw a blanket around his naked, charred body and she and Mr. Eagen raced him to Missoula. When the doctors pulled the blanket off, most of his skin came with it. John died a few days later.

By then many of the prairie's original homesteaders had died or fled the hardships of such a life. Anna and Marie continued on. Mr. Rittenaur began to trust Marie's moxie and strong constitution implicitly. As families left, he loaned her the money to buy their land, for which she paid an average of $4 an acre. Many questioned Marie's "worthless land" buying ventures. Her mother did not. Anna knew land would always be of value and encouraged her daughter's investments. Before each sale, the women conferred in Czech while my father wondered what they discussed so passionately.

My grandmothers might have known instinctively what John Wesley Powell had figured out scientifically—that if farmers were to make a living in the thirsty West they needed large plots of land. Eastern agricultural soil, with adequate rainfall, yielded more grain per acre and fed more livestock. This "Great American Desert" was different. One hundred sixty acres couldn't sustain much of anything. Acquiring miles of it was the only way to survive.

Marie left management of the land to her teenage boys and leased the prairie's country store. The establishment became the valley's hub of activity. There, whites and Indians converged to buy goods, exchange gossip, and drink coffee.

Many native women became regular visitors. At first they came sporadically, then daily to have coffee and visit with Marie—in a tongue that was second language to them all. Each day Lizzy Coutere and Agnes Curley would arrive in their one-horse buggy. Lizzy restocked the exquisitely beaded white deerskin jackets, embroidered leather gloves, moccasins, and belts Marie sold for her. In turn, Lizzy taught Marie how to tan leather and cure venison.

In 1956 Marie Cross died on Camas Prairie. In a country where single women held little bargaining power she had prospered—leaving each son a fine ranch. Those who hung on did the same for their children.

Over the decades these inheritors of the land learned, as Linda Hasselstrom wonderfully describes in her poem "My Last Will and Testament," that a farmer's relationship to the soil is a passionate, consuming liaison:

> *[. . .] You earn the land*
> *after your name is on the title.*
> *The sacraments of inheritance*
> *require payment in blood and sweat.*
> *If you only accept, you lose everything.*

To hold it, you must fight
the plan to dump sewage in the creek,
fight the scheme to dump nuclear waste,
creating jobs
for people desperate enough to take them.

Fight the silence of the frozen land,
struggle to lift tons of baled hay,
fight for the lives of cows
made stupid by pain;
fight fire in winter grass,
stand helpless as hail booms on the roof.

Even if you are homeless, landless,
beware this bequest;
look this gift in its barbed teeth.
If you've never felt the wind
breathe in your lungs,
earth's blood singing in yours,
think before you accept this freedom,
this prison. [. . .][8]

Luckily farmers don't undertake this struggle alone. They assist one another through disappointment and poverty, blizzard and drought. They work and socialize together like those who came before them did. Ranch life has always been a community affair. On Camas Prairie, gatherings still resemble those that the early homesteaders initiated a century ago.

Children in the valley continue to attend the two-room schoolhouse located on the 1912 site. As in decades past, weddings, funerals, and basketball games are held in the old gym that was constructed in 1931. To swim, the valley's residents still meet at Green Springs.

Green Springs is actually more of a marsh than a swimming pool. Hot mineral water bubbles from the ground, creating several large ponds. Cattails frame the water and make a perfect home for the Louisiana swamp frogs transplanted there long ago. The ground surrounding the bog is white with alkali and minerals; the smell is of heat and summer. Hot sand and clay alternate as the pool floor.

When I was a child, my little sister and I loved the privileged occasions when we got to go to Green Springs. Other times, we usually swam in the horse trough back of our barn—filled with water bugs and skippers. Trough swimming was troublesome because first you had to scoop out the scummy algae around the sides and then capture the long-winged bugs that bit your legs mercilessly. Although we delighted in the process, a girl had to admit it was an undignified affair. We much preferred the mud hole at Green Springs.

Farm families congregated at the springs on hot summer evenings. At first the pond was clear. However, after several dives off the board or a mud fight, we stewed rather than swam. Most of the children in the valley learned to swim there because the water was soft and easy to float on. The bottom of the pond was also pliant. In certain areas the hot mire had no indication of bottom. It felt like luxurious quicksand. Those of fearless heart would wedge themselves down into it so far someone would have to pull them out.

On blankets alongside the shore, people visited or repeated what history they knew about this mineral slough. For centuries, the Kalispel had gathered here to hold powwows and religious ceremonies. An old and substantial aura surrounded Green Springs—like the atmosphere of ancient ruins, where you can feel important things have happened—but you don't quite know what they've been.

Places like Green Springs and the stories that unfolded there are becoming rare in this existence. Myths of earth and tradition diffuse in our modern society of fragmentation. We should fight against such disintegration. When the tales of an individual or culture fall apart, both become vulnerable. Humans instinctively rely on memory of personal history, and stories of collective history, to guide them as they think and feel their way through the present.

For thousands of generations our survival depended upon keen attunement to the surroundings through story and encounter. Acute sense helped us notice new or odd developments: changes in animal behavior, unusual footprints, extraordinary weather. Such information signaled danger—or new opportunity. This sensitivity kept us alive and evolving. We turned these observations into story.

Today, we live in a world that has, by and large, lost this inner voice and discernment of the elements. Without such instinct and remembrance, knowledge floats around, impotent and helpless. That's why abstract data about environmental degradation are less likely to change us than more story about, and experience in, the natural world. We must tell tales that make people feel attached to the universe and then they will likely take care of it. The emotions of shame and fear are not as sustainable as those of love and belonging.

This connection will also fill us with purpose. Nothing sparks excitement for life more than feeling we are linked to a larger whole and have something important to do. Nothing makes us feel more hopeless than sensing we do not. Without such affiliation, no amount of success is success enough. We must again see ourselves joined to a past narrative tied up with future narratives, allied to a meaningful sequence of events leading to a significant conclusion. As Baal Shem Tov suggests, "In remembrance lies the secret of redemption."

If we have such a foundation, we can absorb tragedy and suffering without despair. Stories give us context for coming to terms with that which is otherwise unbearable. They allow us to name and reconcile that which otherwise presents itself as misery, absurdity, or chaos. Even the celebrated existentialist Jean-Paul Sartre recognized the meaning story gave to human existence:

> *A man is always a teller of tales, he lives surrounded by his stories and the stories of others, he sees everything that happens to him through them; and he tries to live his life as if he were telling a story.*

Such narrative has enabled those in the West to endure loss and heartache. It also has given them perseverance, joy, and the ability to survive.

Chapter 8

The Undying West

During the twentieth century, the West of Turner, Russell, and Curtis did change significantly, but its people did not lose their character, its population did not burst at the seams, and Indian culture did not die. Contrary to Turnerian predictions, the westerner still possesses spirit and fortitude, large tracts of the region are largely unpopulated, and Indian peoples have increased sevenfold. In 1890 approximately 250,000 Native Americans inhabited the United States; today they number close to 2,000,000.

The tribe's survival is evident in people like Johnny Stanislaw. John is a quiet man who lives alone in the hills of Camas Prairie. He attended school in the valley a few years behind my seventy-six-year-old father. Johnny's older brother Ustus and Dad were friends. Ustus was murdered in the 1950s when he took his summer Forest Service wages to the Dixon Bar to celebrate. After a raucous party, he was found robbed of his money, lying face down on the railroad tracks near Perma.

Johnny, as well, spent time living an untamed life. One evening he got into a knife fight with another man. The fellow stabbed him and then cut a deep slash across his face, almost removing his eye. Nearly dead, it took Johnny months to recover. After he came home, he swore off liquor and today lives a life of peaceful solitude.

Sometimes Johnny walks the twenty miles to town. If my father happens on him, he gives him a ride. A few winters ago, as a terrible blizzard approached, Dad noticed Johnny slowly trudging down Markle Hill. The temperature was dropping quickly, so Dad rushed to pick him up. The eight miles left would have been long ones. Since then, every time Johnny sees my father he thanks him for that particular lift.

Last fall, as the sun made an eerie descent over the blue Camas Prairie hills, Dad and I went to see Johnny. I wanted to ask him about the history of his Kalispel family, the oldest in the valley. In my father's Dodge jalopy we ascended the almost impassable dirt road up into what has always been Indian country. Dogs of every breed barked their warning as we approached—mostly dingoes and mixed-breed mutts, the big ones knocking the little ones aside for an opportunity to bite at the tires.

My father jumped out amid the pack and started toward the aged house. I knew I had been away from home too long again—dogs with a pedigree that included coyote, porcupine, and timber wolf frightened me. I hollered to my father that I would simply stay put until he found Johnny. Not locating his friend, Dad hobbled up toward a new log cabin nestled in the woods. It was a handsome cottage the tribe was building for Johnny, who had refused to let them wire it for electricity. He said he wanted to continue to live in the old way.

While wild dogs circled the vehicle, like a wolf pack in a Charlie Russell painting, Dad disappeared. I peeked through the window at an animal that sported a human face and a porcupine body and sent him a half smile. He stared back. Before long, however, I grew ashamed of my cowardice and stepped out of the pickup.

In complete silence, a large man appeared from the shack and started toward me. A deep scar—that looked as though it might have cut him in two—tore across his face. The dogs danced around him as he advanced. At the same time my father, moving more slowly than I could imagine, emerged from the woods. "Who are you?" Johnny hollered. Dad said, "It's me—Sid." With that, Johnny's hardened face melted into laughter and he said, "I know."

As the sun set in the biting cold, we encircled the warm pickup engine like wranglers around a campfire. Johnny told us about his

Kalispel ancestors who had come from the northwest near Lake Pend d'Oreille and down the Clark Fork River. They camped and fished along its shores with thousands of their own, eventually moving north onto Camas Prairie. He explained the difference between the Kalispel, Pend d'Oreille, and Flathead—all Salish speakers but distinct clans. The tribes also shared many similarities—like their universal respect for Coyote. It was the reason, he said, they didn't trap him. Coyote was a friend to the people—dying and resurrecting to come again to their aid.

The dogs grew silent as Johnny spoke with clarity and good humor. His scarred face reflected wisdom and kindness, intelligence and thoughtfulness. He spoke in his beautiful native tongue, describing its nuance and color.

Salish is a pictorial language. The word for moon translates as "Man with a Shriveled Nose." When there are shadows on its surface they are called "Toads," in which case the moon becomes "A Man with a Toad on His Back." Each month of the year also represents a picture. April is the "Month of Buttercups" while September is the "Harvest of Ripe Things." Even Salish names have meaning and, in the old days, were created from a significant event in the person's life. The name Sxu'-tes-em-exe' means "Grizzly Bear Track."

As the chill cut into my bones, neither man flinched. My father leaned against the pickup to rest his ruined hip and prompted Johnny with more questions. They laughed and reminisced about people they had known and their early days on the prairie, when they said folks "got along."

I watched the old-timers, both chiseled by weather and years, their faces resembling the land around them—brown, eroded, mapped with branching creekbeds and coulees. They were westerners who shared more than they differed, both proud and loyal to the cultures they loved, extensions of the land—survivors of, and yet dinosaurs to, modernity.

After returning to Seattle, I sent Johnny a thank-you note for the wonderful stories he had told. A few days later a letter arrived, written on lovely stationery in exquisite penmanship, stating that he had enjoyed our conversation very much and would always be available to help. For me, Johnny Stanislaw embodies the history of his people.

Although he has suffered, he endures, intelligent, proud, and generous. Like Johnny, my father also manifests this pride and toughness—characteristics both men display in unyielding tenacity.

When I was six years old, Dad appeared at the front door barechested and covered in so much blood I hardly recognized him. That morning he left for the barn to dig postholes while Mom took my older brother, Ben, to a friend's birthday party. My two-year-old sister and I were to stay inside and out of mischief.

In the vast world of dangerous farm equipment, the posthole digger reigns king. Its long spinning rod is covered with blades so sharp they easily grind into frozen earth. Ideally, the operator stays as far away from the monster as possible, negotiating the scalpel staff from a lever on the tractor. Instead of shutting the machinery off that day, Dad impatiently jumped down to pull something out of the blades—which immediately caught his sleeve and began pulling him in. He grabbed a crossbar and held on while the power takeoff cut off his jeans jacket, sweater, shirt, and significant pieces of his arms, neck, and chest—during which time he held his throat inches away from the whirling blades. It took several minutes before the gear tore enough away for him to push free. He stumbled to the house to call his sister-in-law and ask her to take him to the hospital.

When I saw him come through the door, I ran into the living room with Melanie in tow, winding us up together in the drapes so she wouldn't see the blood. I listened as he calmly called my aunt and told her he had been "hurt," then walked into the bathroom to get cleaned up before she got there.

More than physical power kept my father alive that day. It was also his incredible strength of will. After working so hard to build our small farm, a machine wasn't going to end the fight. Over the years, I came to marvel at this brand of toughness, one that he, and the other ranchers in the valley, displayed. They shared a level of determination that unbearable weather, unpredictable farm prices, and repeated disappointments could not destroy. It's why when I read journalistic assessments of the "dependent" American farmer, I simply don't recognize the picture.

Rather than dependency, I have always witnessed another code of conduct. My sister stayed in Montana. She can cook for a crew of thirty while tending to her five children and then go out and castrate a bull faster than any cowboy there. She's also one of the most charitable people I know. She is constantly feeding, boarding, or helping someone.

The nation's farmer embodies this strength and generosity. However, the aloneness of the place can also create a bullheadedness and skepticism about things which they don't see eye to eye.

Some ranchers refuse to concede the wrong inflicted on the Salish and Kootenai and see tribal strength as a threat to their own interests. As the tribe began exerting their rights in the early 1960s, many whites resented tribal authority. Such an attitude seems unjustified in light of the tribe's ancestral claim to the land and the government's nefarious dealings with them. Nonetheless, some local inhabitants won't acknowledge either situation. They are willing to bemoan the government's treatment of the farmer but not the whites' part in unfair dealings with the Indians.

If both cultures are to weather the onslaught of the modern age, cooperation seems important, but before true healing can begin, whites must face their history straight on. It's easy to disregard the past, however, when area schools teach very little of the true story about whites and Indians. During my grade school and high school years on the reservation, almost nothing was taught of Salish and Kootenai history, except to expropriate the tribes' fearlessness for our sports mascot, the "Savage." History classes merely repeated the state's legacy of gutsy populist politicians, rugged pioneers, and black-lunged Butte miners. Frederick Jackson Turner might as well have written every Montana history text I'd ever read.

Although Turner's pioneer story is part of the state's past, Indian heritage predates that of Europeans by thousands of years. Unfortunately, ignorance of, or unwillingness to acknowledge, this fact oversimplifies the state's history and tempts some whites to assume the role soldiers took in Buffalo Bill Cody's Wild West Show—that of "abused conqueror."

Only when westerners are honest about the past, can we gain fuller understanding of western history and form new alliances. So simply believe, however, that we should bury history so it doesn't s up the present—that such bygones aren't pertinent. But they a many reasons. History is the underpinning of our present world. Like yeast to bread, it ferments our entire culture. To deal intelligently with current issues, we must be ever conscious of the past.

Native Americans are justifiably upset about the way they were treated, the breaking of covenants, the disruption of their ancient culture. For some reason, our government believed that treaties with Indians weren't written on the same paper as those made with England or France. If we are to move on to reconciliation, whites must admit their ancestral part in the wrongs and the tribes' right to self-determination on land they still hold today. That will also help us avoid further injustice and abandon ridiculous attitudes of superiority. Then genuine restoration can begin.

Facing the truth does not mean that white Americans can't be proud of the strength and accomplishment of the westward movement. This spectrum of stories provides us with affiliation and fits us into a narrative larger than ourselves. These stories impart strength through identification with the soil and community. We can cling to the nobility and truth that our ancestors displayed—yet be honest as well. Life is always a two-sided coin, and naive simplicity paints people as either heroes or villains—in reality we are rarely one or the other and mostly a little of both. We must be grateful for the honor in our legacy and ready to admit and make right the injustice.

In such an atmosphere, white and native cultures can find much common ground. Indian and farmer are compatriots in the rare ability to listen to the land and to tell stories about their relationship to it. Our shaky, shifting civilization could use this message of earth connection. As native and white emphasize their commonality, they will be able to nurture an association that will help protect one of the last pristine areas of America.

The real danger to the farm community is not Indian autonomy anyway. It's economics. Today, it's the rancher's way of life many deem "vanishing." Yet if the family farm becomes extinct, will the earth benefit from the industry or agribusiness that follows? On the other hand, strong Indian government protects the environment from the disasters progress bring. A shared concern for the land should encourage these cul- to collaborate as they move toward a new century.

Recently graduated together from Hot Springs High School are cousins
Christy Lawson, Stacey Foster, and Joni Bras, ancestral granddaughters of
Hudson's Bay trapper Angus McDonald, Nez Perce maiden Catherine
McDonald, Chief Eneas of the Kootenai, Bitterroot Salish Lona Miles, and
Homesteader Roy Bras. Courtesy of Denison Photography.

As in all historical dialects, few races remain independent or "pure" anyway. They borrow, change, and merge, becoming what they must to survive. Many on the Flathead Reservation are already a beautiful combination of both.

The history of Camas Prairie is a microcosmic story of the West, a cross-stitch of conquest, suffering, and betrayal commingled with strength and survival—a cloth still on the loom with diverse threads weaving an evolving tapestry. The future of this rugged, breathtaking place is as strong, eclectic, and hopeful as the people who live there. It is their bond to the soil that gives residents such hope and courage in the midst of great sorrow. Both cultures have found healing and joy in the land.

This is the message that the West offers modern society. Many times, our scientific heritage explains us right out of anything as unsophisticated as healing in the soil or magic in story. We dismiss any power we cannot codify or control and boil our lives down to possession. Yet our pathos and obsessive need to acquire puzzle us. We bemoan our inextricable march-step toward the devastation of the planet. We force ourselves to think about purpose or stewardship—then hightail it to Nordstrom.

But our problem is deeper than a greater need for resolve. We must have a change of heart—a change in psyche. We must regain a reverence for the mystique of the land and reawaken our belief in its vitality and power to regenerate.

To change our course we don't need more facts or better programs; we need a change in emotional alliance. In prehistoric times humans were energized by cosmic ritual. In this archetypal period the Goddess was worshipped. Her body represented Mother Earth. During this era the magnificent temples at Crete were built and the Great Pyramids arose. The Greeks expressed themselves in the Parthenon. The Mayans and Aztecs erected altars. Humans believed such life force contained enormous power—it was the magic that drove everything—and they sought and embraced it. Their rites and symbols evoked it, sustained it, and channeled it to their communities. Renewal ceremonies held at summer and winter solstices and spring and fall equinoxes helped societies flow with the times of year and the movement of the earth. The basic pattern of existence moved in sync with a seasonally rejuvenated world.

Our biblical heritage was one of the first assaults on such union, not only with its concept of a fallen planet but also its vision of millennial fulfillment in a future age: the idea that ultimate meaning could not be experienced on the earth but only in heaven, or after the Second Coming of Christ. The Christian mentality that "We are in the world but not of it" has been around a long time.

By the seventeenth century, humans were looking for answers outside religion. During the Enlightenment, objective inquiry became the controlling human preoccupation. A scientific priesthood emerged and began weighing and measuring objective truth—which, they proclaimed, was all truth. If we followed universal rules, mystery could be eliminated. Newton's premise was "I make no hypotheses" ("Hypotheses non fingo"), in other words, "My laws are based upon exact experimental evidence—nothing but cold, hard facts." Descartes reinforced this thinking with his image of a mechanistic cosmos. From Descartes and the Enlightenment on, humans saw the universe as a Great Machine. Our job was merely to calculate how it worked. We know that in 1905 Albert Einstein challenged this steady-state model of the universe with his theory of quantum physics. Contrary to Newtonian physics, quantum mechanics tells us that Newton's theories don't work on the subatomic level. We can't predict such phenomena with any certainty—only probabilities. Energy appears as particle one time, the next time as wave.

However, the mentality of the Great Machine remained. The Instrument Universe entrenched itself in the human subconscious. It became our modern myth. This "objective" view infiltrates all of twentieth-century natural science. Our textbooks have adopted it and taught our schoolchildren to see the world through Cosmic Machine glasses.

The school system tends to present this sterile earth as the only viable option. In such a sanitized world, the excitement of existence can't help but be diminished. In *Creative Energy*, eco-theologian Thomas Berry declares, "If a fascination, an entrancement, with life is not evoked, children will not have the psychic energies needed to sustain the sorrows inherent in the human condition"[1]—or, I believe, the inner vision to be caretakers of the planet.

Whereas in Indian culture, children are introduced into the mystique of life through ritual and vision quests, our children no longer feel this magic energy. In *The Mystic Warriors of the Plains*, Thomas Mails describes how ritual transferred this meaning onto Indian youth:

> *From childhood on, the Indian was constantly exposed to the sacred rituals which dramatized and explained his heritage; even more he participated in them and thus was able to feel his place as well as to understand it intellectually. Together with the ancient legends told by the storytellers the ceremonies served to perpetuate the traditional values of the culture of each Plains tribe. Thus in a culture without written literature, the ceremonies became living dramas, which kept the good things of old alive by renewing their memory in an annual cycle of ceremonial rites. In their most profound forms they served to gather the people into an interdependent community. To put it as simply as possible they told the Indian who he was, and what he had to to preserve the culture for future generations.[2]*

Today our children are rarely taught such meaning and identification. Instead, the earth's grandeur is boiled down to a formula. Most of the time, neither school nor community transfers such enchantment onto them.

Both the mechanistic world view and fallen-earth story fail to provide the needed archetype to create future citizens concerned about a healthy planet. Such domination mentalities, practiced by both the scientific elite and religious fundamentalists, will continue to leave us unmotivated. In these anthropomorphic systems, humans are not merely components of the larger whole but stand above it as directors and rulers. We can no longer afford to see ourselves in this position. We must submit and revere all of creation.

As long as humans are left as the focal point of the universe, we will cleave to a fertile vision of consumerism. This "gobble-up" mentality will remain our abiding incantation. Because our world view is rooted in it, society will continue to follow its motivation.

Recently, in a suburban shopping center near Seattle, I parked behind a young man in a beautiful BMW. He opened his car door and dumped an ashtray of cigarette butts and garbage onto the ground. When I suggested that someday his children might wish he'd had more respect for the planet, he looked at me in disgust. As I thought about the scenario later, I felt sorry for him. He appeared to have everything our society tells a young man he could possibly want. I'd guess his lack of reverence for the earth wasn't from inadequate education either. I'm sure he had heard about our polluted biosphere, the devastation of the rain forest, and the compromised ozone layer. It seems, however, these facts hadn't made much of a dent. His affection was tied to a different loyalty. I can't help thinking that there might be a correlation between a twenty-year-old driving a BMW and his lack of reverence for the earth.

Has our consumer mentality served us well? Are we, or the children we have raised on it, happier, more satisfied, wiser citizens? Is our world better off?

We must start making choices based on long-term effect. Native Americans have a criterion for decision making. They ask themselves what their choices will mean to people living seven generations from today. With this kind of foresight, stewardship and preservation take precedent. But how do we regain such sensitivity to the earth?

To revive this relationship, our children must be reacquainted with stories that have meaning—stories of earth, balance, and reconciliation. Introducing them to books like Joseph Bruchac's *Keepers of the Earth: Native American Stories and Environmental Activities for Children* is a good start. This kind of touchable, story-rich education will change their lives. It will burrow into their hearts and nest. They will start to view the world, and how they fit into it, differently. The void will overflow with meaning and not possessions. As Daniel Taylor declares about story, "I am convinced that stories go somewhere to roost, somewhere deep inside our spirits. They settle there, beyond consciousness, to grow, blend with other stories and experiences, and work their influence from below."[3]

We must retell these earth stories and learn to understand the land. To help people in this process, places like the Center for the Rocky Mountain West in Missoula, Montana, have sprung up. Such organizations encourage residents to appreciate the history of their home ground and give them connection to others who live there. In their mission statement pamphlet, the center "seeks to sharpen Westerners' understanding of the region and guide their visions for its future. . . . to celebrate and study the region, and create a forum for reflective, imaginative, and inclusive dialogue among those who are committed to this place."

Last fall I attended a conference sponsored by the center. People packed into the sessions and tackled issues of the environment, history, and future of the area. Indians, ranchers, academics, politicians, and citizens filled the room. In one particularly vigorous debate, a leading environmentalist and a rancher came head to head. The discussion was spirited but remarkably healthy. In the end, much common ground was established. If we are to create such coalition, we must seek this kind of dialogue. Open exchange is the first step.

If we don't have soil of our own to bind ourselves to, we can adopt some. In *The Absence of the Sacred,* Jerry Mander suggests we become bioregionalists. He recommends we try "finding a place the planet, on our street, in our city, in our region, and deciding the place is one we will protect. Learn its natural history and its cultural history. Visit the place regularly. Watch it carefully. If it's threatened, do something."[4] In doing something we will gain this hands-on land knowledge.

There is much hope. A new Earth tradition is emerging amongst us. We can see it gaining momentum in popular culture and even academic circles. New narratives are being told about the importance of alliance with the planet. In the end, love of the land will be learned in the same way western cultures have done it—through experience and storytelling.

I believe both will revive our understanding of creation, like it has been done for those on the Montana prairie. Such keen perception has helped both Indian and white cultures to stay alive, unified, and strong, and—even more importantly—to live in harmony with the earth. We need to seek this awareness and teach our children to do the same.

We can hear once more what we need to learn
in the voice of the mist
in the echo of rain.
In the quiet You will speak again
and tell us what we used to know
in utterances from within the soil
and through the sound amongst the grass
when the wind holds council with the land.

We can hear once more what we need to learn
when our stillness makes
Your whisper clear
like those who have from timeless year.
They've learned to recognize Your song
in the breeze of sage that speaks at night
and murmurs secrets of the earth
teaching them to listen well.

Notes

Chapter 1

1. Wallace Stegner, *Where the Bluebird Sings to the Lemonade Springs: Living and Writing in the West* (New York: Penguin Books, 1992), p. 48.

2. Today more than forty Salish-speaking peoples occupy land throughout the Northwest, some as far west as the Olympic Peninsula. Each has developed their own culture, yet all are tied linguistically. It is debated whether eastern tribes gave the Flathead their name by referring to them in sign language reflecting the flattening of a head or if whites mistakenly attributed the practice to them. The tribe denies ever securing its babies to a cradle and putting pressure on their frontal bones and prefer to be called the Bitterroot Salish. Whenever possible I will do so.

3. Anthropologist Harry Turney-High argued that the Montana Salish migrated from Oregon via the Snake and Clearwater Rivers. However, most anthropologists agree that the tribe was forced south from Canada. The footnoted map has been compiled from the following works: James Teit and Franz Boaz, eds., *The Salishan Tribes of the Western Plateaus: 45th Annual Report of the Bureau of American Ethnology* (Washington, D.C.: Government Printing Office, 1930), pp. 25–395; Carling Malouf, *Economy a Land Use by the Indians of Western Montana* (New York: Garland Publish 1974); Carling Malouf, *A Study of the Prehistoric Sites Along the Clar River Valley* (Missoula: University of Montana Press, May 1982); F Ewers, *Gustavus Sohon's Portraits of Flathead and Pend d'Oreille Ind*

(Washington, D.C.: Smithsonian Institute, 1948); Stuart Chalfant, *Aboriginal Territory of the Kalispel Indians* (New York: Garland Publishing, 1974); E. O. Fuller, *The Confederated Salish and Kutenai Tribes of the Flathead Reservation* (New York: Garland Publishing, 1974); John Fahey, *The Kalispel Indians* (Norman: University of Oklahoma Press, 1986); John Fahey, *The Flathead Indians* (Norman: University of Oklahoma Press, 1974); Paul Phillips, *History of the Confederated Salish and Kootenai Tribes of the Flathead Reservation* (New York: Garland Publishing, 1974).

4. Malouf, *Economy and Land Use by the Indians of Western Montana*, p. 55.

5. Nathaniel Wyeth, *Correspondence and Journals of Captain Nathaniel Wyeth 1831–1836* (New York: Arne Press, 1973), p. 25. According to Hiram Chittenden, *American Fur Trade of the Far West* (New York: Press of the Pioneers, 1935), p. 821, trappers considered eighty beaver pelts to constitute a pack.

6. As cited in Michael S. Sample, publisher, *Montana: The Last Best Place* (Helena, Mont.: Falcon Press, 1989), p. 34.

7. Vine Deloria, Jr., *God Is Red* (Golden, Colo.: Fulcrum Publishing, 1994), p. 67.

8. Linda Hasselstrom, *Land Circle: Writings Collected from the Land* (Golden, Colo.: Fulcrum Publishing, 1991), p. 1.

9. Gretel Ehrlich, *The Solace of Open Spaces* (New York: Viking, 1985), p. 103.

10. William Kittredge, *Who Owns the West?* (San Francisco: Mercury House, 1996), p. 108.

Chapter 2

1. David Alt, *Roadside Geology of Montana* (Missoula: Mountain Press Publishing Co., 1986), p. 35.

2. James Teit and Franz Boaz, eds. *The Salishan Tribes of the Western Plateaus: 45th Annual Report of the Bureau of American Ethnology* (Washington, D.C.: Government Printing Office, 1930), pp. 307–313. Stories of pre-Salish inhabitants or "Foolish Folk" can also be found in Harry Turney-High, *The Flathead Indians of Montana* (Menasha, Wisc.: American Anthropological Association, 1937), summer 48, pp. 15–17.

3. Turney-High, *The Flathead Indians of Montana*, p. 20.

4. Fine works about the edible plants of the Salish include Jeff Hart, *Native Plants and Early Peoples* (Helena: Montana Historical Society Press, 1992); V. E. Booth and J. C. Wright, *Flora of Montana* (Bozeman: Montana te Press, 1959); Ella Clark, *Indian Legends from the Northern Rockies* man: University of Oklahoma Press, 1966); H. D. Harrington, *Edible*

Native Plants of the Rocky Mountains (Albuquerque: University of New Mexico Press, 1967); P. J. Powell, *Sweet Medicine* (Norman: University of Oklahoma Press, 1969); P. C. Phillips, *Medicine in the Making of Montana* (Missoula: Montana State University Press, 1962); and T. White, "Scarred Trees in Western Montana," Montana State University *Anthropological and Sociological Papers* (1954), p. 17.

5. Hart, *Native Plants and Early Peoples*, p. 40.

6. Meriwether Lewis, *Original Journals of Lewis and Clark*, Bernard De Voto, ed. (Boston: Houghton Mifflin, 1953), p. 123.

7,8. Ross Cox, *The Columbia River*, Edgar Stewart and Jane Stewart, eds. (Norman: University of Oklahoma Press, 1957), p. 135.

9. The Coyote and Rattlesnake Tale has been adapted from Joe Hayes, *Coyote & . . . : Native American Folk Tales* (Santa Fe: N. Mex.: Mariposa Publishing, 1983), pp. 57–60.

10. The Kootenai resided from Flathead Lake to Canada. Although they were allies of the Salish and included in the 1855 Confederated Tribes of the Flathead Reservation, they were a completely separate tribe with their own distinct language and culture.

11. Warren Ferris, *Life in the Rocky Mountains: 1830–1835* (Salt Lake City: Rocky Mountain Bookshop, 1940), p. 90.

12. Malouf, *Economy and Land Use by the Indians of Western Montana* (New York: Garland Publishing, 1974), p. 39.

13. U.S. Serial 791 (1855), 33 Congress, 2 Sess., Ex Doc. 91, p. 437.

Chapter 3

1. J. B. Tyrell, *David Thompson and the Columbia River* (Toronto: University of Toronto Press, 1937), pp. 12–14; W. M. Stewart, "David Thompson's Surveys in the Northwest," *Canadian Historical Review*, vol. 17 (1936), pp. 289–303; T. C. Elliot, "The Fur Trade in the Columbia River Basin Prior to 1811," *Oregon Historical Quarterly*, vol. 15, no. 4 (December 1914), pp. 241–251.

David Thompson's travels can be traced in *David Thompson's Journals Relating to Montana and Adjacent Regions, 1808–1812*, Catherine White, ed. (Missoula: Montana State University Press, 1950). See also Jack Nisbet, *Sources of the River* (Seattle, Wash.: Sasquatch Books, 1995).

2. David Thompson, *David Thompson's Journals Relating to Montana and Adjacent Regions, 1808–1812*, Catherine White ed. (Missoula: Montana State Unviersity Press, 1950). pp. lxxxi

3. Thompson, *David Thompson's Journals Relating to Montana and Adjacent Regions, 1808–1812,* p. lxxxii.

4. John Work, *The Journals of John Work, A Chief Trader of Hudson's Bay Company,* William Lewis and Paul Phillips, eds. (Cleveland, Ohio: Arthur Clark Co., 1923), pp. 146–147. Other firsthand accounts of men who trapped on Camas Prairie are found in David Thompson, *David Thompson's Narrative of His Explorations in Western North America, 1808–1812* (Toronto: The Champlain Society, 1962); Francis Ermatinger, *Fur Trade Letters of Francis Ermatinger, 1818–1853* (Glendale, Calif.: A. H. Clark Co., 1980); Alexander Ross, *The Fur Hunters of the Far West,* Kenneth A. Spaulding, ed. (Norman: University of Oklahoma Press, 1956); Alexander Ross, "Journal of Alexander Ross—Snake Country Expedition, 1824," T. C. Elliot, ed., *Oregon Historical Quarterly,* vol. 14, no. 4 (December 1913), pp. 366–388; Peter Skene Ogden, *Ogden's Snake Country Journal, 1824–1826,* E. E. Rich, ed. (London: Hudson's Bay Record Society, 1950); Peter Skene Ogden, *Traits of American Indian Life and Character* (New York: AMS Press, Inc., 1853); Warren Ferris, *Life in the Rocky Mountains,* Paul C. Phillips, ed. (Denver, Colo.: Old West Publishing Co., 1940); Nathaniel Wyeth, *The Correspondence and Journals of Captain Nathaniel J. Wyeth, 1831–1839,* F. G. Young, ed. (Eugene: Sources of the History of Oregon, 1923); Angus McDonald, "A Few Items of the West," F. W. Howay, W. S. Williams, and J. A. Myers, eds., *Washington Historical Quarterly,* vol. 8 (1917), pp. 188–229.

5. Thompson, *David Thompson's Narrative of His Explorations in Western North America, 1808–1812,* p. 297.

6. For a discussion about the location of Salish House, see "Journal of John Work, September 7–December 14, 1825," *Washington Historical Quarterly,* vol. 5 (July 1914), pp. 182–183; Catherine White, "Saleesh House: The First Trading Post Among the Flathead," *Pacific Northwest Quarterly,* vol. 33 (April 1942), pp. 251–263; and Allan H. Smith, "The Location of Flathead Post," *Pacific Northwest Quarterly,* vol. 4 no. 3 (April 1957), pp. 47–53.

7. For information about construction of a "glacier," see George Simpson, *Journal of Occurrences in the Athabasca Department: 1820 and 1821,* E. E. Rich, ed. (Toronto: Publications of the Hudson's Bay Record Society, 1938), pp. 316–317.

8. Thompson, *David Thompson's Narrative of His Explorations in Western North America, 1808–1812,* p. 303.

9. Ross Cox, *The Columbia River*, Edgar Stewart and Jane Stewart, eds. (Norman: University of Oklahoma Press, 1957), p. 187.

10. Thompson, *David Thompson's Narrative of His Explorations in Western North America, 1808–1812*, p. 306.

11. Thompson, *David Thompson's Narrative of His Explorations in Western North America, 1808–1812*, p. 304.

12. In history books written before 1920 about Montana, no mention of Thompson is made. For instance, in Judge Frank H. Woody's *A Sketch of the Early History of Western Montana* (Helena: Montana Historical Society, 1896), vol. 2, pp. 88–106, Woody states, "From the time of Lewis and Clark's expedition up to about the year 1835 or '36, we have no definite knowledge of what transpired in this portion of our present Territory. At a very early date a number of Canadian voyageurs, and Iroquois Indians from Canada, visited the country, and sometime between 1820 and 1835, the employees of the Hudson's Bay Company visited it for the purpose of trading with the Indians and extending the power of dominion of that gigantic company, but these early adventurers left us no available data from which to write their travels and adventures." This information is included in Michael Leeson, ed., *History of Montana* (Chicago: Warner, Beers and Co., 1885), pp. 838–859. Flathead Indian agent Peter Ronan never mentions the explorer in *Historical Sketches of the Flathead Indian Nation from the Year 1813 to 1890* (Helena: Montana Journal, 1890). As well, Montana journalist Dean Stone was unaware of Salish House and David Thompson when, in his "Montana's First Christmas," *Sunday Missoulian*, December 23, 1911, and *Following Old Trails* (Missoula: Montana Press, 1913), he mistakenly attributed the first building erected in Montana by whites as one constructed in the spring of 1813 by Factor McMillian.

    The work of David Thompson was finally revealed to the state at the annual meeting of the Montana Pioneer Society, held in Missoula in 1914. Mr. T. C. Elliott gave an address titled "David Thompson—Montana Pioneer." According to some, it was the first time the work of David Thompson was brought to the attention of the people of western Montana. See also Catherine White, "Introduction," *David Thompson's Journals Relating to Montana and Adjacent Regions*, pp. clvi, cxxx.

13. "Jefferson's Instructions to Lewis, 20 June, 1803," in R. G. Thwaites, ed., *Original Journals of the Lewis and Clark Expedition, 1804–1806*, vol. 7 (New York: Dodd, Mead, and Co., 1905), pp. 247–252.

14. Thwaites, *Original Journals of the Lewis and Clark Expedition, 1804–1806*, vol. 7, p. 335.

15. Thwaites, *Original Journals of the Lewis and Clark Expedition, 1804–1806,* vol. 3, p. 54.

16. The story was told to O. D. Wheeler by Chief Victor's widow, who was present at the meeting. O. D. Wheeler, *The Trail of Lewis and Clark,* vol. 2 (New York: G. P. Putnam's Sons, 1904), pp. 65–68.

17. Bernard De Voto, *Across the Wide Missouri* (Boston: Houghton Mifflin Co., 1947), p. 5.

18. Ross Cox, *Adventures on the Columbia River* (New York: Harper, 1832), p. 118.

19. Ibid., pp. 122-124.

20. Samuel Parker, *Journal of an Exploring Tour Beyond the Rocky Mountains* (Ithaca, N.Y.: Andrus, Woodruff and Gaumtlett, 1844), p. 293.

21. Osborne Russell, *Journal of a Trapper* (Lincoln: University of Nebraska Press, 1955), p. 55.

22. Francis Victor, *The River of the West* (Hartford, Conn.: W. Bliss Co., 1870), p. 48.

23. Bridger established the thriving fort in 1843 on the Oregon Trail. In 1854, during his absence, Mormons raided the fort and burned it to the ground. They claimed the destruction was in retaliation for Bridger's selling arms and ammunition to the Indians. The fire destroyed the trapper financially, burning up livestock, merchandise, furs, buckskins, and buffalo robes worth more than $250,000.

24. David Douglas, *Journal Kept by David Douglas During His Travels in North America* (London: Wesley and Sons, 1827), pp. 270–271; and Edward Ermatinger, *Edward Ermatinger's Journal* (Ontario: Royal Society of Canada), vol. 6, sec. 2, pp. 87–89.

25. Letter from Archy McDonald to Francis Ermatinger in 1844. Francis Ermatinger was Edward Ermatinger's brother.

26. This and other quotations from the account of Ross's Snake Country Expedition can be found in Ross, *Fur Hunters of the Far West,* pp. 206–293.

27. Jim Clyman's journal, as cited in Peter Burns, "The Short and Incredible Life of Jedediah Smith," *Montana: The Magazine of Western History,* Winter 1967, p. 47.

28. Governor Simpson to Dr. J. McLoughlin, July 10, 1826, in *Fur Trade and Empire: George Simpson's Journal, 1824–25* (Cambridge: Harvard University Press, 1931), p. 52.

29. Ross, "Journal of Alexander Ross," p. 35

30. Ogden, *Snake Country Journal,* p. 273; Ross, "Journal of Alexander Ross," pp. 386–388. The expedition that followed was also recorded by Ogden's assistant, William Kittson, *Snake Country Journal,* pp. 209–213.

31. The following account can be found in Ogden, *Traits of American Indian Life,* pp. 31–44.

32. Nathaniel Wyeth, *Correspondence and Journals of Captain Nathaniel Wyeth 1831–1836* (New York: Arne Press, 1973), p. 190.

33. Warren Ferris, *Life in the Rocky Mountains: 1830–1835* (Salt Lake City: Rocky Mountain Bookshop, 1940), p. 199.

34. Gene Caesar, *King of the Mountain Men* (New York: Dutton, 1961), p. 143ff.

35. James Beckwourth, *The Life and Adventures of James P. Beckwourth,* T. D. Bonner, ed. (New York: Harper, 1856), p. 70.

36. Russell, *Journal of a Trapper,* p. 58.

37. Victor, *River of the West,* pp. 51, 111.

38. As cited in John Killoren, S.J., "Come Blackrobe," DeSmet and the Indian Tragedy (Norman: University of Oklahoma Press, 1994) p. 46.

39. Edward Huggins, "MacDonald's Arrival with the Interior Brigade with the Fur Returns of 1854, Arriving by Way of Nachess Pass," manuscript in the Clarence B. Bagley Collection (Seattle: University of Washington Special Collections Library, 1855). Huggins was clerk and bookkeeper at Fort Nisqually from 1850 to 1855 and in 1857 became factor.

40. Francis Prucha, *American Indian Policy in the Formative Years, 1790–1834* (Lincoln: University of Nebraska Press, 1970), p. 291.

41. McDonald, "A Few Items of the West," p. 192.

42. Trappers mentioned who married Native American women and raised children from these unions are David Thompson, Finan McDonald, Alexander Ross, Peter Skene Ogden, Jim Bridger, Joe Meek, John Work, Francis Ermatinger, Osborne Russell, James Beckwourth, and Angus McDonald.

Chapter 4

1. Gregory Mengarini, "Memoria delle Missioni delle Teste Plate, 1848," in Gilbert J. Garraghan, *The Jesuits of the Middle United States,* vol. 2 (New York: American Press, 1938), pp. 238–239.

2. In 1937 anthropologist Harry Turney-High interviewed a Salish Indian who was more than one hundred years old. The Indian told Turney-High that Shining Shirt lived before his great-grandfather's birth. He also told Turney-High about this prophecy. Harry Turney-High, *The Flathead*

Indians of Montana (Menasha, Wisc.: American Anthropological Association, 1937), pp. 41–42.

3. This quote and others from De Smet can be found in Hiram M. Chittenden and A. T. Richardson, *Life, Letters and Travels of Father Pierre-Jean de Smet, S.J., 1801–1873* (New York: Harper, 1905), vol. 1, pp. 327–350; vol. 2, pp. 593ff.; and vol. 3, p. 952.

4. Bernard De Voto, *Across the Wide Missouri* (Boston: Houghton Mifflin Co., 1947), p. 373.

5. Gregory Mengarini, "The Rocky Mountains: Memoirs of Father Gregory Mengarini," Oregon Province Archives, Gonzaga University, p. 59.

6. Fahey, *The Flathead Indians*, p. 79.

7. Father Nicholas Point, "Religion and Superstition," in *American West*, vol. 4, no. 4 (November 1967), p. xx. Quotes from Father Point can also be found in Father Nicholas Point, *Wilderness Kingdom, Indian Life in the Rocky Mountains: 1840–1847; The Journals and Paintings of Nicholas Point*, translated and introduced by Joseph P. Donnelly (New York: Holt, Rinehart and Winston, 1967), pp. 130–135.

8. In 1836 Marcus and Narcissa Whitman established their Protestant mission among the Cayuse in Washington. The settlement soon became a way station for travelers along the Oregon Trail. When settlers exposed the Cayuse to diseases they had no immunity to, scores of them died. After a smallpox epidemic in 1847, several warriors who blamed the deaths on the missionaries attacked the mission, killing Marcus, Narcissa, and eleven other whites.

9. Mengarini, "Memoria delle Missioni delle Teste Plate, 1848," in Gilbert J. Garraghan, *The Jesuits of the Middle United States*, vol. 2, p. 268ff.

10. Fahey, *The Flathead Indians*, p. 88.

11. The Stevens survey report is printed in *U.S. Senate, 33rd Congress, 2nd Session*, Sen. Exec. Doc 78.

12. The following portraits and narrative can be found in John Ewers, *Gustavus Sohon's Portraits of Flathead and Pend d'Oreille Indians 1954* (Washington, D.C.: Smithsonian Institute, 1948).

13. Governor Stevens to the commissioner of Indian affairs, December 29, 1853 (Washington Superintendency, 1853–1874 NA).

14. Article 5 of the Hellgate Treaty. The treaty and its effect on the Salish and Kootenai people can be found in: Robert Bigart and Clarence Woodcock, *In the Name of the Salish and Kootenai Nation: The 1855 Treaty and the Origin of the Flathead Indian Reservation* (Pablo, Mont.: Salish, Kootenai Press, 1996), pp. 9–66.

15. Fahey, *The Flathead Indians,* p. 143.
16. As cited in Richard White, *It's Your Misfortune and None of My Own* (Norman: University of Oklahoma Press, 1992), p. 101.
17. Calvin H. Hale, "Report of the Adjutant-General of Oregon, 1865–1866," p. 18.
18. Joseph, "An Indians View of Indian Affairs," *North American Review,* April 1879, p. 419.
19. James A. Garfield, *Garfield's Diary of a Trip to Montana in 1872,* Oliver Holmes, ed. (Missoula: University of Montana Press, 1934), August 26, 1872.
20. *The Weekly Missoulian,* April 26, 1876.
21. Peter Ronan to Governor Potts, July 10, 1877 (Microcopy 234, Roll 507, National Archives).
22. Several months after the incident, Duncan McDonald interviewed the Nez Perce who had escaped into Canada. His interviews can be found in Linwood Laughy, comp., *In Pursuit of the Nez Perces: The Nez Perce War of 1877, as Reported by Gen. O. O. Howard, Duncan MacDonald, Chief Joseph* (Missoula: Mountain Meadow Press, 1993). (Note: The family name was originally spelled MacDonald when they arrived from Scotland. However, the "a" was later dropped during the nineteenth century in the United States.)
23. The text of the surrender speech is given here as recorded by James Mooney in "The Ghost Dance Religion and the Sioux Outbreak of 1890," Fourteenth Annual Report of the U.S. Bureau of Ethnology, part II, 1892–1893 (Washington, D.C.: Government Printing Office, 1896), pp. 1104–1110.
24. General William Tecumseh Sherman, "Report to the Secretary of War, 1876–77," p. 15.
25. Father D'Aste to Father Dewey, December 29, 1884. As cited in John Fahey, *The Flathead Indians* (Norman: University of Oklahoma Press, 1974), p. 236.

Chapter 5

1. Fahey, *The Flathead Indians,* p. 229.
2. Mary Ronan, *Frontier Woman: The Story of Mary Ronan as Told to Margaret Ronan,* H. G. Merriman, ed. (Missoula: University of Montana Press, 1973), p. 52.
3. Stories of Weeksville can be found in Maurice Helterline, *Horse Plains* (Plains: The Printery, 1986) and *The Missoulian* articles of March 17, 1882; January 26, 1883; January 19, 1883; January 5, 1883; December 15,

1882; February 18, 1883; June 6, 1884; March 8, 1906; and May 30, 1982, as well as in the *New Northwest Deer Lodge,* February 23, 1883, the *Anaconda Standard,* March 8, 1906, and the *Sanders County Signal,* March 15, 1906.

4. Report to the Commission of Indian Affairs, 1883. As cited in John Fahey, *The Flathead Indians* (Norman: University of Oklahoma Press, 1974), p. 231.

5. White, *It's Your Misfortune and None of My Own,* p. 115.

6. H. L. Dawes, "Have We Failed with the Indian?" *Atlantic Monthly,* vol. 84 (1899), p. 281.

7. Moss's report, August 6, 1896 (33647-96, NA). As cited in Fahey, *Flathead Indians,* p. 275.

8. William Smead to District Attorney Rasch, June 16, 1903 (Federal Records Center, Seattle, Washington).

9. Theodore Roosevelt, *The Works of Theodore Roosevelt,* vol. 17 (New York: Scribner's Sons, 1922–1926), pp. 150–151.

10. Fahey, *The Flathead Indians,* p. 244.

Chapter 6

1,2. *The Missoulian,* December 12, 1995.

3. Paul Kane, *Wanderings of an Artist Among the Indians of North America (1859)* (Rutland, Vt.: Charles S. Tuttle, 1968), p. 125. Cited in Patricia Nelson Limerick, *The Legacy of Conquest* (New York: Norton and Co., 1987), p. 188.

4. Brian Dippie, ed. *Charles M. Russell: Word Painter* (New York: Harry N. Abrams, 1993), p. 310.

5. Cited from the web page of the Environmental Working Group, "City Slickers."

6. Karthryn Barry-Stelljes, "Rangeland Can Improve with Grazing," *The Ag Almanac,* vol. 19, no. 11, November 1995, p. 1.

7. Eric Johnson, "Down and Out on the Farm," *Missoula Independent,* August 10, 1995, p. 9.

8. George D. Levin, *I.S.A. Newsletter,* South Dakota Division, p. 2.

9. Charles Johnson, "The Pains and Gains of NAFTA," *Farm Journal,* May/June 1996, p. 3.

10. Harlan Hughes, "Ranchers and Packers Caught in Cost-Price Squeeze," *Livestock Reporter,* June 1996, p. 4.

11. Jon Christiansen, "Bruce Babbitt on Western Land Use," *High Country News,* May 1993, p. 4.

12. Dan Dagget, *Beyond the Rangeland Conflict: Toward the West That Works* (Layton, Utah: Gibbs Smith, 1995), p. 7.
13. Ivan Doig, *This House of Sky* (New York: Hartcourt Brace Jovanovich, 1978), p. 174.

Chapter 7

1. Chris Roberts, *Powwow Country* (Missoula, Mont.: Meadowlark Publishing, 1992), p. 74.
2. Daniel Taylor, *The Healing Power of Stories* (New York: Doubleday, 1996), p. 122.
3. Joseph Bruchac, *Roots of Survival: Native American Storytelling and the Sacred* (Golden, Colo.: Fulcrum Publishing), p. 72.
4. Leslie Marmon Silko, *Ceremony* (New York: Viking, 1977), p. 2.
5. Joseph Bruchac, *The Native American Sweat Lodge: History & Legends* (Freedom, Calif.: The Crossing Press, 1993), p. 39.
6. Jacob Riis, *How the Other Half Lives: Studies Among the Tenements of New York* (New York: Charles Scribners Sons, 1890), p. 11.
7. White, *It's Your Misfortune and None of My Own*, p. 228.
8. Linda Hasselstrom, *Land Circle: Writings Collected from the Land* (Golden, Colo.: Fulcrum Publishing, 1991), pp. 238–239.

Chapter 8

1. Thomas Berry, *Creative Energy: Bearing Witness for the Earth* (San Francisco: Sierra Club Books, 1988), pp. 32–33.
2. Thomas Mails, *The Mystic Warrriors of the Plains* (Tulsa, Okla.: Council Oak Books, 1972), p. 173.
3. Taylor, *The Healing Power of Stories*, p. 11.
4. Jerry Mander, *The Absence of the Sacred* (San Francisco: Sierra Club Books, 1991), p. 394.

Index

(Note: page numbers in italics indicate photographs or illustrations.)

Abenaki, 169
Adams, Sophie, 47
Adolph, 111
Agribusiness, 31, 154–155, 158–159
Aguirre, Ivan, 161
Alexander, Chief, 101–102, *101*, 104–106, 108
Alfalfa, 2
Allard, Charles, 172–177
Allard, Charles Jr., 175
Allard, Louis, 172
Ambrose, 12, 105
American Fur Trading Company, 79, 89
Anthony, Saint, 94
Arapaho, 136
Argo, Arthur, 166–168
Argo, Cecil, 166–167
Argo, Johnny, 167
Argos, xii, 1, 153, 166–168
Aristotle, 94
Arlee, Chief, 16, 111
Arlee (town), 16, 123–124
Arlee, Johnny, 27–28
Ashley, William, 66, 67, 68
Astor, John Jacob, 63, 78
Astoria, 63, 64
Athabasca Pass, 61
Athabascans, 12, 36

Babbitt, Bruce, 158, 159
Badgers, 22
Bald eagles, 17
Bannock tribe, 49
The Barber, 122, 123
Barn owls, 17
Bauer, R. C., 126
Bear Track, 100–101, *101*, 104–106
Bears, 14, 182. *See also* Grizzly bears
Beavers, 17, 45, 63, 70, 72, 74
Beckwourth, James, 81
Beker, Henry, 167
Berries, 39–40, 40–41

Berry, Thomas, 205
Big Canoe, 102, *102*, 104, 106
Big Crane, 1
Big Face, 49
Big Hole Basin, 113–114
Big Hole River, 69
Bighorn sheep, 142, 143
Billy the Kid, 122, 123
Birds, 25, 182
Bitterroot, 25–29, *26*, 40, 159
Bitterroot Festival, 26–28, *28*
Bitterroot Valley, 49, 89, 100, 105, 111, 113, 127, 159
Black Hills, 109
Black tree lichen, 39, *39*
Blackfeet, 12, 16, 37, 46, 49, 67, 78, 91, 92, 96, 98, 101, 104, 105, 106, 117, 135
    wars with Salish tribes, 49, 50, 59, 60–61, 65, 69–70, 75–77, 78–80, 89
Blackfoot Challenge, 162
Blanchet, Father, 92
Blue Jay Dance and Ceremony, 45–46
Blue jays, 45
Bodmer, Karl, 82
Bonner, John, 189
Bonner, P. J., 189
Bonner Springs, 24
Border dikes, 150–151, 152
Branding, 29–31
Bras, Joni, *203*
Bras, Roy, 148, *148*, 203
Bridger, Jim, 66–67, 68, *77*, 79–81
Brown, Tony, 165
Bruchac, Joseph, 169, 183, 207
Buffalo, 21–22, 45, 46, 49, 50, 63, 70, 85, 117, 173–177, *174*, *175*, *176*, 183
    horn cup, *51*
    hunts, 50–52, 60, 92, 100–101
    Salish products, 52–53
Buffaloberry, 39–40

Bureau of Indian Affairs, 125, 138
Burgess, Lou, 190
Burke, Chas H., 134–135
Butler, William, 9

Cabinet Mountains, 19, 121, 143
Camas, 11–12, *11*, 39, 40, 59
Camas Creek, 139, 140
Camas Prairie, ix, x, xii, xiii, 1, 5, 10, 12, *13*, 15, 16–17, 19, 33–35, 60, 61, 68, 71, 78, 79, 85–86, 90–91, *98*, 118, 139, 150, 178, 189, 199, 203
    animals, 17–18
Camas Prairie Gym, *190*, 194
Camas Prairie Indians, 126–127, 130
Camas Prairie School, *189*, 194
Campbell, Curley, 123
Canadian Northwest Trade Company, 55–57, 61–62, 64, 68, 74
Canyon Creek, 115
Cargill, 155
Carrington, Henry, 127
Carter, Jim, 187
Casteel Blacksmith Shop, *188*
Catholic Church, 87–97, 125–127
Catholic Indian Bureau, 125
Catlin, George, 82
Cattle, 17–18, 25
    branding, 29–31
    calving, 22–23
    drives, 153–154
    and effect of NAFTA and GATT, 31
Cayuse Indians, 96, 103
Center for the Rocky Mountain West, 207
Charles II, King, 55
Charleton, Wavie, 187
Charlot, Chief, 111–112, *113*, 127, 130

Cheeneys, 153
Cherokee, 102
Chinese, 121, 122
Chinook tribe, 145
Christianity, 204. *See also*
    Catholic Church
Claessens, Brother, 89
Clark, W. A., 117
Clark, William, 88, 145. *See also*
    Lewis and Clark
Clark Fork River, 12, *13*, 21–
    22, 34, 36, 37, 38, 57, 59, 68,
    91–92, 118, 123, 198–199
Clark Fork Trail, 117
Clyman, Jim, 73
Cody, Buffalo Bill, 146, 201
Coeur d'Alene tribe, 106
Coleman, Jim, 156
Collier, John, 138
Collingsworth, Chub, 190–
    191, *191*
Columbia River, 57, 62, 78
Colville Reservation, 116
Colville tribe, 106
ConAgra, 155
Confederated Salish and
    Kootenai Tribes
    game preserves, 142–143
    land claim, 138
    and Yellowstone Pipeline,
    139–142
Conoco, 139, 140
Conservation easements, 156
Consumer mentality, 206
Corican Canyon, 95
Cottonwood, 40
Cottonwood Road, 187
Country store, 193
County fair, 18
Coutere, Lizzy, 193
Cox, Ross, 42, 60–61, 64
Coyotes, 14, 17, 21–22, 23, 44–
    45, 95
Crazy Horse, 109
Cree, 47
Croghan, Phil, *190*
Crop rotation, 150
Cross family
    Anna Malleck Svoboda
    Lauerman (great-grand-
    mother), 5, 150, 184–186,
    190, *191*, 192–193
    Ben (brother), 152, 200
    family farm, 150–151, *151*,
    162–163
    Gordon Cross (uncle), 6,

190–191, *190*
    Herb Cross (uncle), 186,
    189–190
    John Lauerman (great-
    grandfather), 150, 185–186,
    190, *191*, 192
    Marie Cross (grandmother),
    10, 183, 192–193
    Melanie (sister), 152, 153,
    200–201
    Mother, 3, 150, 152, 187
    Richard Cross (grandfa-
    ther), 186, 192
    Sid Cross (father), 3, 6–7, 8,
    10, 150, 152, 189–190, 190–
    191, *190*, 192, 197–199, 200
Crow tribe, 47, 49, 73, 101, 106,
    115, 135, 136
Culligan, Clifford, 187
Curley, Agnes, 193
Curley, Joe, ix–x
Curtis, Edward, 132–133, 197
    sample photograph, *132*
Custer, George Armstrong, 109
Cut Thumb, 75

Dagget, Dan, 160–161
D'Aste, Father, 117
Dawes, Henry, 124–125
Dawes Act, 124, 130
De Smet, Pierre-Jean, 88–92,
    88, 93, 96, 99, 100
De Voto, Bernard, 64, 90
Deer, 14, 182
Deer Lodge, 177, 189
Defenders of Wildlife, 162
Deloria, Vine, Jr., 29
Demer, Father, 92
Demeter, 24
Denver, John, x
Descartes, 204
Dick the Diver, 122
Dixon, Joseph, 127, 128–129
Dixon Act, 127–128, 130
Dixon Bar, 197
Dog Lake, 118, 187
Doig, Ivan, 163–164
Douglas, David, 70
Drips, Andrew, 89
Droughts, 20
Ducks Unlimited, 162

Egans, 153, 192
Ehrlich, Gretel, 31
Einstein, Albert, 204–205
Elk, 22, 142–143

Enas, Joe, 144
Eneas, Chief, 131–132, *131*,
    203
Enlightenment, 204–205
Environmental movement,
    156–162, 207
Erchul, Joe, 187
Ermatinger, Francis, 70–71, 78
Evaro Canyon, 19
Expansionism. *See* Manifest
    Destiny
Exxon, 139, 140

Family farm, 150–151, *151*,
    162–163
Family tree quilt, 18
Farm subsidies, 151–152
Farmers and farming, x, xii, 1–
    2, 10, 19–20, 151–152, *188*,
    197, 200–201. *See also* Bor-
    der dikes, Cattle, Crop ro-
    tation, Grazing land,
    Homesteading, Irrigation,
    Ranchers and ranching
    and agribusiness, 31, 154–
    155, 158–159
    community, 10, 29–30, 162–
    163, 186–187, 194
    conservation easements, 156
    financial bind, 154–156
    and grasshoppers, 188
    and railroads, 119–120
Ferris, Warren, 49, 79
Field mice, 17
Finley, Agette, 172
Fisk, Elizabeth, 115
Fitzpatrick, Tom, 80–81
Flathead Indian Reservation,
    15, 19, 85, 107, *107*, 139
    and Edward Curtis and
    Eleanor Whitfeld, 133
    and Northern Pacific Rail-
    road, 120–121, 123–124
    opened to white settlement,
    124–131, *128*
    and Yellowstone Pipeline,
    139–142
Flathead Irrigation Project,
    148–151, 152–153
Flathead Lake, 19, 143, 177
Flathead Post, 68, 77, 78, 79,
    82
Flathead River, 2, 36, 68, 74–
    75, 118, 123, 189
Flathead tribe, 12, 15, 26, 36,
    49, 59–60, 74, 78, 104, 199

and horses, 48–49
merging with Kalispel and
Pend d'Oreille, 49
territory, *13*
Foolish Folk, 35–36
Forsyth, Norman, 176–177
Fort Benton, 101, 106
Fort Colville, 92
Fort Connah, 83, *86,* 105
Fort Kearny, 108
Fort Keogh, 115
Fort Laramie, 108
Fort Missoula, 108, 113, 117
Fort Owen, 99
Fort Walla Walla, 108, 117
Foster, Stacey, *203*
Foxes, 22, 74
Frontier, closing of, 134, 145–
147
Fur trade, 55–86, *81, 82*
rendezvous, 67–68, 74, *80,*
81–82, *83,* 88, 89

G, Kenny, x
Gant, Richard, 97
Garcia, Andrew, 114
Gardner, Johnson, 77
Garfield, James, 111
Garson Gulch, 18
GATT. *See* General Agreement
on Tariff and Trade
Geese, 17, 23, 61
General Agreement on Tariff
and Trade, 31, 155
Gibbon, John, 113–114
Gila National Forest, 157, 158
Giorda, Father, 108
Glimp, Hudson, 162
Goddess religions, 204
Gold, 117
Jim Grinder's cache, 178–
183
Goodwin, Phillip, 176–177
Grant, Ulysses S., 108, 111
Grasshopper plague of 1916, 20
Grasshoppers, 20, 188
Gray, John, 62
Grazing land, 154, 160–161
Great Buffalo Round-Up, 173–
177, *174, 175, 176,* 183
Great Depression, 192
Green Springs Pond, 187, 194–
195
Grinder, Jim, 170–178, *177*
gold cache, 178–183
Grizzly bears, 41

Guthrie, A. B., 24

Hades, 23–24
Hale, Calvin H., 109–110
Haller, George, 106
Hammond, A. H., 121–122
Harbert, James, 149
Harvest, 2–3
Hasselstrom, Linda, 30, 193–
194
Heath, Carol, 163
Hellgate, 50
Hellgate Treaty, 100, 105, 107,
108, 127, 138
Henry, Andrew, 64, 66, 72
Heraclitus, 94
Herder, Gottfried von, 167
Hicks, Bill, 142
High Country News, 162
History, 9–10, 201–202
Hoecken, Adrian
Hoecken, Adrian, 88, *88,* 106
Holland, Bill, *190*
Holland, Tom, *190*
Hollands, 1, *190*
Homestead Act, 131, 148, 184
Homesteading, 147–149, *148,
149,* 166–167, 185–186, 191
promotion, *146, 147*
Horses, 25, 36
acquisition by Native
Americans, 47–49, *48,* 50
and Salish, 53–54, 126
Horton, Butch, 162
Howard, O. O., 110, 115, 116
Howard Ranch, 162
Hudson's Bay Company, 55–
56, 68–78, 79, 82–83, 105
Huet, Brother, 89
Huggins, Edward, 84–85
Hungarian pheasants, 17
Hunter, Chuck, 139, 140

IBP, 155
Ignace, 87, 88
Imported beef, 156
Incashola, Tony, 27
Indian Claims Commission,
138
Indian Reorganization Act, 138
Insula. *See* Red Feather (Insula)
International Journal of Wil-
derness, 162
IRA. *See* Indian Reorganization
Act
Iroquois, 68, 70, 71–72, 87

Irrigation, 148–150

Jackrabbits, 17
Jackson, David, 68
Jacobs, Joe, ix
Jefferson, Thomas, 62, 97
Jorgenson, Erick, 186
Jorgensons, 1, 186
Joseph, Chief, 110–117, *112*

Kalispel House, 59, 60
Kalispel Indians, 11–12, 15, 36,
49, 59–60, 74, 101, 104,
197–199
berry harvest, 21
canoes, 37–38, *37*
clothing, 41
fall hunt, 21
and grizzly bears, 41
hunting, 41
loghouses, 38
territory, *13*
vegetable foods and herbs,
38–41, *39*
winter camp, 21
woven goods, 38
Kelly, Hall, 78
Kennedys, 153
Kennedy's Lake, 17
Kinnikinnick, 39, 47, 63
Kiowa, 136
Kittredge, William, 32
Knuffke, Darrell, 160
Kootenai House, 57
Kootenai Indians, x–xi, 15, 29,
49, 59–60, 74, 78, 85, 104,
107, 136, 138, 201. *See also*
Confederated Salish and
Kootenai Tribes
and alcohol, 131–132
and Edward Curtis and
Eleanor Whitfeld, 133
and Yellowstone Pipeline,
139–142
Kootenai River, 57

Lake Missoula, 34, *34*
Lake Pend d'Oreille, 34, 57, 88,
198–199
Lakota Sioux, 109, 115, 135
Land and landscape, xi, xii, 2,
9, 31–32, 195–196, 202, 204,
208
Lansdale, Richard, 106
Lapwai Reservation, 110
Latham, Bob, 142

Lawson, Christy, *203*
Lawyer, 109
Lehman, Bill, 156
Lewis, Meriwether, 41, 62. *See also* Lewis and Clark
Lewis and Clark, 25, 40, 55, 62–63, 66, 99, 100, 109. *See also* Clark, William; Lewis, Meriwether
Limerick, Patricia, 9–10
Little Big Horn, 109
Little Bitterroot Valley, 18, 187
Lolo Pass, 112, 113, 172
Lonepine, 18, 187
Looking Glass, 83, 110, 112, 113, 115, 116
Lord of the Pen, 51–52
Loretto, 79–80
Louisiana Purchase, 62
Lovage, 47
Loyne, Charles, 114
Lozeau, Edward, 37
Lynch, Nip, 187

Mackenzie, Alexander, 56
Mails, Thomas, 205
Malpai Borderlands Group, 162
Mandan tribe, 63
Mander, Jerry, 207–208
Manifest Destiny, 97, 102–103, 134
Marias Pass, 106
Marrinan, Jack, *190*
Marrinan, Mike, 186
Marrinans, 1, 186, *190*
Marsh hawks, 17
Martens, 22
Mason, Charles, 106
Mason, John, 114
McCammon, Joseph, 120
McCoy, John, 190
McDonald, Angus, 83–86, *84*, 87, 100, 105, 108, 112, 144, 173, 203
McDonald, Archibald, 70–71, 83
McDonald, Catherine, 83, 112, 113, 144, 203
McDonald, Duncan, 112, 114, 127
McDonald, Finan, 59, 60–61, 68, 70–71, 72, 83, 84
McDonald, Joe, 144
McLeod, C. H., 129
McNaughton, S. J., 161

McNichols, Charles, 130
Mdawelasis, 169
Meek, Joe, 68, 81, 82
Mengarini, Gregory, 89, 92, 93, 95, 96–97
Merrit, Wesley, 108
Michele, Chief, 104, 178, 186
Miles, Lona, 203
Miles, Nelson, 115, 116
Mill Creek, 103
Miller, Alfred Jacob, 82, 83
Mission Mountains, 19, 88
Missoula, 6, 123–124
Missoula Mercantile, 129
Missoula River, 103
Moise, 100, *100*, 104–106
Montana, ix–x
Montana Clean Water and Public Health Protection Act, 156–157
Montana Department of Fish, Wildlife, and Parks Department, 142, 156
Montana State Penitentiary, 177
Moonshiners, 186, 188–190
Morgan, J. P., 132–133
Mortson, Walter, *190*
Moss, William M., 126
Mullan, John, 98, 99, 102, 104, 105
Musselshell River, 106
Muster, Ed, 186, 187

NAFTA. *See* North American Free Trade Agreement
Native Americans, xi, 1–2, *132, 133*. *See also* Bureau of Indian Affairs, Indian Reorganization Act, individual tribe names, Powwows
acquisition of horses, 47–49, *48*, 50
adaptability, 145
and bitterroot, 25–28, 29
dances, 14–16, 135–138, *136*
early twentieth century, 134–135
increased population, 197
internal sovereignty developments, 138–139
reservations, 15, 19, 85, 103, 104–105, 107, 110, 116, 134–135
reservations opened to white

settlement, 124–131, *128*
spirituality, 28–29, 94–95, 205. *See also* Sweat houses
stewardship, 206–207
storytelling, 168–170
Sun Dance, 135–137, *136*
tribal councils, 138–139
U.S. policy, 102–108, 202
union with the earth, 9
Nature, xi–xii, 2, 32
Nature Conservancy, 156, 158, 162
Neiman, Charlie, 166–167
Neiman, Morland, 139, 140
Nerinckx, Father, 89
Nevada, University of, Reaching Sustainable Agreements Program, 162
Newell, Doc, 82
Newell Tunnel, 149
Newton, Isaac, 97, 204, 205
Nez Perce, 37, 74, 83, 88, 89, 103
flight of, 109–117
Nick, Mrs. *See* Nickerson, Claudia
Nickerson, Claudia, 6–8, 10, 187
Nickerson, Joe, 6, 7, 8
Ninemile Valley, 141–142
Ninemile Valley Preservation Council, 142
Nobili, Roberto de, 90
North American Free Trade Agreement, 31, 155
Northern Pacific Railroad, 19–20, 118, *121*
and Salish Indians, 120–121, 123–124
Northwest Passage, 62–63
Northwest Trade Company. *See* Canadian Northwest Trade Company

Ogden, Peter Skene, 74–77, *76*
Ohio Dan, 122, 123
Olsen, Al, 3
Oregon Volunteers, 108
Otters, 63, 74
Owen, John, 96–97, 98–99, 108

Pablo, Laurette, 172
Pablo, Michel, 172, 173–177
Pablo, Micky, 140
Pablo Dam, 149
Pacific Fur Company, 63–64

Parker, Samuel, 67
Parks, Rebecca, 4–5, 10
Parks, Wade, 4–5
Parks family, 4–5, 10, 153
Parmenides, 94
Paul, John Peter, 143–144
Paul, Phillip, 138
Paul, Saint, 90, 94
Pawnee tribe, 63
PCA. *See* Production Credit Association
Pelkoe, John, 39
Pelley, Phil, 6–7, 8, 10, 163, *190*
Pend d'Oreille Lake. *See* Lake Pend d'Oreille
Pend d'Oreille tribe, 12, 15, 26, 36, 49, 74, 78, 101–102, 104, 105, 199
territory, *13*
Perma, 2, 3–4, *4*, 12, *13*, 68, 118, 123, 139, 189
Bar and grocery, ix, 3
bridge, 2–3
grain elevator, 3
Persephone, 23–24
Peu-peu-mox-mox, 108–109
Phillips, Billy, 189
Pierre, Victor, 186, *190*
Pierre's Hole, 89
Pike, Zebulon, 66
Pioneer Bar, 19
Plato, 94
Podobinik, Jim, 187
Point, Nicholas, 89, 92–93, 95–96
Polson, 189, 190
Chamber of Commerce, 149
Ponderosa pine, 40
Pony express, 112, 117–118, *118*
Pony tax, 126–127
Potts, Benjamin, 111
Powell, John Wesley, 20, 193
Powwows, 14–16, 138
Price, Hiram, 125
Production Credit Association, 17–18
Pueblo, 170
Pursch, Frederick, 25

Quiet, 9

Railroads, 19–20, 98–99, 117, 184
land grants, 119
Ranchers and ranching, 31–32,

155. *See also* Cattle, Farmers and farming
and environmental movement, 156–162, 207
Ratcliff, "Rat," *148*
Rattlesnakes, 17, 44–45
Ravalli, 123, 129
Rawn, Charles C., 113
Reaching Sustainable Agreements Program, 162
Red Crow, 1
Red Feather (Insula), 75–77, 79
Red Wolf, 105
Rendezvous, 67–68, 74, *80*, 81–82, *83*, 88, 89
Ricci, Matteo, 90
Rifkin, Jeremy, 31
Riis, Jacob, 184
Rios, Albert, 168
Rittenaur, Clifford, 192
Rocky Mountain Elk Foundation, 156
Rocky Mountain Fur Company, 79
Rocky Mountain juniper, 42, *42*
Ronan, Peter, 111, 120–121, 124, 125, 172
Roosevelt, Theodore, 130
Roothram, Father, 93
Rosati, Joseph, 89
Ross, Alexander, 63–64, 71–74
Rural West, x
Russell, Charlie, 146, 176–177, 197, 198
Russell, Osborne, 81
Ryman, J. H., 129

Salish House, 57, 59, 64–65, 68
Salish Indians, ix, x–xi, 12–14, 16, 17, 19, 36–37, 63, 85, 107, 138, 199. *See also* Confederated Salish and Kootenai Tribes
acquisition of horses, 47–49, *48*, 50
and alcohol, 131–132
assimilation and opening of reservation to white settlement, 124–131, *128*
and bitterroot, 25–28, *27*, *28*, 29
Blue Jay Dance and Ceremony, 45–46
buffalo hunts, 50–52
buffalo products, 52–53

and Camas Prairie, 126–127
and Catholic Church, 87–97, 125–127
chiefs, 43–44
and colors, 42
council, 43
Culture Committee, 143, 144
dances, 14–15
and Edward Curtis and Eleanor Whitfeld, 133
and farmers, 186, 193, 199, 201, 203
and farming, 19
first appearance on Camas Prairie, 35–36
and fur trade, 58–60, 74, *83*
and horses, 53–54, 126
and Isaac Stevens, 103–106
language, 199
Lord of the Pen, 51–52
lovemaking, 42–43
move to reservation, 104–105, 107
and Nez Perce, 111–112, 117
and Northern Pacific Railroad, 120–121, 123–124
physical and psychological characteristics, 42
and scents, 42
shamans, 45–47, 100–101, 135
spirit quest, 12–14, 92–93, 179
storytelling, 43–45
and Sun Dance, 136, 179
sweat houses, 180–183
territory, *13*
tribal council, 139–144
wars with Blackfeet, 49, 50, 59, 60–61, 65, 69–70, 75–77, 78–80, 89
and white diseases, 49–50
winter storytelling, 21–22
and Yellowstone Pipeline, 139–142
Salish Kootenai College, 144
Salmon, 21–22, 45
Salmon River, 110
Saxton, Rufus, 98
Schafft, Charles, 108
Scientific worldview, 204–205, 206
Semte'use. *See* Foolish Folk
Shaeffer, Billie, 186

Shaeffer, Ted, 2–3
Sherman, William Tecumseh, 116
Shining Shirt, 87
Shortys, 153
Shoshone, 48, 49, 136
Sierra Club, 160
Silko, Leslie Marmon, 170
Simeon, Saint, 94
Simpson, George, 73–74, 78
Sitting Bull, 109, 115
Skagit, 36
Small, Charlotte, 57
Small, Patrick, 57
Small Salmon, Mitch, 40
Smead, William H., 125, 126, 127, 129–130
Smith, Jedediah, 66, 68, 72–73, 75, 77
Snake Country Expeditions, 68–70, 69, 73–78, 79
Snake Creek, 115, 116
Snake Dance, 14
Snake River, 110
Snake tribe, 72
Snohomish, 36
Snoqualmie Pass, x
Sohon, Gustavus, 98, 99, 100, 101, 102, 103
Specht, Brother, 89
Spokane tribe, 74, 106
Spring, 23–25
Sprinkler pipes, 152–153
St. Ignatius Mission, 88, 106, 108, 117–118, 125–126, 143, 144
     Boys' Band, 126
St. Joseph Mission, 88
St. Mary's Mission, 89, 90, 92, 96, 99, 100, 106
Stanislaw, 1
Stanislaw, Johnny, 197–200
Stanislaw, Ustus, 197
Stasso, Lasso, 14
Stegner, Wallace, 9, 162
Stevens, Isaac, 98–99, 103–106, 108, 109, 138
Stevensville, 113
Stewart, William, 82
Stipe, Chuck, xii, 159
Stone, Gene, 139, 140
Storytelling, xii, 10–11, 18–19, 21–22, 43–45, 165–168,

207, 208
Stuckly, George, 50
Sturgis, Samuel, 115
Sublette, William, 68
Sun Dance, 135–137, 136
Survival, 9
Svejcar, Tony, 154
Sweat houses, 180–183
Sweeney, 122, 123

Taft, William Howard, 130
Taylor, Daniel, 168, 207
Taylor, Jim, 141
Teit, James, 35–36
Teller, Henry, 128
This House of Sky, 163–164
Thompson, David, 12, 55–62
     travels, 57–59, 58
Thompson tribe, 37
Toffler, Alvin, 32
Toiyabe Wetlands and Water-sheds Management, 162
Toohulhulsate, 115
Trade and Intercourse Act of 1802, 85
Trail of Tears, 102
Tree bark, 40
Trout Unlimited, 162
Tuekakas, 110
Turner, Frederick Jackson, 134, 145, 197, 201
Two Eagle, 65
Tyrell, J. B., 62

U.S. Department of Natural Resources and Conservation, 156
U.S. Forest Service, 142
U.S. Soil Conservation Service, 150
Umatilla tribe, 103
Union Oil, 139, 140
Union Pacific Railroad, 184
Ute, 136

Vanderburg, Frances, 144
Vanderpol, David, 140
Varves, 35, 35
Victor, Chief, 99–100, 99, 104–106, 108, 111

Wagner, Les, 156
Wahon, 51–52

Walking Coyote, 173
Walla Walla tribe, 103, 108–109
Walters, Mrs., 187
War Dance, 14
Washington, x
Weasels, 17
Webber, Brian, 163
Weeks, I.S.P., 121
Weeksville, 121
     outlaws, 122–123
Wells, John, 108
West, x, xiii, 203
     cultures, xi, 1–2
     land and landscape, xi, xii, 2, 9, 31–32, 195–196, 202, 204, 208
West Elk Wilderness, 162
Western Slope Environmental Resource Council, 162
Wheat, 2–3
Whiskey Trail, 189
White Bird, 83, 110, 112, 113, 116
Whitfeld, Eleanor, 133
Whitman, Marcus, 81, 88, 96
Whitman, Narcissa, 96
Wild Horse Island, 143, 177
Wild Horse Plains, 5, 6, 18, 53, 60, 68, 71, 74, 91, 117, 118, 127, 139, 189, 190, 192
The Wilderness Society, 160
Wilson, M. L., 147
Winans, David, 142
Wind, 3–4, 16–17, 24
Wind River, 73
Winter, 22–23
Wolves, 91
Woodchucks, 17
Woodruff, Thomas, 116
Worden, Frank, 129
Wormwood, 47
Wounded Head, 114
Wyeth, Nathaniel, 17, 78
Wyghant, Lew, 122

Yakima tribe, 103, 106
Yellowstone Pipeline, 139–142

Zeus, 24
Zimmer, Charles, 122

About the Author

*C*arlene Cross grew up on the Camas Prairie farm her great-grandmother homesteaded in 1919. In this remote valley in northwestern Montana, the family's nearest neighbor lived miles away. Today, the family still operates the original homestead as a working ranch. Carlene holds a degree in religious studies from Big Sky College in Montana, as well as a BA in history and an MA in communications history from the University of Washington. She lives with her children on an island in the Puget Sound in Washington. This is her first book.